AF870623

THE PERSISTENCE OF CODE IN GAME ENGINE CULTURE

With its unique focus on video game engines, the data-driven architectures of game development and play, this innovative textbook examines the impact of software on everyday life and explores the rise of engine-driven culture.

Through a series of case studies, Eric Freedman lays out a clear methodology for studying the game development pipeline, and uses the video game engine as a pathway for media scholars and practitioners to navigate the complex terrain of software practice. Examining several distinct software ecosystems that include the proprietary efforts of Amazon, Apple, Capcom, Epic Games and Unity Technologies, and the unique ways that game engines are used in non-game industries, Freedman illustrates why engines matter.

The studies bind together designers and players, speak to the labors of the game industry, value the work of both global and regional developers, and establish critical connection points between software and society. Freedman has crafted a much-needed entry point for students new to code, and a research resource for scholars and teachers working in media industries, game development and new media.

Eric Freedman is Professor and Dean of the School of Media Arts at Columbia College Chicago. He is the author of *Transient Images: Personal Media in Public Frameworks* (2011) and serves on the editorial board of the *International Journal of Creative Media Research* and the advisory board of the Communication and Media Studies Research Network.

"Freedman skillfully reveals the importance of game engines for understanding contemporary video games. And then, he goes one step further, and reveals just how important they are for understanding cities, consumerism, and nearly every other aspect of modern life. This is a must read for every student of the media."

Eric Gordon, Professor of Civic Design, Emerson College

"Eric Freedman has taken a complex and concealed topic – how game engines function to constrain and create possibilities, which helps him consider the impact of code on everyday life – and rendered it visible. Freedman presents a well-written and well-informed critical analysis, using case studies that problematize and facilitate the interrogation of these technologies in their social contexts from multiple angles."

Rebecca Ann Lind, Associate Professor of Communication,
University of Illinois at Chicago

THE PERSISTENCE OF CODE IN GAME ENGINE CULTURE

Eric Freedman

Routledge
Taylor & Francis Group
NEW YORK AND LONDON

First published 2020
by Routledge
52 Vanderbilt Avenue, New York, NY 10017

and by Routledge
2 Park Square, Milton Park, Abingdon, Oxon OX14 4RN

Routledge is an imprint of the Taylor & Francis Group, an informa business

© 2020 Taylor & Francis

The right of Eric Freedman to be identified as author of this work has been asserted by him in accordance with sections 77 and 78 of the Copyright, Designs and Patents Act 1988.

All rights reserved. No part of this book may be reprinted or reproduced or utilized in any form or by any electronic, mechanical, or other means, now known or hereafter invented, including photocopying and recording, or in any information storage or retrieval system, without permission in writing from the publishers.

Trademark notice: Product or corporate names may be trademarks or registered trademarks, and are used only for identification and explanation without intent to infringe.

Every effort has been made to contact copyright holders. Please advise the publisher of any errors or omissions, and these will be corrected in subsequent editions.

Library of Congress Cataloging-in-Publication Data
A catalog record for this title has been requested

ISBN: 978-1-138-35338-1 (hbk)
ISBN: 978-1-138-35339-8 (pbk)
ISBN: 978-0-429-43424-2 (ebk)

Typeset in Bembo
by Taylor & Francis Books

CONTENTS

FIGURES

ACKNOWLEDGMENTS

Many people have guided me throughout this project, sharing their creative, technical and critical expertise while revealing a deep commitment to their respective practices. This manuscript would not have been possible without the generosity of a number of individuals working at game studios in Berlin, Frankfurt, Hamburg and Athens, and those advocating for regional investment in game development. I count among them Collin Bishop, Marc Hehmeyer, Malte Kosian, Johannes Kuhlmann, Sven Ossenbrüggen, Christoph Schulte, Finn Seliger, Alexander Spohr, Johannes Spohr, Christof Wegmann, Philip Weiss, Cornelius Wiegmann, Karsten Wysk, Konstantina Bethani, Thanos Georgoulis, Theodoros Giannakis, Dimitris Koutsomitsos, Lefteris Kretsos, Kate Mataraga, Anna Mykoniati, Tina Pandi, Charis Papaevangelou, Mike Papagathangelou, Marinos Boyko Pehlivanov, Elina Roinioti and Vasiliki Tsiftsian. My research in Germany and Greece (the latter informs a follow-up study beyond the purview of this book), and in particular my conversations with game developers, programmers, artists and public servants invested in supporting regional and national game development communities highlights the specific labors of those working within the game development pipeline and their negotiations with larger global industrial forces—the specificity of writing code, building assets and developing games, and the more generalizable lessons of doing this work. This is not simply a landscape of products, a field to be read, but a landscape where individuals are faced with the real pressures and consequences of having to keep their games and their studios afloat in an increasingly competitive field of play. Even as the tools are becoming more democratic and more accessible for entry-level game developers and younger collaborative studio enterprises, the marketplace remains one of careful calculation. Working at the intersections of art, technology and commerce, the passionate engagement and deep knowledge of those creating assets, designing games, working with code and building software programs shaped my perspective and contributed significantly to my understanding of game-based architectures.

I thank those faculty colleagues in the Interactive Arts and Media Department in the School of Media Arts at Columbia College Chicago, who took the time and had the patience to discuss the intricacies of game programming. Portions of Chapter 8 were published as part of a related essay in a special issue of *Game Studies: The International Journal of Computer Game Research*, edited by Bonnie Ruberg and Amanda Phillips; their insights greatly improved my contribution to their volume and contributed to this book in its current state, pointing me toward seminal texts in queer game studies and independent game communities that inform my approach; and the feedback I received from participants at the 2017 Queerness and Games Conference, a vibrant gathering of queer game scholars, developers and players was invaluable, as it provided a broader perspective on both the games community and the games industry, and signaled the importance of engaging with any number of exclusionary or limiting practices. As well, Mary Kearney and Michael Kackman furthered the foundations of my work with their editorial feedback as part of the publication of my contribution on software studies to *The Craft of Criticism: Critical Media Studies in Practice*.

I would be remiss if I did not acknowledge the fantastic body of ideas being tested out by scholars and practitioners that I have encountered along the way while conducting my research and writing this manuscript, at gatherings that have made significant strides in creating spaces to talk about research in critical game studies, including the video game scholarly interest group affiliated with the Society for Cinema and Media Studies, and those who have shared their work at the Digital Games Research Association, Replaying Japan and Media in Transition; these gatherings continue to highlight the vibrancy of contemporary video game studies, the significant cultural and industrial weight of the field, and the complexity of its channels of influence. I also thank my external reviewers, among them Eric Gordon and Rebecca Ann Lind for lending their critical eyes to my research and pushing me to clarify my arguments; their feedback strengthened the manuscript by making me a more thoughtful writer. Of course, the strongest editorial voice came from my original editor Erica Wetter at Routledge, who expressed enthusiasm for this project at its outset and shepherded the book forward with Emma Sherriff at the press. Finally, I thank my husband, Ryan Ratliff, who has for the second time been a strong voice of encouragement without ever asking me about my progress or my deadlines.

1

GAME ENGINE CULTURE

This book project traces the industrial development, migrations and ideological inflections of video game engines. Providing one point of analysis in the game development pipeline, the game engine, as an object of critical inquiry, can be used to illustrate the synthetic power of computing and the instrumentality of code in everyday life. Game engines have promoted a new cultural economy for software production; while the formative impulse for the separation of engine and assets in the early 1990s was to cultivate communities of collaborative production (working with common source code structures), open source software has yielded to a business model that privileges fixed forms of interaction with stricter technological and relational constraints. This project explores the bounded relations between technologies and their social contexts, grounding its social impact statements in a focused intellectual history of computing.

What is a game engine? In the most reductive terms, the engine is a single piece of software that produces common functionality for multiple games; a game engine includes a tool suite or content editor (for game creation and object-oriented asset manipulation) and a runtime component that is active when a game is played. As a software abstraction of a graphics processing unit, engines are development tools for interactive digital content creation, and code frameworks that determine and control the attributes of the field of play across platforms and devices. The birth of engines in the early 1990s fostered a split between core functionalities (components such as the rendering engine, the physics engine, sound, scripting and artificial intelligence) and game-specific content, building on the already extant separation of source code from assets and resources. This split also fostered a division of labor (one of socio-economic consequence) between programmers creating systems and artists filling in the parameters of those systems, with the most segmented organizational subdivisions in triple-A (large in scale and budget) development. This industrial division also shaped the field of game studies, placing more focused attention on visual analysis, ignoring certain material relations to study narrative, genre, seriality, and other literary and cinematic conceits.

Game engines manage the computational tasks that are central to many digital media production pipelines, and their value lies in the rapid prototyping and development of real-time interactive content. Engine development by its very nature has led to the widely accepted practice of separating core software components (for example, rendering, collision detection and audio systems), from game art (commonly referred to as assets) and the rules that govern play, though the line between the game and the engine may shift within any one development studio and across a studio's intellectual properties (Gregory, 2009, 11). This developmental practice has also led to commonly held divisions of labor in the game development pipeline; in large team environments, distinctions are often drawn between designers (responsible for the governing play concept, including gameplay rules and structures), artists, programmers, level designers, as well as other discrete talent classifications (for example, sound engineers).

The engine is a data-driven architecture, a software framework, while a game contains hard-coded logic or special-case code to render specific types of assets. The game engine can best be understood as a foundation, though the engine itself can be subdivided between runtime components (the subsystems required when a game is executed) and a tool suite (for digital content creation) that suggest even more deeply bifurcated fields of production and analysis. The engine lays down the framework for both game development and gameplay. Engines contain a large number of subsystems that govern game logic, memory management, networking, rendering (generating animated graphics), audio, physics and artificial intelligence; and their ease of use is both a product of their programming language and scripting (how they are written and how gameplay is structured and customized, with scripting as a higher-level construct to call out underlying code functions) and the simplicity of their editorial graphical user interface. As a software foundation, most engines are iterative; they can be used as a base for multiple games without undergoing extensive modification to their programming, and their versioning is commonly limited only by major changes to a hardware platform. Whether they are game consoles or mobile devices, most engines encounter a limit to their reusability as processing environments move forward. By knowing the engine and the unceremonious and decidedly non-visual machinations and industrial labors of software, we may untangle the multiple paradigms of game studies and find the roots of those affordances that are commonly (mis)understood as characteristics of play—when, in fact, everything matters in the game development pipeline.

For those unfamiliar with game engines and uncertain as to why they matter, this book turns to a number of case studies drawn from game culture, consumer culture and contemporary media industries that reveal exactly how game engine logic is impacting everyday life; game engines are embedded in the infrastructure (and the business models) of those media and information industries that depend on algorithmic exactness. Amazon, Apple, Capcom, Epic Games and Unity Technologies are all building their own engine-dependent software ecosystems; engines are transforming the commercial landscape of film and television, and becoming central to new media economies and new experiences in augmented and virtual reality. Game engines are responsible for running most simulated environments, and while they may be complexly layered software development tools, composed of multiple subsystems, many have become so visually oriented that they allow content developers to avoid the complexities of code. Game engines are the building blocks for efficient real-time visualization; and they signal quite forcefully the colonizing influence of programming, of software on digital and physical experience. Game engines are powering our visual futures, and engine developers are rapidly iterating their products to tackle new markets, where data and visuality continue to converge. A number of key technology shareholders are looking to dominate the field of engine-driven social experience, and are capitalizing aggressively on the common language borne from the video game industry. Game engines are part of the larger field of code; they can be understood as entities where code has coalesced. Given that engines undergird contemporary media and information systems, it is important that we make them more visible; because technology is so central to our social systems, shaping and organizing daily life, declaring our identities, interpreting and answering our queries, and impacting how we see and know the world around us, it is important that we understand what engines and similar code objects are doing.

The difficulty of holding on to mechanics and aesthetics is compounded by the semantic and practiced openness of game engines as well as their importance not only to game development but also to the field of play. The game engine, as a complex software structure, is comprised of a number of substructures. We might begin by separating the core engine (a collection of product-facing tools used to compile games to be executed on target platforms) from any number of associated user-facing tools. The core layer of the engine handles low-level base systems that typically include rendering, collision detection and response, physics and character animation, which are interlinked to gameplay systems that include scripting, artificial intelligence, player mechanics, cameras and sound, and data handling systems that include networking, streaming, memory management, file reading and threading; this is an oversimplification of game engine architecture, as many game engine developers also rely on engine abstraction to simplify hardware and software platform dependencies, writing an abstraction layer that sits on top of the specific operating system code. These system layers are usually wrapped by user-facing development tools or a more robust integrated development environment populated with common editor windows.

This study is focused primarily on 3D (three-dimensional) game engines (engines used to generate real-time interactive 3D animated content), and is based on a particular conception of the game engine as a software framework that contains both a core engine (a more static, "hardwired" operating system—the engine's root persona) and a user interface system that offers the necessary plasticity associated with game design and development—the production of a unique intellectual property. Within this field, there are both general-purpose game engines suitable for building a broad range of game genres, and special-purpose game engines, often designed by individual studios—proprietary software builds targeted at specific titles, genres, aesthetics, game mechanics or industry-defined implementations. Game engines, as system-dependent tools, often function alongside a number of middleware offerings. Most game developers depend on more than one product, and follow a decision-tree that begins with selecting a game engine, then choosing additional software supports (middleware) that might include a multiplayer solution (to support networked play), a backend solution (for hosting), an analytics platform, an advertising platform, and a product to manage in-game purchases. The developer is also dependent on a publisher. There are multiple opportunities for specialized engine-based middleware development and integration along the game production pipeline, as most game engine developers use middleware to satisfy certain conditions of their engines; and while even the most comprehensive game engines can accommodate middleware, several of the key engine manufacturers have built-out ecosystems of convenience, with tightly-integrated interrelated middleware components, and have strategically positioned themselves to drive the game development market.

The video game industry is not simply a sum total of its software enterprises and its serialized intellectual properties; it is also an arena of hardware and software development and licensing. Brand names are attached not only to game franchises, but also to the engines that govern the physics-based properties of characters and, by extension, those players who read and engage with them. With most engines, success is measured by the naturalness of the relations across engine, asset, controller, character and player—relations that are circumscribed by the historical, technical and material conventions of the game industry. While a game engine may be known in developer and player communities by its distinct mechanics, abilities and features, in most video games the dynamics of play and the constellation of transactional engagements with the game world work to conceal the engine's core mathematical logic; and the signature look of a developer or studio commonly masks any particular aesthetics that might otherwise be associated with the engine.

With its focus on video game engines, this manuscript proposes how an analysis of code space, and the engine-based labors and technologies that undergird the objects of contemporary screen culture, can strengthen more generalized discussions of the impact of code on everyday life. Understanding that a game engine is a particular type of code object, the goal of this manuscript is to help media scholars and practitioners to "locate" software; given its relative immateriality, software is a rather challenging "non-object" that is nonetheless central to contemporary cultural experience. Software is not simply a tool, it is also a structuring transaction, actuated with little debate or understanding, and difficult to tackle alongside an informed textual or industrial analysis of any media form; yet software is the medium and the context of convergence culture. The goal is to unravel the material outcomes of code through a detailed examination of video game engines, and by examining several case studies that make clear their pervasive use across a broad range of industries.

We live in a software culture, which we can begin to approximate first by gathering together our everyday software and then expanding our scope outward to consider the toolsets that impact our lives, even if they are beyond our reach: search engines, social media systems, mapping applications and global positioning systems (GPS), blogging platforms, instant messaging clients, online shopping portals and their offline warehouses, assemblies and distribution systems, aeronautical and military systems, platforms that allow the writing of new software (including APIs—application programming interfaces), and game engines. We may differentiate between software programs (applications) and software environments (application contexts—for example, within an operating system, as part of a database system, or framed by a suite of development tools), between common use software that connects industries and user groups (technologically integrated market sectors), and software deployed in micro-industrial contexts (such as Amazon's inventory management system, and middleware deployed in peer-to-peer architectures for systems integration). Collectively, these reference points produce a sense of computational ubiquity that is lived and material, and may be broadly framed as part of increasingly complex information space, of context-aware, data-rich connections between software and the physical world. Game engines are part of the coded landscape; they can be integrated into a company's backend systems and used to model touch screen experiences, set to work for previsualization in live action filmmaking, and woven into the data flows of architectural visualization; extending the parameters of real-time 3D rendering beyond video games, their graphical capabilities can be leveraged in both animation and simulation.

There have been a number of intellectual efforts to secure the relevancy of code and its associated artifacts. Lev Manovich (2013) has taken an ontological approach, outlining the intrinsic properties of software objects. Lawrence Lessig (1999) focused on the commodity value of code. Theorists such as Adrian Mackenzie (2006) have examined the machinations of labor (and the production of identity and subcultural formations) associated with the work of hackers, programmers, and those bound up in the consumption of their knowledge capital. Each of these frameworks considers code at a particular juncture, rather than holding on to the complex interactions of code; code operates along a continuum, as a site of negotiations involving commodity production, organizational life, technoscientific knowledge and industrially-aligned geopolitical territorialization. Code carries power relations, distributes agency, shapes communication, contours personhood and organizes everyday life; yet it readily disappears behind functional surfaces and their more immediate gratifications. David Golumbia (2009) suggests that while computation occupies a privileged place in critical discourse—as a popular metaphor for illustrating the intersectionality of technology and everyday life—the precise role of computation on human patterns of interaction and belief systems is often underanalyzed. While the rhetoric associated with computation often points to a radical historical rupture (from analog to digital, and toward new organizing principles), I argue that the rise of computation follows other cultural flows—a network of changes in public discourse, in our institutions, in corporations, and in governance, as well as in cultural expression. Golumbia notes, "Too often, computers aid institutions in centralizing, demarcating, and concentrating power" (4). One of my goals is to illustrate those power relations, and to do so requires moving beyond a conversation about the broad strokes of computation; instead, we need to look more deeply at computation in context, and the shifting alignment of the functionalities of physical computers (and their respective languages) with the ideologies of computationalism (a state-based, mechanistic view of cognition—a computational theory of mind).

To further the fields of media studies and game studies, this manuscript considers the manner in which the engine, code and 3D design, purposefully bound together in the game production pipeline, introduce operational limits that link those correspondences (between computation and cognition, as part of the industrial labors and efficiencies of game development). For developers, game engines present a necessary mechanical order, but they also facilitate rapid development and cross-platform deployment. Game engines make the process of development more economical. This presents a trade-off between order and possibility that organizes the field of play and establishes the player's relative freedom. The writing of an engine requires that larger development teams work through the idiosyncratic approaches (to writing code) of individual programmers to arrive at a common codebase. The proprietary game engine is illusive; beyond the editor environment, it is pure code (though some engine editors feature integrated visual scripting tools to foster collaboration between artists, designers and programmers). The engine provides the syntax to allow the insertion of an infinite variety of assets that may perform in the same way. The engine controls the soft and hard physics, determines the relative utility of exploration, and emits the signals of agency. The engine determines the relative impact (and realness) of our (avatar's) presence in the world we inhabit, and the general push in engine development, asset creation and game mechanics is toward realism in effect and affect. The engine produces the relative openness of the game universe.

Game demos and trailers may reveal or conceal the mechanics of the engine itself—celebrating the attributes of interaction and occasionally showcasing machine-based physics, or illustrating the narrative impulse or the signposts of agency. The core technologies of the engine drive embodiment; they are the locus where static and dynamic elements are defined and world chunks are delimited. By knowing the codebase of the engine, we come closer to understanding the relative mutability and stasis associated with software, and we are pushed to reconsider traditional studies of new media that treat internal data structures as static formalizations of attributes that can simply be read (Mackenzie, 2006).

As they are software "objects," video game engines may be considered within the purview of software studies—an interdisciplinary field that has emerged since around 2006 (with the gathering of the Software Studies Workshop in Rotterdam) as a creative and critical approach to the theories and practices of computing—to understand the core yet underexamined role of software in both culture and society. Software can shape subjectivity, social agency, politics and aesthetics; and it is produced, activated, theorized and reinscribed by computer scientists, engineers, hackers, consumers, artists, technologists, philosophers, entrepreneurs and industrialists. The limits of participatory culture, where tech-savvy consumers are also empowered producers, are tethered to the relative openness of coded architectures; as software applications become more complex, their scripts become more specialized and inevitably de-democratized.

Software studies has continued to gain traction within educational circles as core curricula have opened up to include information and computational literacy (and liberal arts fields have expanded to embrace the digital humanities), and beyond the academy as the labor market has revived skills-based initiatives in high-tech fields including software programming, mobile application development, data analysis and user experience design. These two impulses have foregrounded to varying degrees the material layer of software as a matter of language and engineering, and its ideological layer as an instrumental part of social formations.

Software is at the center of the global economy, culture, social life and, increasingly, politics; it lies at the heart of various institutional operations that need control mechanisms, data management and assessment tools, from social service agencies to hospitals to universities to scientific research labs, corporate retailers, and municipalities (which deploy a number of digital tools for mapping, data visualization, data-informed decision-making and large-scale infrastructure projects). Software undergirds contemporary systems of representation, communication, organization and interaction; software is the substrate and context of media. Every software program has distinct architectures of coding, scripting and programming that govern basic linguistic processes, the specificity of contextual actions, and the implications of device control. We may understand the impact of software on material culture (software is not simply a metaphor), but what methodology do we use to scrutinize the immaterial layer of code?

Game engines have become integral to our information economy, and are central agents in a number of often interrelated media and media-dependent development pipelines. They are a part of broader industrial arrangements that depend on the organizing power of code, though they are most often directly associated with video games. Game engines are central to the production of meaning in games and other engine-driven experiences and software-driven objects; and as such, one of my goals is to introduce the design process as a rich textual field that can work comfortably alongside more traditional textual analysis. By introducing process, my hope is to close one of the gaps that exists in critical game studies—the separation of production from analysis—and to bridge the divide between the equally important work of game producers and theorists. To do so, I am drawing attention to a pipeline model and interrogating creative labor at multiple points in the development cycle, as a way to see the evolving ideological imperatives and complexities of code—to understand code as a process. By introducing design as a process into game studies, we can more properly locate the relevant discursive tensions that emerge as game developers negotiate a number of distinct and demanding cycles—publishing cycles, cycles of hardware and software development and versioning, the cyclical nature of studio labor and studio organization and ownership, as well as the evolution of culture (and screen culture) at large. Game engines act as an industrial shorthand, and they speed up the build, iteration and release of interactive properties. Game engines are built from a logical framework that guarantees consistency, continuity and communicative certainty, and their value has allowed them to colonize a wide range of industrial economies. By studying the design process, I hope to shed light on the underlying mechanics of these emerging culture industries, and to contribute to the procedural literacies of media theorists, designers and consumers looking to more forcefully work in, play in or simply navigate this terrain. Illustrating how game engines interact with assets is easier than demonstrating the interaction between game engines and the broader field of play. The former is revealed in the editor—in the visual scripting tools used by game artists. The latter, however, requires a more nuanced understanding of the relationship between code, programmer, tool, artist, intellectual property and audience (even in the case of open source engines that alter this transactional pipeline, allowing the engine to operate more freely as a content creation platform) to signal what Henry Lowood (2014) refers to as "the messy interplay of intentions, users and the marketplace" (196).

What is to be gained from studying game engines and, more generally, software? If the goal is to understand the ideological trappings of new technologies, and our operational horizons as citizen-consumers, we must understand the architectures and pipelines of hardware and software development. To do so, we must be equipped with the requisite technological literacies, and must know how to position our readings of software within a meaningful critical frame—one that is reflexive and not merely procedural, mechanistic or pseudo-scientific, and one that may not follow the familiar outlines of media studies.

This book pulls together histories of technology and the associated fundamentals of computer science and machine-based learning, related scientific studies and their literatures, as well as a broad range of artifacts that punctuate the landscape of applied material innovation and the application of software to a number of participatory learning and design models (situating game engine environments in a number of discrete industrial and municipal sectors, including education and civic life). I weave together these primary and secondary materials across a number of game engine case studies to illustrate the complex relays between science, technology, industry, information, media, culture and community, and to highlight several key pressure points between personal and collective agency and industrial design. Why study game engines? They are abstract core technologies with cross-industrial applications far beyond the operational directives of gameplay. With its focus on game engines, and through a series of case studies of individual engines and their applications, this manuscript unpacks this circuit of relations and furthers the important task of turning a critical eye toward examining the ideology of software. It is within this context that I consider the more dominant commercial engines, alternatives to these engines, and the more expansive field of non-game engines that drive other culture industries.

Code is the new horizon for media studies. We are living in a machine-readable world that can be acted on by software independent of human control. The power of code is significant. Turning our attention away from information and communication technologies and their associated artifacts as things to be read, or perhaps simply looking more deeply, software studies allows us to consider the role of code in setting transactional limits, to scrutinize the understated organizational power of code, and to expose code as a constant in a changing formula of experienced social relations. This manuscript uses the video game engine as a pathway for media studies scholars and practitioners to navigate the broad terrain of software practice, and is intended to encourage both communities to mind the gap between content production and game production (linking visual culture to its mechanics or infrastructure). Through a series of case studies this manuscript lays out a methodology for reading "immaterial" objects, as part of a broader lesson about connecting algorithms to material outcomes. There are lingering gaps in game production research—gaps that are not always solved by bringing an academic lens to communities of practice. One of the foundational questions guiding my research is to understand exactly how to properly situate game tools, a difficulty matched by the complex nature of the game production community—an uncertain descriptor with unsettled contours.

Software studies does not simply map the techniques of critical media studies on to software objects; it calls for us to consider the transformative nature of digital technologies (and not simply digital media) across visual and aural culture; software studies cuts across radio, film, television, video games, mobiles, and other media forms and environments. Software studies situates digital technologies in their cultural contexts as part of broader emerging media and information ecosystems, examines specific artifacts of code and their operations (a strand of inquiry often referred to as critical code studies), elevates the industrial labors of programmers and the machinations of programming languages, and outlines the contours of the technological imagination. Software studies can be focused on code, language, network, environment, interface or design (while the study of computing systems—a series of unique relations between hardware and software—is commonly considered platform studies).

Software studies consistently links the technical considerations of software to economic, political, cultural and ideological concerns, and connects software as object, material and medium to software practice. Platform studies shifts our attention to the materiality of media technologies, though it works with many of the same theories and methodologies as software studies, and considers the underlying "possibilities" of code. In their inaugural contribution to the MIT Press "Platform Studies" book series, Nick Montfort and Ian Bogost (2009) read across hardware and software, situating the Atari Video Computer System in its cultural contexts. The texts in the series follow this focus on hardware systems (and several attend to other game systems, including the Super Nintendo Entertainment System and the Nintendo Wii) in order to reveal the technical, cultural and artistic affordances of each successive software environment. Yet, as Aubrey Anable (2018) notes, by creating a concise history of technology, these successive studies offer little insight into the complex relationships between bodies and technologies; perhaps as an unseen consequence of technical rigor, the formalism of platform studies almost always erases matters of difference. Anable suggests, "Imagining media platforms as sealed 'black boxes' reinforces a similar scaling off of subjectivity, agency, race, and sexuality" (137).

Software studies confronts the tension between our understanding of computers as technologies of visibility (of seeing, connecting and acting across a network or within a rich field of possibility—our experience of living in an Internet of Things where any device can be connected and seamless data flow can be used to build smart cities) and the opaqueness of their internal operations. The tension is invoked yet underexamined in a culture affected so broadly by computerization, and so fluidly connected. Wendy Chun (2004) notes that computers have created a paradoxical commitment to visuality and transparency. We evidence the former in the sheer volume of digital images, assets and code objects that are shared across networks. The latter quality, transparency, is the net effect of the combined work of database systems (where consumers are "known" by Google, Facebook, Amazon, their cable companies, and other agencies in the business of commercial surveillance and consumer desire), artificial intelligence and interface design to produce unobstructed transactional engagements, effortlessly linking inputs and outputs without calling attention to the language of software. The task at hand is to situate a certain form of textual analysis—one that traverses both visual and non-visual artifacts—within this uneven terrain. To study software is to understand any interface as a mediating environment that cannot be untethered from the more obviously critically inflected signposts of content or the subtler trails of core technologies that transform space, place and time into data points; an interface stands between these foreground and background layers of narrativity and the engine. We may understand this, as Alexander Galloway (2012, 72) points out, as a "layer model" with mathematical logic at its core; Galloway suggests that this model unlocks our ability to see software as a symbolic system that operates across several distinct yet necessarily integrated registers, and in this case complicates (or necessarily contextualizes) the operational imperatives of the engine's source code, which needs to communicate across discrete machine layers that bind engine software to middleware within a particular operating system, bound to particular and dynamic representational objects, and for a particular interface environment with a particular form of device control. To read engine software also necessitates comprehending the limits of studying its object status, as "software is both scriptural and executable" (Galloway, 2012, 73). Writing the engine is distinct from running the engine—the source code exists prior to its execution, though it is written with a view toward its future executable state, and under the conditions that a developer/programmer must consider the user experience. One often overlooked complication in software studies is the matter of how we read code. Reading code (and understanding the why and the what in deciphering scripted intent) is more difficult than writing code; most programmers know this, and it explains why in many build environments a programmer may choose to write entirely new functions rather than try to make sense of and rework legacy code. This study of engines can perhaps simplify the analytical problem—that code is a symbolic system (in its purest sense), and that reading code for ideology can be a flawed process of translation that requires narrativizing its machinic imperatives while erasing the conditions of its labor. The cultural power of code is often arrived at only in those moments when its use runs counter to the stable and predetermined mandates of its execution (Galloway, 2012, 71); this power is illustrated most readily by game designer Anna Anthropy (2012) in her writing and work that stridently challenges and expands the field of video game design, and transgresses the industrially-sanctioned limits of the form. Hacking and modifying games requires exposing the code, understanding an engine's properties (3D architecture, mechanics, physics, sound, camera system and so on), and changing the rules (by rewriting the code or by using a level editor). Yet, as these software exploits highlight the functional nature of the engine, they do not belie that functionality; the goal is, after all, to keep things executable, and to build a playable experience. Independent games, when they take advantage of existing infrastructures to create new stories, do not run counter to the mandates of machine logic, but do require a keen understanding of the basic functionality of code and its representational limits.

Knowing what code does, what it executes, is not knowing what code means. Mark Sample (2013) draws a distinction between the procedural and evocative powers of code, separating the performative dimensions of code (its functional logic) from the traces of its historical context (its personal or institutional signature—its idiosyncrasies). The game engine is a coded software architecture as well as a meaningful system filled with "extra-functional significance" (Marino, 2006).

By studying the engine as infrastructure, we can see code at a particular moment when it has coalesced and attached to a singular narrative impulse, even as we understand that the engine as communication is always transactional, carrying operations, relaying interactions, and connecting and transforming inputs and outputs. The engine, as an artifact, can illuminate the act of machine writing, and is a point of convergence between functional imperatives and expressive tendencies. The engine is, perhaps, the point of convergence between layers.

The field of video game studies has expanded into deeper studies of the coded mechanics of play; but even as it has expanded to consider platform and software (as distinct points of production and analysis), it has not fully attended to the discursive tensions of game development. This study is designed to encourage broader intellectual and creative consideration of the role of game engines in an industry commonly read as a series of fixed assets (playable intellectual properties); and my attention to labor and the design process is an attempt to call into question the stability of game engine architectures, and by extension, digital platforms. Despite corporate pronouncements of orderly technical progress, most game makers experience development environments and platforms as fundamentally messy affairs—as points of friction that push against individual agency.

This book is not a history of games, nor is it focused on players and designers. But it is focused on certain critical questions related to change that inherently bind together designers and players, and provide some insight on the evolution of the industry. The goal is to establish connection points between game studies and other fields of inquiry—including media, cultural and technology studies. The project at hand may have its strongest affinities with the materialist analysis undertaken by Paul Dourish (2017) in his seminal text, *The Stuff of Bits*, for such an approach "opens up a new space for examining social and cultural life in a world of technical objects, a space in which we can (indeed, must) recognize the intractable configurations of those objects outside social processes of design, interpretation, distribution, and appropriation" (Dourish, 57). Within this framework, the game engine has a unique valence, its affordances have influence; as I have already privileged convergence as a functionally reductive term (one that suggests a successful synthesis—of intersecting media, of media and computation, and of computational structures), let me balance that perspective by calling out a more situational notion of convergence (convergence as a functionally expansive term), as the game engine is a site where historical, social and political concerns and determinants are brought into temporary alignment (Dourish, 2017, 57) in the service of seamless machinic discourse. The execution power of the engine is a product of cultural confluence. Despite my claim that the engine may be considered a site of convergence, the work of critical media studies runs counter to this impulse to understand things synthetically; critical analysis requires that we unravel the complex relays held within the materialities of information and consider the relationship between human practice (in part, the work of the developer/programmer), digital materials (the language of computation, as well as software and hardware bodies), and representations (video games and video game objects). These relationships continue to evolve, and the versioning and re-engineering of game engines is one signpost of that evolution.

I began my study of game engines in 2007 with the Xbox 360 release of *The Orange Box*, a video game compilation containing five distinct games developed by Valve Corporation and drawing on a common software framework that governs each of these first-person single-player and multiplayer experiences. All of the games in the set run on Valve's proprietary Source engine, which debuted in 2004 with the release of *Counter-Strike: Source*. Valve's Source engine is the successor to the company's GoldSource engine, released in 1998 and constructed as a heavily modified version of the Quake engine (released by id Software in 1996 and subsequently licensed to Valve) with a number of engine subsystems, including artificial intelligence (AI), written from the ground up by Valve programmers. As with many engines, Source was built as a deliberate evolution, a branch, from an existing codebase, as that code was forked to work toward new technical specifications and features without abandoning the older engine altogether. Most contemporary engines are built to evolve incrementally to keep pace with shifts in hardware and associated technologies, and individual subsystems can be updated independently without "breaking" the engine (though versioning occasionally pushes the limits of and undoes backward compatibility). The Source engine has multiple branches, most of which are attached to new supports and features, some dictated by changes to system processors, operating systems and other external determinants, and others by internal choices attached to new forms of gameplay associated with specific game releases; for example, the Left 4 Dead branch of the Source engine was released in 2008 with the game of the same name, and introduced several new development features, including changes to AI, scripting, and shader and effect details (to match the performance of a broader range of graphics cards and central processors).

Back in 2007 my study was more of an observation leading to a series of mental notes that guided my game choices as I scoured game retailers for other Valve titles. Getting into the thick of each branch of the Source engine was taking me down too many paths; as I attempted to map the structural changes in the engine, I began to lose the more holistic view of gameplay. As a media scholar, I remain interested in looking not just at code, but also at a game's design gestalt. One of the features of the Left 4 Dead engine branch is "swaying trees" (a property that is attached to the $treeSway command), a material parameter that produces the modest effect of trees swaying in the wind—more precisely, the script morphs a material by responding to the parameters of an environmental wind entity (acceptable parameters are detailed in Figure 1.1 the online Valve Developer Community).

Yet to view the effect in isolation was to lose sight of my experience of playing the game—isolating and analyzing the imprint of code as a visual effect seemed to be a limited rhetorical gesture, harkening back to my work as a film scholar engaged in close textual analysis. To focus on one visual effect was to drop too many other critical threads—to drill down to the unit model was to obscure other foundational considerations, the industrial labors of game design, and the

```
$treeSway                          "0" "1" or "2"
//Changes the treesway effect. 0 is no sway, 1 is classic tree sway, 2 is an alternate, radial tree sway effect.
//Tree sway mode 2: Hacks to use tree sway code on rectangular sheets of plastic/tarp attached at the four corners.
//Inverts the sway scale radius to be 1 at (0,0,0) in model space and fall off radially towards the edges of the
model.
//The model is expected to be built lying in the X Y plane in model space, with its center at the origin.

$treeSwayHeight                    <float>    //The height in which the effect is applied. Default 1000.
$treeSwayStartHeight               <float>    //The height from the origin in which the effect starts blending in.
Default 0.2.
$treeSwayRadius                    <float>    //The radius from the origin in which the effect is applied. Default
300.
$treeSwayStartRadius               <float>    //The radius from the origin in which the effect starts blending in.
Default 0.1.
$treeSwaySpeed                     <float>    //The speed multiplier of large movement such as the trunk. Default 1.
$treeSwayStrength                  <float>    //The distance multiplier of large movement such as the trunk. Default
10.
$treeSwayScrumbleSpeed             <float>    //The falloff of the effect on small movement such as the trunk. Higher
means a more stable center. Default 0.1.

$treeSwayScrumbleStrength          <float>    //The speed multiplier of the small movement such as the leaves. Default
0.1.
$treeSwayScrumbleFrequency         <float>    //The distance multiplier of the small movement such as the leaves.
Default 0.1.
$treeSwayFalloffExp                <float>    //The frequency of the rippling of a sine wave in small movement such as
the leaves. Default 1.5.
$treeSwayScrumbleFalloffExp        <float>    //The falloff of the effect on small movement such as the leaves. Higher
means a more stable center. Default 1.

$treeSwaySpeedHighWindMultiplier   <float>    //Speed multiplier when env_wind triggers a gust. Default 2.
$treeSwaySpeedLerpStart            <float>    //Minimum wind speed in which a gust triggered by env_wind will start
affecting the material. Default 3.
$treeSwaySpeedLerpEnd              <float>    //Minimum wind speed in which a gust triggered by env_wind will fully
affect the material. Default 6.
$treeSwayStatic                    <bool>     //Whether or not to instead use a static wind value instead of the
values from env_wind. TF2 and GMOD (as of April 2019) only.
```

FIGURE 1.1 $treeSway parameters.
Copyright 2017 Valve Developer Community.

more generalized persistence of code across cultural objects. Getting lost in these parameters was to not see the forest for the (swaying) trees. Nonetheless, my experience with the Source engine in *Portal* and *Half-Life 2*, two titles included in *The Orange Box*, had unlocked a certain pleasure that I associated with the mechanics (more precisely, the physics) of both games—mechanics that include the impact of bodies on the game world and its environments, and the interaction of distinct material assets (all of which are governed by underlying parameters). As a game, *Portal* is primarily a process of learning about a core gameplay mechanic; the level design is structured around implementing that mechanic to solve increasingly complex environmental puzzles (Roberts, 2017), while setting (the Aperture Science Enrichment Center) and characters (the player–character protagonist, Chell, and her rival the AI system known as GLaDOS) are signified but minimized (though they are humorously developed over the course of the game's primary two installments). The primary challenge in *Portal* is developing an understanding of the game's physics—building kinetic energy through the creative use of portals to maneuver through the game's many test chambers. This playable effect is determined at the level of Source's built-in 3D physics simulation engine, referred to as VPhysics. More precisely, VPhysics is an engine library that controls the motion of in-game entities. And, delving more deeply, the objects simulated by VPhysics fall into two categories—rigid bodies (whose parts maintain their relative positions—these objects cannot deform or change shape) and deformable bodies (bodies that are subject to distortion—they are malleable and breakable). Without getting lost in the codebase, it should suffice to say that the pleasure of *Portal* is about observing the differences between these bodies. To some degree, as the game's central conceit is moving (or more properly, propelling) the body through space, *Portal* functions as a body genre because of its codebase. Certain bodies are destroyed, while others carry on.

The pleasure I experienced playing through *Portal*, a game that is sharply focused (and within certain levels, literally laser-focused) on the algorithmic possibilities of unique bodies, was complicated by my affinity for more traditionally-defined body genres that situate the body as both subject and object—notably science fiction and horror. In science fiction and (survival) horror video games, the affective dimensions of gameplay (and visuality) are just as important as scripted material effects. With this duality in mind, I turned my attention to titles by other developers to more properly map the relationships between game affect and effect, to more fully consider the limiting conditions of the game engine. This led me to *Dead Rising*, an open world survival horror game developed by Capcom and released in 2006; for the *Dead Rising* franchise, Capcom integrated the Havok physics engine with the developer's own engine (the newly built MT Framework). In *Dead Rising*, the Havok physics API produces realistic interactions between in-game entities to humorous effect, as players can choose from any number of environmental weapons (for melee and ranged combat) scattered around the game's main setting, the Willamette Parkview Mall. Following suit, after completing *Dead Rising*, I searched for other titles made with or featuring the Havok physics engine. Once again, I associated the engine with a certain pleasure that seemed to be aligned most intimately with the in-game physics and play mechanics, and the absurd spectacle of everyday objects impacting material bodies—behaviors carried across the *Dead Rising* franchise.

My approach to game engines pulls together what Rob Kitchin and Martin Dodge outline as distinct instances of code; in *Code/Space*, Kitchin and Dodge (2011) differentiate between coded objects, coded infrastructures, coded processes and coded assemblages (6–7), moving from the particular and isolated software-dependent object to those phenomena, environments and systems where multiple coded elements converge and are interdependent. I am invested in studying particular instances of engine-based mechanics, but my goal is to situate these instances in broader and richer textual and cultural fields, to build a more nuanced understanding of the operational and ideological imperatives of game engines. Game engines exceed absolute categorization; they exceed the boundaries of their object status (though engine development is a process with identified versioning points that suggest various moments of closure, of boundedness, however temporary). Game engines operate as a continuum across multiple textual fields, as they execute functions and animate proximal assets. This complexity, this messiness, requires that we look beyond the utilitarian nature of software, and consider computation as something more than a system of controls, and of real-world modeling. To study software, and in this case, the game engine as an enunciative agent, we must bring other approaches to bear on the matter of computer science. Andrew Goffey (2014) notes that "those aspects of software that are marginal in the formal-logical, epistemological views of computing science take on a major importance when considered in other fields of knowledge and other kinds of practice" (35). The structurally significant aspects of software can be called out by changing our perspective; we must hold on to the functional starting point, the context of discrete programming practices, and the termination point (or more properly, the other end of the feedback loop) located at the moment of play. But we must understand each of these points as a powerful moment of enunciation, driven by the complex interplay of industrial, technical, economic, social, political, cultural and historical forces. In short, a techno-scientific view of the game engine cannot adequately capture the pleasure of play (Goffey, 2014, 38). My personal attachment to specific engines, the choices that independent game developers make when adopting (or building) an engine, and even the industrial labors of more dominant game engine developers, are driven by the evolving contours of pleasure and desire—the desire to experience, to know, to transform. I firmly believe that by studying the game engine and its imprint, we can advance those critical concerns that are often wrongly dismissed as playful distractions.

Game engines are multifaceted tools with a broad reach across multiple industrial and municipal sectors; they are being used by a wide array of industries and agencies to educate, train and shape human perception of the world around the contours of play. Game engines matter; understanding precisely what they are doing is the task at hand. By examining how video game engines (efficient reusable development platforms) are used across a broad range of industrial vectors, and laying out a clear methodology for studying the game development pipeline, the central goal of this book is to help media scholars and practitioners to understand the instrumentality of code in relation to personal and collective agency, while foregrounding the cultural value of computational literacy. Through a series of case studies, this book highlights the connections between algorithms and material outcomes; my goal is to provide a productive entry point for those unfamiliar with the mechanics of code. There is a scarcity of critical literature on game engine architecture, though there are studies of engine subsystems (such as artificial intelligence) and technical treatments of engine design and build—practical approaches to writing or modifying software. Moreover, games engines are a combination of software components, of interdependent and quite specific subsystems, some of which are common, while others are unique to specific engines (and types of games); and as game engine analysis is a critical consideration of code, we must tease apart engine code from game code. There is no single architecture that binds together all game engines, though there are common imperatives, common logics that drive gameplay. This point will become clearer in my discussion of small-scale engines built by independent developers, designed to solve particular problems or satisfy unique game conditions. Custom engines, built by individual developers for a single studio's games, are commonly designed with custom tools that meet specific uses, realize unique functionalities and satisfy a particular set of technical demands; they may be tailored for a specific experience, or a form of interaction that supports a specific mode of storytelling, world building or play. Governed by these localized considerations, custom engines may lack the tools and documentation that make large-scale engines more versatile and accessible. In-house engines allow developers to build only the tools they need, and they establish a regional dialect of sorts—an interface, a coding model that is understood by a local community (of programmers, developers and artists). There a large number of currently active game engines, and these range in their complexity and accessibility. This book is by no means a *catalogue raisonné* of engines and developers; rather, through a series of case studies, my goal is to highlight the pervasive instrumentality of game engines and the more common conventions that make them extendable, adaptable and reusable. Game engines are part of rapidly evolving game-based and non-game-based ecosystems; and tracking changes in the field is a monumental task. Valve, for example, is not simply a game developer. In 2003, the company launched Steam, a digital storefront that has evolved into a digital distribution platform that holds a significant share of the PC gaming market. Steam acts as a community, a publisher and a developer (offering Steamworks, a suite of game-related tools and services). In 2015, Valve attempted to capture a share of the home console market with an integrated collection of Steam hardware devices. And in 2016, the company launched SteamVR, a platform for VR (virtual reality) content creation and distribution. Software and hardware technologies are tightly interwoven, and it would be short-sighted to isolate the code-intensive dependencies of engine-based development from the media industries that envelop it and give it meaning.

My first book (on public and private photographic practices) borrowed the concept of transience to capture the fleeting and migratory nature of personal images, while this book borrows the concept of persistence to capture the durable yet malleable nature of code. Persistence has a more precise meaning in the field of computer science. In game-based operations, runtime objects are inherently transient; they are created during program execution only to vanish as the field of play evolves (an object is an instance of a class, one example of a formal structure drawn from a larger blueprint). However, the data and the data architecture of game-based operations must demonstrate persistence (together, the data and the data model define objects, their values and behaviors); game data must be accessed continuously during gameplay and remain intact even after the program is terminated. I draw out this distinction between transience and persistence, as my attention in this book is focused on the latter—on those persistent architectures that have established patterns of migration. While the objects may change and the field of play may shift, the data model, the game engine architecture is a constant that can be interrogated. I am not discarding the matter of representation but simply taking a different path as I consider the persistence of code in a culture that may be defined in part by its (game) engines. Game engines negotiate inputs and outputs; they are structured (by a programming language) and they provide structure. Game engines organize data, arrange the visual field, and shape interaction; and they follow an underlying logic. Game engines are efficient and economical, and they have generated new industrial arrangements, bridged existing media forms and shaped new patterns of information flow. Game engines are rapidly becoming a privileged architecture for non-game experiences, and it is critical that we understand their influence on everyday perception and knowledge. Engine-driven worldbuilding is no longer simply the provenance of gameplay and development, and the matter at hand is to provide a critical counterpoint to the far-reaching transformations of game engine mechanics.

2

THE MECHANICS OF PLAY: SITUATING GAME DEVELOPMENT

Video game engines are part of design, build and deploy ecosystems. Engines are localized software "objects," yet part of broader emerging media and information environments. Engines, though largely invisible, have pervaded our culture; they are implicated in sociocultural relations and inherently positioned as protocols for control—the driving force of play, a signpost of the increasing colonization of play by the culture industry, and a necessary mechanism for the production of simulated machine-readable culture. Game engines are at the center of data-driven environments and engagements, which are now a dominant frame for seeing, understanding and interacting with artifacts, events, social and political processes, history and culture. Engines establish the relationships between (data) points, and they create hierarchies; engines depend on overdetermined distinctions between classes or entities, and they control how these elements transform and interact. As simulation agents, and as the architecture for data visualization in the broadest sense, engines drive how we see the world and they guide our projections of its future. We should not underestimate the use value of the core technologies of the video game industry. I state this with some reservation, and some reflection on precedents, given that both media and cultural studies have established histories of developing new reading strategies, for setting consecutive field-specific principles as privileged sites of meaning.

Game engines depend on two opposing forces—uncertainty and knowledge production. At the discretion of their design principles, classification systems and algorithms (as relational databases), they invite open-ended decision making but deliver a fixed set of outcomes. To this end, their form may be unique, but their nature is not. While they should be understood for their technological specificity, they should also be understood more generally as analogous to other structuring practices and tools.

Game engines have influence beyond any localized field of play. Games are major sites of corporate exploitation (Dyer-Witheford, 2009) and part of the flow of global capital. They are a lynchpin in the military-entertainment-educational complex (Huntemann and Payne, 2010). And their engines are often found at the center of cultural exchange as part of larger software ecosystems. While freedom and control are commonly read through the lens of familiar narrative game tropes (character, environment, plot, story and interaction), they are more pointedly attached to the imperatives of software mechanics, well beyond the (explicit) field of play; that is to suggest that engines are making an impact well beyond traditional game space.

As an entry point to studying the role (and coded rules) of play in everyday life, this chapter interrogates the dual investments of multimedia companies in the building of serialized intellectual properties and the engines that govern them. These two interlocked pursuits govern the broader landscape of transmedia storytelling. By situating engines in the game development pipeline (and within game history) and in the broader production pipelines of diverse play-centric industries, this chapter positions video game engines as a distinct corrective in contemporary media studies, connecting studies of code to studies of visual culture, political economy and the broader field of play. This chapter examines the function and transactional limits of video game engines, and frames engines as both software and metaphor—as historically situated commodities that can undo historical agency. Its goal is to set up later case studies in this volume that focus on how, specifically, game engines are being deployed in non-game industries, and as an aspect of convergent media practices, both to build assets and to run those assets.

Several of the major 3D authoring tools, including Unity and Unreal, and their respective parent companies, have had a significant impact on contemporary visual and consumer culture. The most prolific game studios produce their own core engines, even as these engines must engage in a complex relay with the software development kits of other companies, to streamline the development process and the flow through centralized distribution pathways (online and as part of mobile and console systems). And independent game developers in search of players must navigate the available distribution channels and choose from existing engines (or labor to design their own), each with its own properties, advantages and limitations. As well, other media and information industries are increasingly dependent on engine-based operations to drive their distinct modes of production, distribution and exhibition. The coded rules of engagement (the script that drives the interface, forging the computational rules that shape the consumer's physical and mental attachments in the context of reception), form a fundamental part of the industrial processes of development and fabrication in a broad array of industries; each codebase, though invisible and ephemeral is no less important than the physical machinery that encases the processor, runs the game engine and frames the interface. As we make code visible, we also make visible the people who write it, and we begin to situate their labors, precarious as they may be, as a valued part of the (game) culture industry.

This chapter provides a history and a critical context for game engines and surveys the software architectures of several major international game engine developers, including id Software, Epic Games and Unity Technologies. Several of these engines (as well as a number of others) will be considered in more detail in later chapters. This chapter is not a technical history of engine development; instead, the focus is the development and deployment of these engines and their use values within circumscribed historical, technological, industrial and cultural contexts, as well as their alignment with the purposeful acquisition of middleware tools by multinational technology companies looking to expand their footprints and build self-sustaining ecosystems. This is also not an exhaustive inventory of available and retired engines. In *Game Engine Architecture*, Jason Gregory (2009) provides both a robust historical overview of the development of video game engines as well as a deep dive into their mechanics. While my review is intended to bridge theory and practice, it is not intended as a detailed manual of game programming, and it may frustrate software engineers. My intent is to examine the pressure points between game engine software and the more obvious signposts of the work of critical media studies—where surface and substrate become meaningful, where programming shows its influence. Through a series of case studies on the use of each engine (in video game production or as a codebase for other culture industries), this chapter highlights the particular normative influence of each parent company and situates each engine as a by-product (and asset) of broader speculative business goals and deeply entrenched corporate philosophies.

Writing and Reading History

Game engine history could be read as a series of object lessons that slowly reveal the call and response of programming languages and computing technologies. Game engine history could also be read through the lens of authorship, as a series of signature systems written by individual programmers or realized through collaborative development teams either within or adjacent to the studio system. Game engine history, uniquely, might also be reverse engineered; it could be understood as a series of solutions to localized technical or aesthetic problems realized during the ideation or production of a particular game title. The most reductive histories of game engines situate these properties (and their associated codebases) as distinct developmental points along one longitudinal narrative that suggests game engine development chases realism through ever-more-precise simulation and the associated aesthetics and tactics of immersion. Several of these approaches find their parallels in media studies—in theories and methods wrapped around other media objects (film, television, and so forth).

To study game engines in relationship to game history is to expand the concept of media literacy as it pertains to game culture. Media literacy is grounded on meaning making and the cultural contexts of media consumption (educated consumption), and quite often engages with understanding the tools of the trade (educated production); this is truest in those instances where it looks to transform educated consumers into empowered, critically attuned content producers. To situate game literacy within the broader field of media literacy, it only makes sense to consider the context of production and consumption. Game engines are a critical part of that knowledge framework. Rather than construct a linear history of game engine development, and in an effort to move digital media literacy forward, this chapter is organized around a number of mechanical principles. Its goal is to sketch out a potential ontology, however limited, and thus to cover some of the fundamental pursuits that seem to govern the build, iteration and succession of engines. It is of course somewhat counterintuitive to adopt an ontological approach to game engines. Game-based technologies are integral to machine learning—to systems that are designed to change. As the context for engine-based work evolves, so do the systems associated with that work. For all of these reasons, system ontologies must be flexible. Nonetheless, this history foregrounds several general qualities that seem intrinsic to game engine design and development: modularity, efficiency, adaptability, expandability and reusability. These are not technical terms *per se*; they do not refer to the fundamental components of game engine architecture. Rather, they refer to the guiding principles of well-designed engines that, as a result, have a longer shelf life. Game programming design and organization is remarkably complex, and there are a number of distinct approaches to data-oriented design (the two most notable software architectures are object-oriented programming and entity-component systems). The large number of variations on game engine architecture make it difficult to build a comprehensive technical history; for this reason, the history outlined here is focused on the most common tendencies that inform the code writing process.

Traditional engine-based histories of video gaming locate *DOOM* (1993) as an origin point, reading the game franchise and this first installment in the series not only in terms of its position in moving two genres (horror, the first-person shooter) forward, but also in terms of the game's graphic capabilities which are the product of its underlying software system, designed to maximize contemporaneous computing power. Developed at id Software, *DOOM* is the result of the collaborative work of two of the studio's founders, drawing from John Romero's design acumen and John Carmack's programming ability. The legacy of *DOOM* is perhaps most firmly established by understanding the game as a showcase for the power of engine-based game creation, and the value found in the future licensing of its core technology. A full reading of the game should consider its engine, and locate gameplay, assets and architecture within this emerging mode of engine-based production, and its contribution to the evolution of the industry. With the release of *DOOM*, and the reveal of its source code, efficient, adaptable, expandable and reusable technologies became the backbone for most game development studios. Significantly, game and code are purposefully bound together throughout subsequent industrial approaches to advancing playability and should be similarly tethered in critical histories of play (tying together structure, content and the narrative impulse). As Kurt Squire (2005) notes, "an equally important part in the story of *DOOM* is how id released level editing tools, and eventually the game's source code, making it possible for consumers to create custom characters, levels, games, and in-game movies (machinima)" (10). The game was released in 1993, with the source code of its engine available to the public four years later (for not-for-profit use). But even before the release of the engine source code, in fact as early as January 1993 in a public press release, id Software was celebrating the capabilities of the engine and touting the promise of an immersive open game, leading with the by-line: "Revolutionary Programming and Advanced Design Make for Great Gameplay." The January press release speaks in engine-laden terms, detailing advanced graphical features made possible by the engine: texture-mapped environments, non-orthogonal walls, light diminishing/light sourcing, environment animation and morphing, palette translation. As much attention was placed on the game's attention to realism, fetishizing the codebase, as was placed on gameplay in a fantastic interdimensional texture-mapped environment (plot by way of setting—the hellish, creature-filled landscape of the *DOOM* universe). Drawing out the overdetermined nature of the engine, *DOOM* was situated as an evolutionary step forward from its predecessor (and its engine), *Wolfenstein 3D*, released in 1992. Linking effect and affect, press materials for *DOOM* warn of the visceral and kinesthetic power of the engine, while speaking to the game community through and beyond the precise language of game design:

> Texture mapping, for those not following the game magazines, is a technique that allows the program to place fully-drawn art on the walls of a 3D maze. Combined with other techniques, texture mapping looked realistic enough in *Wolfenstein 3D* that people wrote Id complaining of motion sickness. In *DOOM*, the environment is going to look even more realistic. Please make the necessary preparations.

With the public release of its source code, and the invitation to modify and level build, *DOOM* has established its own creative ethos within distinctly identified game communities that form part of industrially sanctioned, participatory culture. The openness of this model (the literal openness of source code), and the invitation to co-creative play, is expressed to varying degrees throughout game history, although the call to community is often one with limits, some of which are explicitly drawn out in licensing agreements.

Game engine history beyond *DOOM* can be read as a laundry list of distinct intellectual properties (and several additional engines or engine variants developed by id Software for subsequent games, including *Quake*), but engine history is not so tidy and such a reading conceals the number of starts and failures, and the quieter yet still significant moments in engine design (as many independent game developers find themselves building their own engines to solve unique design challenges); however, each named engine is itself the product of a protracted development pipeline and the labors of a large number of named and unnamed programmers and developers. And while game engine history may be read in a linear fashion, in a forward movement toward a desired outcome (efficiency, graphical power, realistic effect), game history is not similarly unidirectional in its technical drive; multiple engines are always running at any one moment, and engine choice is commonly driven by the nature of the game under development. And it is shortsighted to approach engine history from a strictly techno-scientific perspective; the *DOOM* engine (commonly referred to as id Tech 1) is notable not only for pushing new graphical limits, but also for its attachment to a genre and for its role in the larger development of 3D first-person shooters. It is a showcase for next generation id technology, for the genre and mode of play, and for a new software licensing model. As Squire (2005) notes, to properly situate *DOOM*, we must read the game (as a text), understand its mode of production, and locate it within the genre; with access to its source code and to its level editor, we must also understand the game as a mutable object, an agent of participatory culture (10). This semantic relay can be used to unlock the operations of other engines. A more nuanced reading of engine history needs to consider the evolving relationship between engine developers, game developers and "produsers" (independent game developers and development communities). The elegance of an engine, found in its efficiency and the creative dynamics of its code, remains an abstraction until its framework architecture is wrapped by a conforming game layer, and while level design can provide deep insight into an engine's core mechanical principles, gameplay more generally can reveal an engine's style, as a gestalt of the mechanics of embodiment.

As we contextualize each engine, and make the infrastructure visible and meaningful, we need to avoid overdetermining the attachments of the engine; there is a certain tension in attaching a narrative to an engine, in reading the system for intentionality. Specific engines are often aligned with specific video game genres, as they are built to meet the specific technical or aesthetic demands of a story type. Traditionally, first-person shooters call for immersion, and depend on an engine to render a detailed and large hyper-realistic world that can keep pace with the player's movements; the genre also calls for specific movement types in particular environments, whether it be on-foot locomotion or a roaming vehicle (Gregory, 2009, 13). These movements are dependent on localized physics and collision detection, and rendering that is optimized for the type of environment that circumscribes the field of play. Other genres privilege other play aspects and depend on a different set of technical demands; for example, massively multiplayer online games (MMOG) depend on speedy, efficient communication across a network of servers to maintain the authoritative state of the game world and bind together the experiences of a large number of simultaneous players (Gregory, 2009, 23–24). With the marketplace for engine development and deployment becoming more centralized in the hands of a few larger developers (such as Unity Technologies and Epic Games), these generic distinctions between engines are rapidly becoming obsolete, as large-scale engine developers are invested in the overall optimization that is associated with hardware, and developing overly robust engines that can meet the demands of disparate hardware platforms and software environments (Xbox One, PlayStation 4, Nintendo Switch, Android, iOS, Windows, MacOS and so forth) and the aesthetic conceits of a broad range of gameplay experiences. In fact, many small game studios find mainstream engines such as Unreal too robust for their needs; they are too processor intensive or too memory hoarding for the efficient deployment of smaller game applications on entry-level devices, often a concern for mobile game developers. Artists at both large and small game studios understand that visual effects (and, more generally, game art) are often driven by the demands of the programmer's workflow. Speaking to this tension through the lens of *Quake* development, programmer Michael Abrash notes,

> Instead of lighting polygons as they're drawn, we light and cache the whole surface for a polygonal area ahead of time. Then when we draw the polygon, we don't have to light it. By decoupling lighting and drawing, we're not locked into the lighting that can be done while drawing a polygon. This enables more complex lighting at high speed.
>
> *(Laidlaw, 1996)*

The evolution of engine-based game development can be read as an attempt to align art and technology—as an effort to propel both speed and graphic quality, maximizing the abilities of the development team and the runtime platform.

A history of game engines needs to consider the complexities of the common concept of evolution. How precisely do game engines evolve? Do they evolve to satisfy a new purpose? Do they evolve in a manner that is unique to the engine as a subsystem? Is the video game industry the driving condition of their evolution? Is their evolution analogous to that of other media and information systems? Is their evolution tied to other tools, hardware and devices? Is their evolution tied to new forms of knowledge? Cloud-based services are changing the patterns of information flow, connecting engine-based systems imbued with machine learning to broader information networks. The drive toward mobility continues to open up new arenas and modes of play. Black box systems, such as integrated smart home technologies, are situating engines in new economies with more casual interfaces. Agile methodologies are changing the fundamental nature of collaborative software development. These are just several of the surrounding social and technological shifts that are impacting next generation game engines. The work of charting an evolutionary history of game engine technologies is complicated by the broad array of environments in which they are conceived and built (and later scaled and redeployed); for example, the context for creating and iterating commercially licensed engines is distinct from that of proprietary in-house engines, and from that of free open source engines. Moreover, what we know about these engines varies with their accessibility and the relative openness of their code.

What birthed the term "engine"? Lowood (2014) attaches the term to Carmack and Romero in the early 1990s, and the development of a shared codebase for a series of *Commander Keen* games that was referred to as the Keen engine. The engine described a single piece of software that allowed the team to produce common functionality across the *Keen* trilogy, and subsequently attempt to license the engine as a standalone product:

> But why call this piece of game software a game *engine?* Carmack and Romero were both automobile enthusiasts and, as Romero explained, the engine "is the heart of the car, this is the heart of the game; it's the thing that powers it … and it kind of feels like it's the engine and all the art and stuff is the body of the car."
>
> *(Lowood, 2014, 186)*

DOOM promised to push back the boundaries of what was thought possible on computers, organizing the components of computer games by separating the core functionalities of the game engine from the creative assets that filled the space of play (Lowood, 2014, 181). Game design and game engine development share their history with computer history (in particular, the development of the PC) and that history's convergence with media history—the purposeful reapplication of personal computing beyond traditional processing and workplace productivity, beyond labor into entertainment and leisure. Of course, Carmack and Romero did not invent the term "engine." Although their automotive analogy may be unique, the term has parallel application in similarly automated mechanical processes, such as Charles Babbage's nineteenth-century proposals for the difference engine and the programmable analytical engine.

The *DOOM* engine was not the only viable engine of its time, and id Software had built several engines prior to *DOOM*, although they were not all released to the public, nor were they all available through commercial licensing agreements. Id's earlier engines were founded on two-dimensional design principles; grid-based level design simplified each game's computational complexity. *Wolfenstein 3D* (1992) runs on a raycast engine that can quickly and efficiently render 3D perspective from a 2D map. Although the codebase of raycast technology was written to match generational hardware specifications (the personal computing marketplace of the early nineties), the engine dramatically pushed those limits: "What id Software did in 1991 was not just program a machine—they repurposed a tool built to do office work and turned it into the best gaming platform in the world" (Sanglard, 2018b, 22–23). Id's software developers were negotiating the threshold of existing computing technology; in many ways, their work followed the lead of dedicated game console developers who were working within the existing parameters of television screen technologies and at the same time interrupting a series of ideological and practiced assumptions about the medium by proposing new forms of interaction and engagement, new viewing spaces and, more broadly, new forms of (tele)visuality.

As early as 1994, Bethesda Softworks had developed a raycast engine for *The Elder Scrolls: Arena* to support the game's open world environment, which was drawn to look three-dimensional (Miller, 2010). The company followed the *Arena* raycast engine with the XnGine, a true 3D engine that was first used in *The Terminator: Future Shock* (1995). Each subsequent custom iteration of the XnGine was designed to keep pace with rapid changes in operating hardware and followed the burgeoning console market (Miller, 2010). Apart from responding to changes in the technology, many of the associated game titles simply extended the existing play attributes of earlier first-person shooters. In his review of *The Terminator: Future Shock*, critic Phil Bedard (1997) notes, "I hate to say this but it is another 3D First person perspective game a-la *Doom*, but with some things thrown in that make it different." Popular video game criticism generally draws attention to style and substance, and in particular, play mechanics and performance, and by calling out the mechanics of play (the responsiveness of the control system, technical performance issues such as slow frame rates, collision geometry bugs, poorly designed camera systems, long loading times) most critics are implicitly referencing the operational successes and failures of the game engine. "Frustration" is a common critical shorthand for enduring technical failure, calling out the negative impact of performance on playability and pleasure. Most reviews of Bethesda's *Terminator* draw from various critical registers (visual, technical, interactive, narrative) to assess the overall quality of the game. Tal Blevins' (1996) review opens with the recommendation, "Even if you have somehow avoided the hulking mass of first person shooters until now, you should consider checking out *Terminator* for its variety of play styles and its overall quality." Assessing the game's play value, Blevins goes on to summarize the game's central premise: "*Terminator: Future Shock* is a TRUE 3-D shooter that combines three types of action: walking, driving, and flying. Of course, in every scenario your main objective is to blow away hordes of mechanized horrors."

While not all reviews are equally enthusiastic about the game's mechanics and, in particular, its character controls, they are generally focused on assessing the quality of the game world and less invested in considering the game's themes and attitudes. Indeed, most first-person shooters, including *DOOM* have been critiqued for their high levels of graphic violence. The Entertainment Software Rating Board, formed in 1994, handed out its first M rating for the Sega 32X version of *DOOM*. While my intent is not to eschew a more nuanced reading of the content of these games, it is important to attach the matter of representation back to the underlying architectures of the game and its genre, and understand the aggressive visual register of the first-person shooter as, in part, connected to its codebase (the determinant of perspective, graphic effects, and the underlying geometries of bodily assault). I will expand on the matter of the representational politics of code in subsequent chapters. The fetishization of the technology found in the critical reviews I have outlined above is also a product of the industry's gender politics; it is a system dominated by male producers and reviewers, and prone to the cyclical affirmation of heteronormative masculinity.

During this same period, game developer 3D Realms had acquired the Build engine (created by Ken Silverman), which was also constructed on two-dimensional geometry (with an additional height component to simulate three dimensions). The Build engine was first used by 3D Realms for the first-person shooter *Duke Nukem 3D* (1996). In advance of the game's release, 3D Realms president George Broussard noted:

> The main advantages the Build engine has over something like Doom are that you can walk over bridges, have true rooms above rooms, swim underwater, have mirrors on the walls, have translucent objects, ride in vehicles like shuttle cars or subways, look up and down, duck, crawl, jump, fly …
>
> *(Next Generation, 1995, 100)*

From its infancy, game engine development has relied on computational geometry to solve the problem of space. And in the field of play, this has translated into reliable and responsive mapping, subject–object relations, artificial intelligence and in-game mechanics. Early engine-based history and criticism highlights these code-driven elements, not by speaking through the language of programming, but instead by using the language of visual spectacle and quotidian movements—the surface effect of game-based subsystems. In his review of upcoming Build engine game titles, Broussard notes, "It's a measure of how fast the technology of videogames is moving that even before Build is finished, it's already obsolete" (Next Generation, 1995, 102). This formative video game commentary, written from a perspective that foregrounds the technological progress of competing developers and publishers, connects content, experience and code in rather rudimentary ways; however, it does call attention to larger material considerations, situating game software in the larger industrial context of computation and computational hardware.

The birth of game engines can also be traced back to the development of independent middleware modules in the late 1980s and early 1990s that were designed specifically to handle video game graphics. Giuditta De Prato et al. (2010) suggests, "These modules represented the first generation of third party graphics engines or renderers, as until their appearance video games were built mostly as single hard-coded applications" (72). As game applications became more complex, developers built increasingly robust engines to manage a wider array of tasks, pulling together graphics, artificial intelligence, physics, audio and other game components. Contemporary game engines adhere to a component-based architecture, a design scheme that allows the iteration, substitution and reintegration of any number of specific subsystems or swappable middleware modules without disrupting the engine's core codebase. This arrangement reflects the cyclical fragmentation and reconnection of the game production pipeline. It is a landscape of both specialized middleware providers capitalizing on modular technologies that follow a small number of proprietary standards, and those developers (such as Epic Games and Unity Technologies) focused on complete cross-platform game engines and integrated production and programming environments.

The Language Gap

Engine development is dependent on computer language development, which gained traction in the 1950s, and on the convergence of media and computing machines that dates to the 1830s and that was essential to the functioning of modern mass societies (and the distribution of image, text, audio and ideology using standardized communication tools and infrastructures). Engine development is also dependent on the early 1980s home computer market that, as Marino (2014) suggests, "led to the creation of a generation of programmers who would be tantalized by the power of programming." These systems highlighted the interconnectedness of computing and creativity, and connected the once distinct domains of business, education and play. Marketing campaigns for the Commodore 64 speak to these intergenerational conceits, openly celebrate the inclusion of basic programming languages, and situate game space within computing space. Ads for the Commodore VIC-20, one of the first successful home computers and the predecessor to the C-64 ask, "Why buy just a video game?" This query framed a proposition that sold families on the multifunctionality of a personal computer, making it stand apart from dedicated cartridge-based home video game consoles like the Atari Video Computer System. The development of the home computer market opened up the programming environment and a space for more robust game development (the Commodore 64 supported multiple programming languages, from low-level machine language to high-level languages such as BASIC, Pascal and Fortran). Dedicated game consoles were notoriously difficult to program and most titles were written and designed by single programmers skilled in assembly language that could speak directly to the unique requirements of platform-specific system hardware.

But game design and engine-based mechanics also have their own history—one that is driven by an awareness of affordance and is often read as a linear pursuit that follows certain technological dependencies (faster processors, greater graphics power, larger system memory) and psychosocial attachments (to realism, to nostalgia, to other emotional work). In his pragmatic approach to writing game history, Stephen Kline (2014) recounts that the study of a game's limitations became its own site of fascination—the realization of design constraints instituted by the game's algorithm (28). The experience of game space—of the boundedness of an avatar, of possible transgressions within a built environment—are all moments at which the player confronts the algorithm and the designer: "Confronting the algorithm is meant to remind us that video games, like real cities, are designed places which are paradoxically forgiving of playful transgression even while they narrow the possibilities of consumer choice" (29).

My use of the term "affordance" as it applies to human computer interaction is closely aligned with psychologist James Gibson's (1979) model. Gibson defines affordances as "action possibilities" latent in the environment, objectively measurable and independent of an individual's ability to recognize them, but always in relation to agents and therefore dependent on their capabilities. For Gibson, the existence of an affordance is binary (it either exists or it does not). But the complication is its association with the actor's experience. An affordance is a relation between an object or an environment and an organism.

In that the concept of affordance is related to the actor's knowledge and ability, it is intimately connected to considerations of procedural literacy—at its most fundamental level, "the ability to read and write processes, to engage procedural representations and aesthetics, to understand the interplay between the culturally embedded practices of human meaning-making and technically mediated processes" (Mateas, 2005, 101–102). Rather than parsing the field of literacies to determine which reigns supreme, procedural literacy should be properly situated among multiple, complementary literacies and should inform other, often more privileged (in that they are more commonly articulated or more popularized, if only because on the surface they seem accessible, more central to popular media discourse, and therefore more forcefully democratic) literacies. In her critical analysis of the history of UNIX, Tara McPherson (2012) draws attention to the difficulty of reconciling (and synthesizing) the history of culture, gender and race, and the history of programming and computing—a rather unique yet consequential inflection of the digital divide. McPherson urges media scholars to excavate screen space and to consider the relative complicitness of code. To thus consider code in relation to culture is to avoid performing an overly reductive, formalist read of operating systems, and in the case of this analysis, game engines. On the subject of multiple literacies, McPherson notes, "We need database literacies, algorithmic literacies, computational literacies, interface literacies" (35). This requires new forms of synthetic critical work. The difficulty is tracing the specific influences of code (and unraveling the complex array of distinct algorithms) at the level of visual representation, play and cultural performance, and the specific influences of the culture industry on code, though the broad strokes of engine development, adoption and dominance are fairly obvious. On the matter of procedural literacy, Michael Mateas (2005) suggests at the very least media scholars should be able to understand "the more general tropes and structures that cut across all [programming] languages" (102), and in so doing escape the foundational problem of speaking of programmed objects as material artifacts and arrive at a more nuanced understanding of the relationship between author, code and audience, and the relational practices of code work.

A gameplay system—a system of rule-based interactions, entities, objectives and signs of progression—is both more and less than the sum of an engine, hardware, drivers, a machine-specific operating system and peripheral device controls. While a gameplay system is a function of the sum total of these components, it is experienced as a series of states, managed at the level of code, inherited from an abstract base class and handled by a game engine. States are data-driven operations that drive the animation pipeline and allow rapid iteration (Gregory, 2009), call out entity properties and functionalities (transform actions), and more generally situate gameplay, binding together characters and events. The more one examines these data-driven imperatives, the more one notices the common grammatical constructs that govern the game development landscape, a common syntax of finite options that serve to organize labor and provide the necessary communication protocols across any given gameplay system. The structured determinacy of objects is matched by the structured determinacy of their transformation, of possibility, of interaction and outcomes. This is the structuring logic of the game engine, the foundation for a series of intellectual properties that can be redeployed without major modification.

The Economics of Reusability

The normativizing imperatives of the game development pipeline foster a certain interpretive inertia, an absence of true agency, that operates across every game state and is written at the level of code; the constraints on materiality set by industry practices and corporate politics impose limits on technological affordance. The ideological implications of these standards are most evident at the level of representation (for example, in game animations). In their critique of the (artificial) limits of technological necessity, Alison Reed and Amanda Phillips (2013) turn their attention to game studio BioWare's "tight economy of animations" (135) in the *Mass Effect* series (the first *Mass Effect* game was released in 2007) to suggest that the pursuit of computational efficiency is highly racialized; the procedural and economic imperatives of syntactic exactness, of defining and recycling common states, is not simply a matter of software engineering but of radical containment, of conforming otherwise diverse digital bodies to a common vernacular.

Video game developer BioWare was founded in 1995, and the studio gained recognition for its role-playing games. Like most large studios, BioWare developed a number of in-house video game engines to serve as the technical base for their titles; some of these technologies were then licensed to other studios to develop their own games, and some came with modding toolkits that provided the fan community with entry into the modification and build process. BioWare led with the Infinity Engine (1998–2002), which was succeeded by the Aurora and Odyssey Engines (2002–2010) and the Eclipse and Lycium Engines (2009–2011). The company was acquired by Electronic Arts (EA) in 2005, and from 2013 forward all BioWare game development was based on EA's Frostbite engine as part of a general move toward a unified technology foundation across all EA development studios and properties. This changeover also aligned with BioWare's interest in moving beyond the render limits of the Eclipse Engine to support larger open world environments and build the necessary framework for multiplayer gameplay. Each engine revision in the BioWare development timeline was attached to a particular shift in technology in order to meet the demands of new technical criteria. For example, the Eclipse Engine was built to support the development of *Dragon Age: Origins* (2009), to take advantage of a shift toward multicore chip architectures that occurred early on in the development process (programmers, designers and artists had to work through the challenges of multicore development, and the Eclipse Engine supported significant iteration over the development cycle to facilitate collaboration).

Mass Effect predated BioWare's move to EA's Frostbite engine and was built with both Unreal Engine 3 and a number of in-house components. Without revealing the specifics of the BioWare codebase, Casey Hudson, the project director for *Mass Effect* notes:

> With these additional components, we're able to deliver an experience that's like being immersed in a big-budget movie, where you have freedom to develop the story however you like, regardless of whether you're fighting spectacular battles, interrogating aliens, or exploring uncharted worlds.
>
> *(Max73, 2007)*

Within this world, the game features a detailed character customization system, and the freedom of story development is intimately connected with the freedom of character development. Yet freedom has its limits, and as the game world is built on a database, character class and attributes cannot defy categorization. They must be tied to the system architecture, and, indeed, character classes are linked to discretely packaged abilities that can be unlocked through gameplay. Stated more forcefully, Reed and Phillips (2013) expose the material technology of *Mass Effect* as a rigid point of determination, highlighting "the tendency to map generic movements onto a range of different characters" (135). While a character's appearance may be relatively fluid (although gender remains binary), the procedural animation is locked to the mechanics of the engine, yet even the former is determined by a unit model, the product of a modular, component-driven subsystem. The viability of the Unreal Engine, the foundation for *Mass Effect*, is tied to its ease of use, its expandability, adaptability and reusability. As a consequence, the engine's financial forecast is linked both to the relative freedom of its architecture and the relative stability of its codebase; many large game developers work with custom versions of the engine.

In 2011, Bethesda Softworks followed the XnGine with the Creation Engine by developing a fork (building a new software package from the source code of an existing software package) of the Gamebryo engine owned by Gamebase. The history of game engines is complicated by the fluidity of code. Engines are iterative; they are constantly modified and not consistently renamed (or they are named internally, to track version history, but not publicly). In many instances, certain features of an engine are developed alongside a game to meet unique technical or aesthetic concerns, or the runtime requirements of the hardware systems that have been announced to arrive at or near the game's release date. And in some cases, the open source code of proprietary engines is shared across developers, and custom frameworks are added to legacy code (a function of a game engine's modularity), often as third-party middleware and libraries, along with hardcoded game-specific alterations to the engine's architecture to support new or enhanced gameplay features. Early previews of Bethesda's *The Elder Scrolls V: Skyrim*, released in 2011 and built on the Creation Engine, tie the new gameplay experience to new systems for lighting, foliage, precipitation and artificial intelligence (Bertz, 2011). Game developers hold onto and continually modify existing code for good reason—to hold onto their edge in the marketplace. It can take years to develop a new engine and to create a stable codebase that can react to market demands. To throw away code is to throw away years of programming work, years of collected knowledge gathered through testing and bug fixes, and years of collaborative learning.

The Limits of Adaptability

Game development is a highly risky business, with most games not recouping their development costs or failing altogether. Much of the cost of game development is incurred in the build and implementation of highly optimized but non-game specific functionality (the game engine) that is vulnerable to changes in hardware architecture (Tulip et al., 2006, 9). While the high cost of developing game engine middleware can be amortized over many games (9), the hardware cycle does not always align with the generative impulse of an engine, which is to extract the maximum performance out of any given implementation platform. Beginning in 2005, the move to multicore processing in PC and gaming platforms began to significantly impact game development and forced significant shifts in engine design. The game industry was grappling with the end of the existing processor cycle and slowly pivoting to parallel development in order to take advantage of multicore processors and chips (while continuing to realize performance gains). While the functional parsing of runtime elements had led to a fairly standard modularization of game engine functionality (the core game framework and its programming structure can be understood as distinct from resources, inputs, game logic, and rendering), these tasks were redistributed in multithread engine design (a move from serial programming to data parallelism), and this changed the development workflow, reorganizing the work of programmers, artists and designers.

The Labors of System Design

These sweeping changes in the game industry and the adaptive practices of large development studios had an impact on small team developers. While it may be an uneven comparison to consider proprietary triple-A engines in relation to the technologies used by indie game developers, in many cases large team and small team developers work with the same toolsets, and even large game studios should be understood as intimate communities of practice (collaborative enterprises that include teams of producers, artists, engineers and designers) that must negotiate the versioning of their respective engines. The Unreal Engine is a tool used by a broad range of studios, taught in many higher education game programs, and utilized by many independent developers versed in its programming language. This circuit of producers and users of a common software package "constitute a network of parties that share a common interest in its destiny" (Damsgaard and Karlsbjerg, 2010, 66). They are mutually committed to the program's refinement and success, and work to co-create its norms. The Unreal Engine Marketplace formalizes (and commodifies) this act of co-creation, as it facilitates the sharing of game-ready content and code, while official Unreal forums provide a space for developers to engage in collaborative problem solving. When Unreal made the leap to multithreaded engine design with the release of the Unreal Engine 3 (first showcased in 2004), developer Epic Games was able to guide its various communities of practice through the transition and shepherd them toward a new approach to programming.

Engine history, far from being understood as a number of technical developments or a series of graphical limits, can be read as an aesthetic pursuit, as a narrative about the nuances of programming and code, and as a conversation about design processes (the iterative work of versioning). As she begins to outline a relational approach to the study of infrastructure, Susan Leigh Star notes: "It takes some digging to unearth the dramas inherent in system design creating, to restore narrative to what appears to be dead lists" (377). It takes effort to foreground what for some are backstage elements and what for others are distinct problems to be solved. The degree to which game engines are necessarily privileged objects of active labor or analysis is always relational, dependent on the dominant paradigm or regime (of seeing, of knowing). As a proper complement to studies of science and technology (STS) that consider the relationship between scientific knowledge, technological systems and society (connecting technological innovation to other social developments, including public policy, ethics and culture), game engine history can and should be framed as part of a broader commercial narrative; as one stream in the flow of global capital, as evidence of the steady push of vertical integration within multimedia conglomerates and the hidden and often exploited labors of programmers, artists and developers; as a significant point of industrial convergence that connects media, information and technology; and, as an ongoing cultural shift toward new forms of knowledge production made possible through algorithmic manipulation. The concept of infrastructure is a useful lynchpin between media studies and science and technology studies, and for my purposes it provides a unifying axis for organizing an otherwise messy taxonomy of distinct game engine architectures. In an effort to differentiate infrastructure from other organizational practices, Star and Ruhleder (1996) suggest a relational approach to infrastructure that focuses on a number of shared qualities, including embeddedness, transparency and reach (381), and a number of transactional properties: they are "learned as part of membership," they shape and are shaped by communities of practice, they are "built on an installed base," and they evolve in "modular increments" (381–382). Game engines fit within this model for understanding infrastructure in that they are situated architectures—organized code embedded within a localized development framework (the production pipeline) and "encased" in other software products, information networks or technologies (reaching across servers, cloud-based systems and local devices). Engines are transparent in nature, not in the sense that they are visible architectures, but by virtue of their invisibility. One can look under the hood of a software system to expose the engine and examine and (in many cases) modify its code, but the beauty of the engine is that it can simply be adopted rather than invented. Engines can be used across a series of intellectual properties and across industries; they have a broad reach. In fact, their use value is found in their reach; they are designed to be reusable and redeployed until they are exhausted—a limit set by external forces, as other hardware and software systems evolve.

The practiced nature of an engine—as a common work environment within a studio or a common platform used across development communities—is a sign of the importance of membership, of communities of practice that share code and convention and traffic in common signs. And as these communities of practice respond to and refine the codebase of any given game engine (which is the particular case for open source engines), and even as development companies begin to understand the often-divergent workflows of artists and programmers, engines too evolve; they are inherently shaped by the conventions of practice. That engines are built on an installed base suggests that any inertia in game development practice is in part a product of the economics of engine build and deployment—a resistance to abandoning an engine before maximizing its value, or to pushing the limits of an engine if the hardware itself and the electronic circuity (the central and graphics processing units) have not evolved. Multicore platforms require new engine architectures—new forms of programming that shift from procedural tasks to tasks that run concurrently (parallel programming). Yet parallel programming challenges the way that programmers think, as it requires a different level of program complexity. Parallel programming is a requirement for next generation consoles (including the Xbox and PlayStation) as their source development kits are designed to split tasks between cores; code that has been separated into components that operate independently can be updated to run in parallel. However, many indie game developers lack the technical knowledge to build true parallelism. That engines evolve in modular increments is a product of their coded nature and dependent on their relative complexity; many can be rewritten line by line, or updated using a component manager, rather than abandoned altogether. Video game engines are structured as multiple interacting subsystems (physics, artificial intelligence, geometric computation, scene management, graphics, etc.), and every loop iteration initiated with each player input requires multiple component updates. These subsystems often have sequential dataflow dependencies (one task produces data for another task), interactive dependencies (tasks share data) and real-time dependencies (a time-sensitive task) (Tagliasacchi et al., 2008, 47). There are a number of computational tasks taking place within each frame.

The operational imperatives of game engines suggest they may be read as part of the disciplinary frameworks of critical code studies, and also as (operating) systems that are proximate to software studies. Following the lead of critical code studies, in order to understand the broad array of engine-driven digital and material artifacts and engagements, we must also understand the constraints and capabilities of specific authoring tools. This is the matter of engine choice and versioning. At the same time, the cultural proximity and power of engines (as well as their entanglements with production, distribution and exhibition, and their status as commodities, as objects borne of the labors of a unique development pipeline) situate them within the broader purview of science and technology studies. It is within this framework that we should consider game engines in relation to a number of ethical questions—questions about labor, about consumption, about identity—that can be folded into a broader consideration of the relative affordances of game engines (where free expression is contoured or compromised, clearly an ethical quandary). The ethics of game engine development cannot be readily equated with the ethics of game engine design as the latter is often associated with game content, and the communicative and expressive choices that game developers make as they build their properties. The ethics of game engine development are inextricably bound to project cycles and protocols. However, development by design is, in the contemporary marketplace of most engines, built around the material reality that engine licensing has changed the industrial landscape of the video game industry, as most developers opt to modify an existing framework rather than build an entirely new one.

The first-generation Unreal Engine, developed by Epic Games founder Tim Sweeney, debuted in 1998 with the release of the first-person shooter *Unreal*. Within a year, the engine was being used by a number of other studios licensing the engine. According to Sweeney,

> The big goal with the *Unreal* technology all along was to build up a base of code that could be extended and improved through many generations of games. Meeting that goal required keeping the technology quite general-purpose, writing clean code, and designing the engine to be very extensible.
> *(McDonald, 1998, 43)*

Licensing the technology became a critical component of Epic's business strategy, placing it in direct competition with id. The emphasis on "clean, general purpose tech" was intended to fuel game development, to simplify the build process and shift the focus for independent developers from technology to content.

Unreal Engine 4 (UE4) was first revealed at the Game Developers Conference (GDC) in 2012; and at the March 2014 GDC, Epic Games released UE4 through a new subscription-based licensing model that gave developers access to the full engine and its source code, but also charged a 5% royalty of gross revenues on any released product made with the engine. In September 2014, Epic made UE4 licenses free to colleges and universities, "including personal copies for students enrolled in accredited video game development, computer science, art, architecture, simulation, and visualization programs" (Davis, 2014). And one year later, at the March 2015 GDC, Epic moved to a free licensing model for all users by establishing a selective royalty schedule for products making more than $3000 per calendar quarter in gross revenue, and taking a percentage of sales from user-generated content made available on the Unreal Marketplace. In the company's latest change in revenue structure, with the December 2018 opening of the Epic Games Store, the company has once again altered its revenue fee structure. These changes are reflected in ongoing revisions to the Unreal Engine End User License Agreement (EULA).

Epic Games and other large developers have the necessary in-house resources to continuously rewrite their engines (Epic employs programmers to work full time on the engine), holding on to the basic infrastructure and architecture as long as possible, while rewriting selective subsystems such as the rendering code. Building for cross-platform deployment allows these developers to spread their costs and risks across the lifecycles of multiple consoles and devices. The EULA is comprehensive, and covers the engine code, and establishes a pipeline model written into the core game systems of independent developers—a labor model that in many cases originates in the classroom. The Epic Games blog promotes the academic release of the Unreal Engine by touting the logic of industrial production:

> Learning the fundamentals (and advanced techniques!) of game development with the same tools used by professional developers to ship successful games is one of the best ways to maximize your chances of starting your own development career. To help accelerate this we provide numerous free content samples, tons of video and written tutorials to explain all the major tools of Unreal Engine 4, and extensive documentation of all features.
>
> *(Davis, 2014)*

Significantly, the EULA situates the engine as a requisite for success, connecting the educational merits of programming and procedural literacy to overtly aspirational career goals.

Unreal was not alone in creating a new labor model or in its (licensed) approach to adaptability and expandability. The cross-platform Unity engine debuted to the public in June 2005 at Apple's Worldwide Developers Conference as a Mac OS X-exclusive game engine. Unity has been partially responsible for the rise of independent game production since its release, realizing the company's goal of democratizing development. Unity has become part of the standard desktop of game development programs at many academic institutions around the globe, and in many independent game communities, as the engine and its development environment has lowered the technical know-how required to build interactive projects. Following the logic of encapsulation, the Unity engine conceals much of its technical labor, as a plug-and-play approach to programming, and allows developers to focus on creating content. This approach, with its accompanying scalability (2D, 3D, low-level to advanced programming), has allowed Unity Technologies to expand its purview and bring its technology to a broad array of other industries that can benefit from real-time 3D development such as automotive design, film and television, architecture and engineering. And Unity is driving the majority share of virtual and augmented reality content design and deployment; the company's first-quarter 2018 press materials suggest that the Unity engine is powering more than 60% of all content, placing it at the center of the evolving extended reality ecosystem (Unity Technologies, 2018).

On the Matter of Complexity

My efforts to summarize the work of large development studios in game design architecture, and to construct a linear history of game engine design that might suggest one software object (and one developer) is distinct from another, are complicated by the parallel migration of other technology companies into the same terrain, including Amazon's build of the Lumberyard engine (which I discuss in the next chapter) and Microsoft's acquisition and development of the Havok engine, which it acquired from Intel in 2015 (which had first acquired the Dublin-based company in 2007 to add Havok's software development tools and physics technology to its own inventory). Game engine history is also complicated by the matter of system interdependency; engine build and acquisition does not always lead to self-contained ecosystems. The industrial networks are intricately interwoven. Most studio engines have other dependencies that are satisfied through licensing agreements. In 2009, Havok announced a partnership with Capcom that added the Havok Physics engine to the Japanese developer's toolset, and at the 2019 Game Developers Conference, Havok announced a partnership with Unity to integrate its physics engine into the Unity ecosystem. Such deals depend on the ready integration of multiple engines into one cohesive game development pipeline, the relative ease of comingling their respective codebases, and carefully written contractual agreements that provide culturally responsive, globally aware technical support and service.

These agreements form part of increasingly complex patterns of ownership; in June 2012, the Chinese technology company Tencent made a minority investment in Epic Games, following its majority acquisition of Los Angeles-based Riot Games the previous year (Riot Games sold its remaining equity to Tencent in 2015). As it has expanded its game holdings, Tencent has also become the primary point of access to China's vast gaming market, and has been able to negotiate lucrative shareholder agreements with Activision Blizzard, Ubisoft and a number of other developers. These partnerships and alliances have clear cultural and political implications, as they cut across distinct regulatory zones; and while the industrial implications are rooted in the readily assessed value of the software systems that have been folded into Tencent's growing portfolio of video game properties, regulation binds technological to social influence at the material layer of game culture.

Linear game engine history is also complicated by the coexistence of multiple engines; what is perhaps most striking in this regard is understanding how individual and team developers are funneled into particular development environments. The pathway for independent game developers is established early and is governed by the adoption of particular (programming) languages. The availability of low-cost open source tools has provided some counterbalance, but the educational marketplace is dominated by Unity and Unreal licenses. GameMaker, a program first released in 1999, has had limited cross-platform and 3D functionality; while Twine, a free and open source tool initially released in 2009, is designed for interactive fiction, and is built on a visual structure akin to hypertext that does not carry with it the programming demands of a 3D engine. At the same time, tools such as GameMaker and Twine are important because of their difference. The structure of both tools—the absence of an engine's subsystem layers—lends itself to a certain ease of expression and to more ready manipulation of graphical elements; that very structure also opens them up in an egalitarian way to a broad range of artists, working with identity and expressivity at the limits of a linear, segmented production pipeline.

Standardization through engine design represented a significant industrial shift from the beginning of the 1990s, when each new game was essentially built from the ground up by a team of engineers, programmers and designers. Engine development involved the creation of a more transparent pipeline that included simplified build tools and a turn toward object-oriented programming; this shift lowered the technical hurdles for artists, designers and independent communities of practice. To be successful, engines must be iterative, rather than static pieces of software, and they must support a broad range of visual strategies and creative practices. While engines move toward greater efficiency and performance, and their subsystems are developed with a general propensity for realistic effect, the most marketable engines are not tethered to a particular style or studio workflow.

Within this abbreviated history of game engine architecture, I propose that the most notable engines (not all of which are covered here) provide seamless experiences, which I intend as an open concept unattached from a particular graphic or technical conceit, and instead aligned with unique design principles, play experiences and product goals. Internally, the best engine designs lead to team building and effective communication across stratified personnel, while externally they lead to meaningful play that acknowledges the player, connects actions to outcomes, and creates a space for expressive possibility. For many consumers, the technology is most noticeable when it fails, interrupting the experience of immersion or the psychological and sensory pleasure of play, and while engines are complex systems, subject to any number of open critiques by those who build with or play with them, any history of their development needs to consider the codebase, the multiple industrial and cultural frameworks that guide their design, and most importantly what players are actually doing.

3

RESIDENT RACIST: EMBODIMENT AND GAME ENGINE DESIGN

To develop a more meaningful history of video game engines, we must, as I have suggested, build a materialist analysis. That requires a methodology for examining the relevant discursive tensions that emerge between the non-visual text of an engine (the matter of production) and the decidedly visual properties of game assets (the matter of play), and for holding onto two seemingly contradictory impulses: first, the orientation toward efficiency and performance that defines how coders and game engines work, and second the messiness and the communicative and expressive openness of collaborative design processes, subjectivity, and play. By posing certain functional limits while celebrating certain capabilities, the engine contours the discourse. It not only shapes the characters, the field of play, and the environmental and procedural mechanics, it also shapes the player's interaction by contouring the visual and physical experience. To fully understand how material relations are manufactured by the culture industry, we must consider the interface as a nexus of several complex interactions that produce embodiment. Joseph Thompson (2012) notes,

> If we can acknowledge the hardware/software elements of a game as their own functioning assemblage, as vital and material (not just vital in its digital emulation of human-envisioned agency), then we can better trace vitality that escapes established routes of agency.
>
> *(89)*

Play is subject to the contingencies of hardware and software performance, and these limitations are not wholly undone by the inclusion of, for example, customizable character attributes; the latter are limited acts of embodiment that work on the surface of things (on the matter of representations), acts that are ultimately bound to machinic determinations. What unites our two potential reading strategies—one that privileges the engine and the other that privileges the representation (bodies that are played with and through)—is that they are both parts of the more general field of play and they are both, even more broadly, information systems realized as material objects. What distinguishes them, however, is the specific material properties of each, properties that, as Dourish and Mazmanian (2011) note might include "mutability, persistence, robustness, spatiality, size, durability, flexibility, and mobility" (4). The information work of the engine determines and is always connected to the rendered runtime object; yet the animated game object is a distinct material form. These matters are distinct in that they are encountered, used and transformed in unique ways, by unique affinity groups—developers, "produsers," players (Dourish and Mazmanian 2011, 4). These matters are bound together in that they are determined by the same sets of information (that form GameObjects or entities). Game engines are not development tools that are simply put away at the end of a build cycle; they remain attached to fully realized game properties. The game engine remains at the core of the game, always defining how players interact with the game system (Charrieras and Ivanova 2016, 339).

Developers and players are connected through the infrastructure of the game engine, a concept that is often lost in histories of the technology. Robert Nideffer (2007) points out that the game engine is not simply a value-neutral software object, rather "it is software that reflects and embodies the cultural conditions symptomatic of the developers of the system, as well as the end users of that system" (230). The game database and the game aesthetic are bound together in the development pipeline, and within the software infrastructure, which sets the stage for the mutually defining work of artists and programmers. While game engine infrastructure has been consistently driven by the concepts of modularity and reusability, the degree to which these concepts have been realized forms a significant part of game engine history. While early engines were built from distinct reusable modules, many of these core elements were not completely independent from their games; a higher degree of detachment was realized only gradually, from the mid-1990s forward, allowing the fully realized engine to circulate among other game titles and into non-game applications.

Through a review of Capcom's engine development pipeline (from the MT Framework to Panta Rhei to the RE Engine), and Konami's acquisition of parallel engine technologies (the Fox Engine), this chapter proposes how we might engage with the study of a relatively immaterial or "difficult" object. This case study in the representational politics of centralized engine development focuses on race, gender and sexuality across Capcom's serialized *Resident Evil* franchise and ties together the concomitant evolution of the company's associated game engines. The goal is to complement traditional studies of video games that might focus on their representational politics, their audiences and their production communities by introducing the matter of software, and to consider the degree to which we can situate representation as information without depoliticizing gameplay. More broadly, my intent here is to develop a method for fully understanding and evaluating the core technologies of visual (game) culture. Runtime objects are not representations that can simply be read; they are data-driven entities that reflect dual agency—the relative agency of both developers and players. The agency of developers is determined by their programming skills and by the native language(s) of the game engine; the programming paradigm of the engine determines how the developer interacts with it. We may see greater agency in individuated game engines (engines that are built in-house or licensed and customized) if we look "inward" to the level of software and understand the significant decisions that were made about the organization of the engine (as a software system) and its interface, and then move from our close scrutiny of the programming language back "outward" to see software design and architecture (Garlan and Shaw 1993). And within this organizational work, we must also understand the unique divisions of labor, and the respective agency of programmers and artists, as the former are trusted with algorithmic design and the latter with the design of dynamic game assets. Moreover, artists and animators are not simply working with the suite of development tools that provide entry into the body of the engine; they are also working with a suite of external design tools for digital content creation that might include Autodesk Maya (for 3D animation), 3ds Max (for 3D modeling), Pixologic ZBrush (for 3D sculpting) and other software applications, as they build assets that are then integrated into the game engine and rewritten by the engine's algorithmic infrastructure to satisfy the conditions for real-time manipulation. Agency is a complex relay that flows through the game engine; and as for the engine itself, and the evolution of its software subsystems, "the growing complexity of the software infrastructure brings new actors to co-becoming with its own formation" (Charrieras and Ivanova 2016, 352).

Game objects are containers that hold multiple components and have varying data dependencies; to study a game's representational politics, we must take note of the language of its objects. The two main programming paradigms, object-oriented design and component-based data-driven design, offer distinct approaches to object handling and the game engine interface (Charrieras and Ivanova 2016, 337). These approaches influence how game developers interact with the engine and determine the relative freedom that game artists and designers experience when creating game objects. The freedom that artists and designers experience in the game development pipeline is determined by many intervening labor conditions, yet regardless of the organizational logic of the workplace, their efforts always remain governed by a high-level scripting language that structures their interactions with fixed object classes or dynamic data objects.

A Case Study in Software Systems: Capcom

To consider how developers and players negotiate across an engine, I turn my attention to Capcom, one of the larger game industry stakeholders. Capcom is (among other enterprises) a Japanese game developer and publisher that has, over the lifespan of its investments in video game development, committed to building and recycling the company's own technologies; to some degree, Capcom's earliest efforts in game design were inefficient, with internal development teams designing their own engines and tools. Capcom uses overseas affiliates to create larger networks of human, intellectual and social capital as it taps the assets of other companies, and it has had to develop a series of data standards to regulate its global operations. Capcom built its first named engine, the Onimusha Engine, in 2004, as part of the design of the third game in the Onimusha series. The engine allowed the development team to build 3D backgrounds for the PlayStation 2 console, which was released in 2000. Following the Onimusha engine, Capcom moved to a standardized environment for its developers, with the build of the MT Framework. The MT Framework was designed for the 2006 releases of *Dead Rising* and *Lost Planet: Extreme Condition* but became the company's default engine even as new consoles, most immediately the Xbox 360 and PlayStation 3, were released. The MT Framework remained at the center of Capcom's game development environment until the more recent build of the RE Engine. The newer engine includes several modifications to the graphics and render operations of the MT Framework, most of which are designed to produce greater realism: new shader methods, dynamic shadows, and render outputs to support 4K resolution, HDR (high dynamic range, which offers better contrast and a wider color spectrum for overall enhanced image detail) and virtual reality. The advancements in the engine are, of course, dependent on advancements in runtime platforms and display technologies; for example, Microsoft's Xbox One S is the first console to support HDR gaming, while Sony's PS4 Pro supports both 4K and HDR, and a firmware update to Sony's original PS4 brought HDR to the earlier console release.

Capcom was established in 1983 and entered the home game development market in the 1990s, armed with its previous experience in arcade game sales and an emergent "single content multiple usage strategy" that gained momentum with the *Street Fighter* franchise; the property originated at Capcom in 1987 as an arcade game, was followed by a 1988 release for the Atari, Commodore 64, and other home systems, was redeveloped for the Super Nintendo Entertainment System in 1992, and has since expanded to other platforms. Capcom's business holdings include the development of digital game content, arcade operations in Japan, and two market sub-segments (both dedicated to arcade-based technologies) that utilize content from its home video game properties. As a corporate supersystem, Capcom's unique business model connects corporate, economic and social values; the company's value proposition includes an appeal to the "inbound effect from raising consciousness around gaming culture" (Capcom 2017, 4). The move toward engine design and the increasing public visibility of its engines (which are now featured as part of the company's annual reports) serve to support the solidification of Capcom's development ecosystem. With a stable game engine at its core, the company has strengthened the synergies across its intellectual properties (the Capcom supply chain) and brought into alignment those devices and display technologies that are not part of its portfolio. Capcom's labors remain firmly attached to a global chain of products and services, and the engine provides a conduit for that connectivity as a stable and privately controlled communication infrastructure that can speak to distinct operating systems and implementation platforms, keep pace with these intersecting technology sectors, and reduce the time to develop, test and go to market.

The game engine is a critical component of the Capcom ecosystem; the engine showcases the power of advancing technologies. The engine draws attention to itself, and in doing so raises consumer consciousness; the engine showcases corporate tech and espouses the virtues of Capcom's other intellectual properties. The engine also assures that Capcom's game developers are speaking the same (programming) language, with engine development and game development teams working in close coordination, upgrading the engine to meet the data requirements of new games, new world building methods and new consoles. Capcom's ability to globalize is dependent on its software practices. The build of a common development environment presents a certain difficulty for reading Capcom's output against the grain of Japanese culture, yet the company's diversified holdings allow it to operate as a global game developer and publisher with significant regional influence (much like Konami, which has investments that include video games, casino games, and a nationwide network of sports facilities in Japan).

Writing the Game Engine

One of Capcom's most well-known video game franchises, *Resident Evil,* sits at the center of its own transmedia network of live-action and animated films, comic books, novels, audio dramas, merchandise, and even a temporary theme park attraction. The franchise is a dense intertextual field, actively held together by multiple structuring practices—marketing, public relations, narrative work, the representational conventions of genre (horror) and, in the case of its video games, a series of proprietary engines. As is often the case with many long-running game titles, over its lifespan *Resident Evil* has been built on more than one engine. And while put in the service of multiple installments of the same franchise (the first *Resident Evil* game debuted in 1996 for the PlayStation console), the development arc of Capcom's engines has been largely tied to the singular pursuit of representational (graphical, physical and environmental) realism and the most stable attributes of the survival horror genre, although the game has strayed from its roots in the genre at various points throughout the franchise's history.

Much of the technical history of the video game industry is bound to improving how games run rather than radically disrupting the thematic conceits of financially lucrative serialized intellectual properties. Writing about the future of PC gaming from an early vantage point on game engine design, critic Steven Kent (2002) forecasts, "tracing the development of computer and video games is simply a matter of watching what's been available to developers in the form of memory, processing power, and polygons that can be rendered on the screen at once." It is not surprising then, that while Capcom has iterated the MT Framework and designed the RE Engine over the course of the *Resident Evil* franchise, the larger plotline—the focus of which is a secret organization experimenting with biological weapons on an unsuspecting populace—remains fairly constant. Any experimentation within Capcom seems wedded to infrastructure work rather than the build of truly transformative applications. The functional attributes of Capcom games remain remarkably consistent, even as the company's engines are radically transformed. If we are aware of this divide, we can more properly situate Capcom's object trouble; this is the matter of representation. To fully consider the ideological work of video games, we have to acknowledge that ideology is conveyed through multiple fronts—representation, narrative and operating systems—all of which can be governed by industrial practice.

Software allows us to consider code as a material practice, as one possible design of organized computation (Mackenzie 2006). Yet as it coalesces as a material practice, proprietary engine design looks to conceal its inner workings. In object-oriented programming (OOP), GameObjects, behaviors and components (rendering, collision, physics, etc.) are tightly coupled. In entity–component systems (ECS), entities and components are decoupled, although their data interacts; in a real-time interactive system framework, an ECS pattern separates high-level engine algorithms from the object structure of (low-level) simulated entities, and by doing so consistently reveals the semantic traits of the engine (Wiebusch and Latoschik, 2015). In OOP, encapsulation or information hiding can conceal the internal representation, or state, of an object from the outside, and keep it from being publicly editable. Encapsulation also allows the programmer to provide stability and consistency to a game's objects; basic object classes governed by specific organizing principles can be used to generate other classes. Information hiding is one limit in a game system, aimed at securing the integrity of an object (preventing invalid states) as well as reducing system interdependency and complexity. At this limit, there are no open object classes nor are there non-conforming states. Encapsulation does not drive ECS; instead ECS distributes the behaviors of player characters across multiple component systems (separating behaviors from entities). In OOP, encapsulation conceals the inner workings of objects; in ECS, decoupling entities and components has the same obscuring effect, as it replaces bounded objects with the distributed articulation of entity data. Working with bounded or distributed objects, both design approaches obscure how player characters are defined and function. This is the normativizing effect of the proprietary game engine at its core, and the root of the problem as we work to thoroughly decode the matter of representation.

Jacob Gaboury (2015) notes that theories of the digital image, and of three-dimensional simulation, are historically grounded in a particular understanding of the construction and interaction of objects. This particular ontology requires that as we approach computer-generated graphical images (and digital visual representations more broadly), we "must account for their status materially as both image and object" (44). On the subject of materiality, we must consider that computer-generated images are linked to particular evolving program structures, each with its own agenda. To locate meaning and pinpoint ideology requires reading across images and systems of representation. In the case of game engines, developers are seeking distinct solutions to parallel problems (of image production, transformation and interaction), some of which are driven by common languages, though each may have a unique syntax and algorithm. While the final image produced by the broad array of available and emerging engines may fit within the same visual regime, "each is materially distinct from the other, the product of a unique set of interests and concerns" (56) governed by publishers and developers.

The developer's selection of a game engine and a design approach serves as the most significant transactional limit. When engines appear in public demos, they stand as conflicted texts, as self-contained and readily analyzed objects, with their properties and their data architectures momentarily revealed. They also serve as a symbol of the development pipeline for unfinished games that lack specific release dates, as representative of narratives and forms of interaction and, in many cases, as a forecast for the build of as-yet-undetermined intellectual properties. As such, they stand in a unique critical position, speaking to the distinct binaries of developer and audience, hardware and software, engine and interface as uniquely mutating, queerly open objects. Indeed, a more nuanced approached to game studies should consider both the relative fluidity of the work in progress as an unrealized body as well as the formative conditions of core game technologies.

Reading the Game Engine

Capcom's proprietary engines, like those developed by other corporations, provide a common work environment for the company's global network of developers, programmers, directors and sound designers while simplifying the development process across multiple platforms. Engines set transactional limits on storytelling, fixing and controlling assets. Software mechanics delimit the field of play, and are central to securing the dual investments of companies such as Capcom in the build of serialized intellectual properties and the engines that govern them within the broader landscape of transmedia storytelling.

Capcom's MT Framework (based on multi-thread, meta-tool and multi-target build concepts) is a proprietary multiplatform engine. The MT Framework features an internal library (a framework is commonly understood as a collection of libraries, while a library is a collection of code assembled to perform a specific task, such as graphics, rendering, physics, audio, and so forth) that can output game content in a format that is optimized for each targeted console. The MT Framework radically reshaped Capcom's workflow by supporting the integrated development of games for multiple platforms. Engine building marks a shift in approach for Capcom, displacing the relative independence of the development team with the formularized game studio unit. Engine development is part of a comprehensive strategy for economic growth that includes maximizing the utilization of proprietary content within new operational models.

The first version of the MT Framework (1.0) was used for the *Dead Rising* zombie game, released in 2006, with new versions of the engine released from 2007 through 2010. Changes to engine source code yield changes in design architectures (for example, in the materials editor), fostering the need for ongoing conversations between designers, artists and programmers. The goal for Capcom (and other studios) is to continue to realize greater efficiencies in the game development pipeline (marrying code and design) and to mitigate the dependency on the middleware of other software developers (such as Havok, known for its Physics engine).

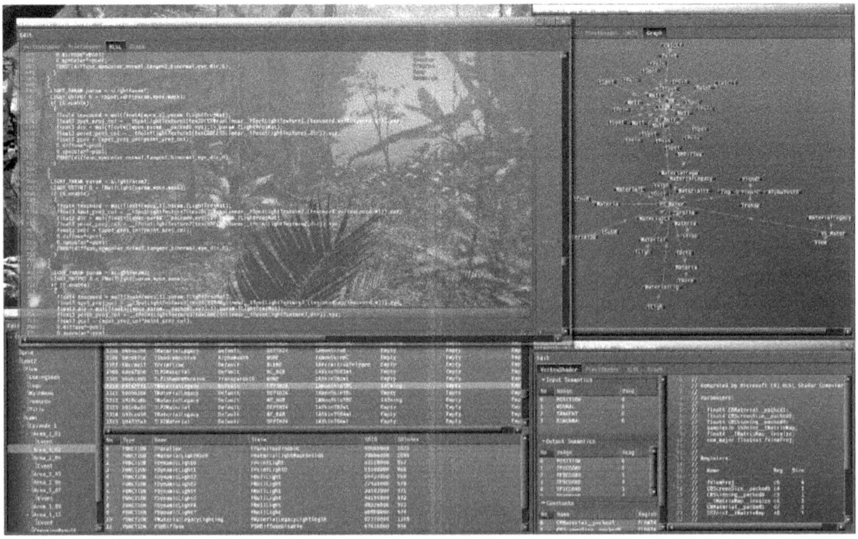

FIGURE 3.1 MT Framework development environment.
Copyright 2008 Capcom Co., Ltd.

Released in 2015, *Resident Evil: Revelations 2* runs on the last version of Capcom's MT Framework (2.0). The game returns to the roots of the survival horror genre and has significant stealth elements, although it also implements cooperative gameplay across two characters. While one character is equipped with traditional firearms and melee weapons, the other is more vulnerable, limited to using environmental weapons such as crowbars and bricks. These secondary characters can also find hidden items: one is equipped with a flashlight, while the other has special perceptive abilities. Enhanced vision binds these two female protagonists, whose narrative and mechanical functions are primarily altered forms of looking. There are two such pairings in the game (Barry Burton and Natalia Korda; Claire Redfield and Moira Burton), introduced across its chapter-like installments. In both cases, this basic gameplay mechanic produces a purposeful tension between narrative and environmental agency, and while gender politics are writ large across the character pairings (the young girl Natalia and Barry's daughter Moira embody two fundamentally passive game mechanics—stealth and distraction), any concomitant shape shifting across character genders does not inherently produce a queer subject. From the perspective of play (of interacting rather than looking), the game holds steadfastly onto its third-person perspective and its acute attention to the physical environment (the body is situated with purpose); for the player, body swapping foregrounds the fluidity of dynamic controller mechanics and the generic rewards of mastery, rather than any true body politic. These bodies keep their pre-determined object status, and remain defined by the broad array of game engine subsystems even in acts of transformation.

FIGURE 3.2 *Resident Evil: Revelations 2* gameplay.
Copyright 2015 Capcom Co., Ltd.

In similar fashion, the game's heads-up display (HUD) maps and flattens the terrain; as an environmental shorthand and unifying signifier, it functions the same way across everybody. Michel de Certeau (1984) suggests that maps are typical forms of fixation of the flux of everyday life, which try to pin it down by abstracting heavily from it. In game level design, maps are defined by their functions, and by the clarity and readability of their associated shape language; environments are understood not simply by their appearances but also by their affordances. Environmental mesh is concealed by environmental game art and translated into a shape language that signals the possibilities of gameplay either explicitly (a user interface button prompt tells us how and when to interact with an object), or through learned affordance (we can infer how to act based on our cumulative knowledge of the game's rules and systems).

This is an object lesson in procedural literacy (problem solving with programming, systems and play) and the liminality of code, of operationalizing the queerness of code by purposefully remapping it. Code is fluid; it lacks any inherent mechanical or anatomical fixity, although these possibilities become increasingly constricted throughout an ever-narrowing production pipeline and, as I have mentioned, through the choice of a specific data architecture. Code is perverse in that it submits all assets to the same inscrutable logic, and conversely, code is normative in that it limits what the body can do as part of a fixed circuit of material relations that is the governing logic of successful game production and gameplay. There is an unseen gap between the algorithm of the game and its appearances, between basic environmental mesh and the art and language of affordance. The game mechanic must make sense, and it must work without failure. The control schemes linked to the controller and the control schemes linked to the software and hardware-based manipulation of the character's body are tethered by the engine, a hub that also determines the potential kinesthetic energies ascribed to the player's body in the production pipeline and released in post-production praxis. Algorithmic manipulation composes and moves the body, and structures its interactions with environments and other objects. Performance and appearance may seem distinct, but in the digital domain they are subjected to the same controls.

Resident Evil: Revelations 2 privileges physical function(ality) over form but does not altogether erase the symbolic function of narrative. The seriality of the franchise accustoms players to engage in cross-gender identification in order to play through in a completist fashion. Many of the *RE* games challenge players to play through as both male and female characters, either in a story mode that repeats the same narrative premise but equips the player with different skills or weapons, or in a challenge mode that foregrounds environment over narrative. As part of an industrial imperative to create replay value that is often aligned with both game-specific and platform-specific rewards frameworks, the *RE* games that allow multiple character choices situate those choices as a form of functional mastery commonly structured as sequentially unlocked gameplay (a prerequisite to proceeding to newer levels or modes of play). In *Resident Evil 5*, players who complete the game as the lead character Chris Redfield can elect to play through again as Sheva Alomar, who is otherwise controlled by AI in single-player mode. Shifting gender, race and ethnicity from Chris to Sheva (who hails from an unnamed West African country), the latter is sequenced as a secondary subject position, once again locating character choice as a sign of functional mastery. A completist approach to gameplay can also unlock Sheva's alternate "tribal" outfit (a leopard print bikini, white body paint and heeled sandals)—a costume that marks and exaggerates her status as an exotic other. To locate queerness and communicative openness in requisite body swapping is an unsatisfying proposition. To locate the limits of queerness and free expression in locked character attributes (where unlockable costumes are similarly linked to underlying object-oriented achievement algorithms) moves us closer to understanding the critical value of code. But to fully understand the imperatives of code, we must extend our analysis beyond the franchise's serialized narrative and situate game mechanics (as mutable design decisions) and interfaces within the framework of the conventions of a genre and as part of the broader industrial arc of engine development.

Setting aside for the moment a game's visual and aural matter, the in-game mechanic is perhaps the most readily accessible sign of an underlying engine mechanic. However, the game mechanic is one step removed from the engine's underlying processes, providing more immediate insight into game design than game programming. Artificial intelligence is another accessible sign of an underlying engine mechanic. For example, evidenced-based decisions that impact game outcomes are made possible through an engine's underlying artificial intelligence frameworks. While one can situate decision-making as a form of ethical ideological engagement, to some extent most gameplay can be understood as a cycle of interaction that leads from information gathering and analysis to decision-making and interaction. While game AI is associated with mechanics (attached to characters, it is fundamental to producing embodiment), it is a property of the engine. As an algorithm developed by the programmer that can be associated with data management, it nonetheless creates clear signposts of intentionality. Indeed, if we consider AI as a component of a character or a game object more generally, we should do so in relation to the physics, render and transform (position, rotation and scale) components of the same object. To develop a fuller understanding of a game object, we need to take note of how these components are governed by software systems that may couple or uncouple data and behavior. These relations are specified by the engine. We might focus, as Eva Hudlicka (2009) suggests, on the relative generation of affective behavior in game engine design, expanding game AI to include "symbolic representational methods and classification algorithms for emotion recognition" (300) that could in fact redefine the parameters of the game object, converging the design of game engine systems with the data-driven processes of virtual assistants to understand the known states of the user through context-dependent game feedback.

In the case of *Resident Evil: Revelations 2* and many of the titles in the *RE* franchise, in single-player mode (distinct from cooperative gameplay) character-linked AI is a narrative imperative; each time the player switches bodies, for example, from Barry to Natalia, AI follows, occupying the body that is freed from device control. Yet the player must manage both bodies; in a form of psychological projection, the player must attend to the well-being of each character pair, even when one half of the unit lingers just off screen. At the same time, AI also controls the game's enemies. While a form of emotional projection binds together the game's central protagonists, despite the mediating influence of machinic embodiment (the game's protagonists are all delimited by a codebase, and are all subject to varying degrees of AI control or determinacy throughout the game narrative), the same type of projection does not extend to those bodies that, although similarly inhabited by AI, are defined by their appearances and actions as enemies. The contextual operations of AI across these distinct bodies is driven by a number of underlying conditions, embedded in the codebase, that, to varying degrees, prompt player identification, call forth distinct actions and, by nature of their animations and vectors, allow for a distinct set of transformations.

Consistently throughout the *RE* franchise, we are asked to consider the health of our bodies, and to know just enough about each game's underlying algorithms (how far we can stress the body, the environment, the interaction) to avoid triggering a death animation. Each character model is rendered with a set of materials, each of which contains a shader and the values for that object's properties. Gameplay code, in turn, feeds several values into the object shader, which are then processed to create an additive offset to the object's vertex coordinates (moving, rotating, transforming). In simpler terms, gameplay code supplies an object's shader with values that signal the changing state of the object; in the *Resident Evil* universe, as in most games, the physical imprint of code is not simply found in character builds, but also in the impact of the game environment on the character model. The changes to an object's vertices reveal that body's state of duress—the location of a weapon's impact, the vector of the impact, and the radius of the impact. In the case of *Resident Evil: Revelations 2*, health status is not registered on the protagonist's body but translated into a disembodied visual signature; as players take more damage, the screen itself begins to redden. Countering the seemingly singular pursuit of graphical realism fostered by repeated versioning of the MT Framework, this title translates the physical register into a game-specific code, as is common with heads-up displays and the broad array of health meters associated with survival horror games. These signs of damage can also yield to a finite set of more traditional death animations—of pre-rendered vector displacements. Once the playable body meets its damage threshold, the controller is temporarily disabled.

Algorithmic knowledge (a facet of procedural literacy) is a fundamental skillset across the *RE* series. As successive titles have stretched the fundamental mechanics of survival horror to emphasize both melee combat and conventional weaponry, players have been tasked with making critical choices across firearm classifications (handguns, shotguns, machine guns, rifles and magnums) to consider firepower, and reload speed, capacity and "critical hits." These nuances impact game progression and shift our attention from bodies to weapons as the origin points of ritualized pleasure, making enemy combat more or less challenging, and requiring constant consideration of resource allocation (community-authored enemy health cheat sheets have made this calculation much more explicit, indicating the amount of damage needed to overtake specific enemy classes). In every case, the enemy body becomes knowable as a data set: vulnerability is quantified. Perhaps to remind us of the importance of the physical realm, to guide us back to the surface of things, vulnerability is often called out by a visual sign—an obvious weak point—on an enemy body. Visual and narrative pleasure in gameplay can be found in consistently executed rule-based cause and effect—a form of realism aligned with the predictable functioning of algorithms.

Beyond the seamless operation of AI across multiple bodies, the push in engine design is driven by the pursuit of the real in visual representation, while the push in narrative design has led to the proliferation of reductive branching narratives, where choice has an impact on character relationships and story. Certain gameplay choices in *Resident Evil: Revelations 2* affect the campaigns of other characters, and as with most of the titles in the franchise, different choices produce different endings. Yet these decision trees are limited displays of affect and agency, all of which are structured by underlying conditional statements. As such, they do not signal a unique turn in engine development. In any game property, narrative design, interaction design and object design are linked to a common data set, and driven by a shared engine.

The More Things Change: Negotiating Design Bias

Capcom's Panta Rhei engine, the follow up to the MT Framework, was premiered at a PlayStation 4 unveiling event in February 2013 alongside the engine's release title *Deep Down*, yet the engine's development was apparently halted after several later tech demos (and the status of *Deep Down* remains uncertain). As with many Capcom properties, engine development and game development had proceeded in tandem, and as with earlier engines, the goal of Panta Rhei development (which began in 2011) was to keep pace with the evolution of industry hardware. With the introduction of the Panta Rhei engine, Capcom sought to address the new architectures of the PlayStation 4 and Xbox One, and the increasing demands placed on system processing and memory by a broad array of technological enhancements and changes in system architecture, as well as in-game environments, mechanics, management and address systems; the goal was to maximize the rendering power of new hardware.

FIGURE 3.3 *Kitchen* gameplay.
Copyright 2016 Capcom Co., Ltd.

With the development of *Resident Evil 7: Biohazard* (released January 2017), and after abandoning its Panta Rhei engine, Capcom began the build of the successor to the MT Framework: the RE Engine. Developed for the release of an installment in a longstanding franchise, the engine's full name, "Reach for the Moon," captures Capcom's ongoing pursuit of heightened graphical realism. The RE Engine premiered at the 2015 Electronic Entertainment Expo (E3) in *Kitchen*, as part of a tech demo for Sony's virtual reality headset, Project Morpheus. *Resident Evil* 7 was already well under development at the time of the *Kitchen* demo and the two properties are connected to the same storyline and setting; the demo content was repackaged as part of the playable *Resident Evil* 7 teaser, *Beginning Hour*, a prologue to the main game. Director Koshi Nakanishi has indicated that *Kitchen* was developed in parallel with *Resident Evil* 7 as a proof of concept of the RE Engine and VR specifically. In the company's 2016 year-end report, Capcom's Lead Programmer of the Technology Section Tomofumi Ishida suggests the development of the RE Engine was fueled by the company's investment in speeding up the development process while realizing new VR functionalities and building photo-realistic assets to match the specifications of next-generation game consoles. For Capcom, photo-realistic effect is aligned with a broadened approach to localization, extending the act of translation beyond language to include non-textual elements. As *Resident Evil* 7 is set in the United States, Capcom's promotional literature suggests a sensitivity to "design intentions"—a responsiveness to the culture and climate of location. Significantly, Ishida (2016) acknowledges the common negotiations at work between artists and programmers:

> Creating an interesting game should not be hindered by development engine constraints. If an artist expresses a desire to do something, the engine must evolve to make it happen. For this reason, all of us on the engine development team work in constant close contact with the game development team to promote improvements.
>
> *(5)*

For Capcom, the push toward heightened graphical realism in VR meant transitioning to a physically based workflow for *Resident Evil 7* that included advanced photogrammetry, a technique that constructs detailed 3D models from densely populated photographic data (images of a subject are taken in rapid succession from multiple viewpoints) and marries this work with Autodesk Maya, the core of the asset production pipeline, before outputting to the game engine. Referring to the RE Engine as "an engine enabling the artist to fulfill their every wish," Ishida (2016) suggests the RE Engine was designed to deliver efficient large-scale data management and embed more reliable team-based supports in the production workflow, and was regularly modified throughout the *Resident Evil 7* build cycle, allowing Capcom to meet the uncertain challenges of ongoing VR development.

The experimental impulse that drives engine development at Capcom, with the company's concomitant call to creative wish fulfillment, has not led to a similar experimentation with game design and content, nor has it led to a profound

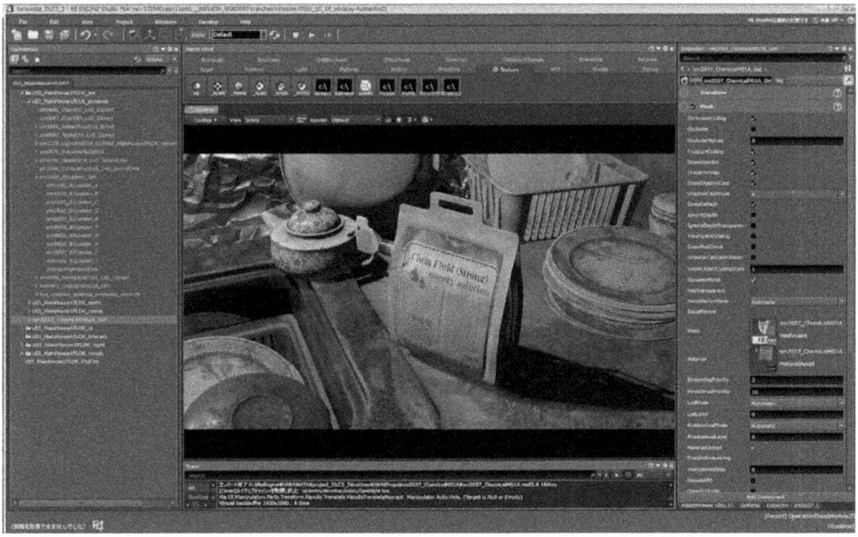

FIGURE 3.4 RE Engine development environment.
Copyright 2018 Capcom Co., Ltd.

responsiveness to specific sociocultural contexts. Engine development has not fundamentally expanded the critical and conceptual boundaries of play, although it has continued to foster new forms of interaction. Rather, as I have stated earlier, there is a generic sameness to Capcom's intellectual properties, with much of the promotional fanfare dedicated to showcasing the company's technology, equating the pleasure of free play with the pleasure derived from enhanced system performance and new tactics of immersion.

The *Resident Evil* franchise has been consistently plagued by its racial, ethnic and cultural politics; the games have repeatedly represented marginalized populations as grotesque victims of transnational capital and global genetic, ecological and militaristic enterprise. The controversy surrounding *Resident Evil 5* (which runs on the MT Framework 1.4) is one significant flashpoint, and originated with the premiere of the game's trailer in July 2007. The earliest backlash was built around the game's cinematics and in-house demo footage, rather than actual gameplay, and read the imagery for what seemed obvious clues to its disposition. In the trailer, the game's white American male paramilitary protagonist (Chris Redfield) runs around gunning down hordes of Black African villagers. The images evoke primal fears of contagion (both viral and racial) associated with the "dark continent," and seem to align the game's action and mythology with broad sweeping cultural paranoia, such as the historical legacy that has grievously aligned Blackness with monstrosity and otherness. More favorable readings draw out the narrative attention to capitalistic and militaristic exploitation, a premise that emphasizes the plight of a victimized African nation. *Resident Evil 7* furthers this narrative dualism by mapping the central conflict onto two opposing forces—a civilized protagonist and an infected backwoods family (the new monstrous other)—at a derelict plantation in Louisiana (the new site of abject horror). And the *Kitchen* demo, a fragment of the *Resident Evil 7* storyline, features a bound male protagonist who is violently attacked by a mad (and presumably infected) woman—yet another embodiment of viral contagion. By foregrounding these narrative tropes, which form the primary pleasure (the central conflict) of gameplay, Capcom naturalizes the operational imperatives of its engine (the secondary pleasures of visual and kinesthetic spectacle—the field and mechanics of conflict). Though the mechanics and the environments evolve with the potential of each engine, a common dramatic impulse binds the franchise together.

The negotiations at those game studios that are similarly invested in dual proprietary properties (game titles and engines) are about the different workflows of artists and programmers; the imprint of the engine on play is consistently found in the interstices between teams and technologies (between tool suites and runtime components, between assets and processes, and between storytelling and level design) as design tools such as shaders can literally be written into source code. Each iteration of the engine marks a point in an ongoing negotiation between programmers and artists over their relative freedoms, while the build and stabilization of a common engine binds together all of a company's developers. Development teams are quick to note the points of friction between artists and programmers, as the efficiency and clarity required of an engine means flattening out many of the idiosyncratic approaches to writing code (Stuart 2009); at the same time, naturalistic game mechanics often involve departing from the fundamental principles of applied physics, much in the same way that animation commonly stretches reality to be more convincing in both effect and affect. The consequences of the evolving development environment, in addition to introducing mechanical difference, extend beyond the hidden labors of the development team. The MT Framework, for example, has custom toolsets—resources that have been used across those titles built with the engine. While the engine was primarily used by Capcom from 2006 to 2015, it was also the foundation for more recent remasters of earlier Capcom titles, including *Resident Evil Zero* (2016) and *Resident Evil: Revelations* (2017), and for several new titles including *Monster Hunter: World* (2018). Capcom has highlighted several technical improvements with each successive version of the MT Framework; MT Framework 2.0, developed in 2008, introduced more dynamic environmental effects, and other enhanced graphics properties including deferred lighting, optimizing the handling of in-game data in the service of immersion. Reflecting on enhancements to the engine in version 2.0, programmer Taro Yahagi (2012) notes:

> This time we've focused even more effort on shaders and implemented even more functions. It's now possible for us to display various kinds of interactivity in our graphics—characters can be shown totally drenched in water or with their clothes scorched.

Capcom's engine development suggests an ongoing investment in the visual spectacle of bodies and environments (achieved through algorithmic exactness), though not in expanded forms of identification and embodiment (an expressive limit that would require algorithmic uncertainty).

Game Engine Reveals: Software as Visual Spectacle

When developers reveal engines in public previews, such as Techland's Chrome Engine 4 demo (2009), they present isolated on-rail displays designed to illustrate rendering power through visual spectacle, rather than the coded depths of each software layer or the mechanics of storytelling. Most render demos posit a relation to a particular game title, even as they have an uncertain status as objects belonging to, but not of a game: for example, the Chrome Engine 4 demo calls out its use in *Call of Juarez: Bound in Blood*, but the pre-rendered clip displays only living environmental elements.

FIGURE 3.5 Techland Chrome Engine 4 Demo.
Copyright 2009 Techland.

Engine reveals are notably different from their associated game reveals. Techland's *Dead Island* February 2011 announcement trailer is a promotional film created by UK (Glasgow) animation studio Axis Productions. The trailer highlights the demise of a typical nuclear family vacationing on the island (the game's principle setting) and, in dramatic reverse time, slowly reveals their undoing by a zombie contagion. The trailer illustrates neither engine nor assets, and it contains neither cinematics nor gameplay. It is a distinct short form animation project. As such, it is a phantom limb of critical inquiry, detached from the body of the game and disassociated from the production pipeline. Unlike the game, it stands as a closed text to be read, laden with cultural value simply in terms of its representational politics (of viral heteronormativity disrupted from without and within, as the young daughter literally tears her father apart) and not in terms of more complex forms of embodiment. As such, it lies outside the primary vectors of critical game studies and does nothing to assist any procedural analysis of either the game mechanic or the game itself. The narrative direction of the trailer runs counter to the temporal unfolding of the open world game, even though the game's setting, a tourist resort on a tropical island, evokes a similar tension between the modern and the primitive. The trailer's cinematic language is far more seductive than the game's limited first-person perspective.

Dead Island was developed with the fifth iteration of Techland's proprietary Chrome Engine, which was first used in 2003. The most forceful critiques of the Chrome Engine codebase are narrowly defined forensic investigations that align most readily with singular game objects. Nonetheless, these are significant interventions that demonstrate the importance of reading script against narrative agency, and of positioning code in relation to game world tropes. Such findings are close approximations of the overall power of script. In the case of *Dead Island*, the rogue "FeministWhorePurna" placeholder text for a subsequently renamed "Gender Wars" skill points to an obviously racialized gender bias in the game narrative and in the game mechanic (Yang, 2017), but also points to a bias in the game development pipeline (where files are named by programmers). The original skill name, which refers to the female lead Purna Jackson, was buried in the file structure of the non-retail Steam release, and sealed over in a fully patched version of the game.

As a similarly conflicted object, *PT*, a playable teaser and promotional vehicle for an unreleased game property developed by Kojima Productions and published by Konami, showcases the mechanics of an engine, but has an uncertain relationship to its parent property. Released for the PS4 in August 2014 as a free download on the PlayStation Network, *PT* served primarily as an interactive teaser for the game *Silent Hills*, a cancelled installment in the *Silent Hill* franchise to be directed and designed by Hideo Kojima in collaboration with Guillermo Del Toro. After the cancellation, Konami removed *PT* from the PlayStation Store and eliminated further installs or re-installs of the game through its network and onto its consoles. The teaser plays as a series of ever-changing hallway loops that the player navigates from a first-person perspective, with each pass marked by environmental changes and cues that, when sequenced correctly, unlock a final cutscene revealing the nature of the game and its role in the franchise. With the cancellation of the game, *PT* exists as a self-contained intellectual property, a game in itself, with an uncertain status as a video game, demo, or teaser, as the mechanics of the full property were never defined (although the playable loop, with its puzzle-solving mechanic and its narrative and environmental emphasis on the haunted and the supernatural is squarely tied to other *Silent Hill* installments). As a playable environmental loop, *PT* is a fairly close visual approximation of the spatio-temporal gradients and the power of its engine, although its closing cutscene reattaches it to an already value-laden serialized intellectual property, fixing its status as something other than a mechanics-driven environmental problem (a puzzle) to be solved.

PT was developed with the Fox Engine, a proprietary cross-platform, cross-generational game engine built by Kojima Productions (under lead architect Julien Merceron) for use in Konami games, including *Metal Gear Solid V*. The engine was presented in demo in 2011 at Konami's pre-E3 conference. Like most engines, the Fox Engine contains a level editor, animation editor, cutscene editor, FX editor, UI editor, sound editor, motion editor and other toolsets. The engine features physically based rendering, with support for reference models from real-world cameras to test the effects of linear space lighting and to maximize its photorealistic effect, and both 3D and photo-based scanning to create photo-realistic character models. The engine can be coupled with other software tools, such as Marvelous Designer, a 3D modeling program for clothes and fabric, to effectively broaden the reach of simulated pattern-based design. The goal of the Fox Engine is realistic, physically accurate output, realized by studying and measuring the details of the world outside the game (a balanced design approach that draws from handling everyday objects) while still situating photorealism in context—defined by the material rules of the game. One promotional piece for the engine positions two sets of images of a Kojima Productions conference room side by side—one set of digital photographs and a second set of screenshots rendered in the engine—and frames the paired images with the prompt, "Is it REAL, or is it 'FOX'?"

Engine, code and 3D design, bound together in the game production pipeline, introduce operational limits that can yoke those correspondences in the service of realism. In their analysis of the Fox Engine, Stephanie Boluk and Patrick Lemieux (2017) suggest that the ongoing push toward (hyper)realism has led to a visual economy in which "all assets are equal and even the most banal subjects require graphical overkill" (129). In their analysis of Fox Engine artifacts and game assets more broadly, Boluk and Lemieux productively extend the concept of realism beyond the formal pursuit of mimesis to the ideological conceits of mastery—over the tools of production, the engine-driven traces of the natural world (for example, modeling and texturing, lighting and shading), and over the player's cognition and perception. To extend the concept even further, we need to call out the role of scripting as an essential aspect of all games: defining and classifying object types, connecting object types (for example, game objects and components) and messaging between object types to activate, deactivate and create new instances of an object.

Ideology operates across the coding and decoding of assets, the core mechanics associated with the field of those assets, and the broader discourses of industrial production (the pursuit of more forceful correspondences between games and everyday life made possible by advancing software, hardware and devices). But our attention to this vast network of informatic code (Galloway, 2006a) is often fleeting, undone by the more seductive and unruly politics of representation and the more overt imperatives of engagement and interaction. Subsequent demo images of the Fox Engine, including a presentation led by Hideo Kojima at the 2013 Game Developers Conference ("Photorealism Through the Eyes of a Fox: The Core of *Metal Gear Solid: Ground Zeroes*"), feature rather unfortunate racialized choices, as pre-built characters are dropped into the simulated Kojima conference room; demonstrating the core technology of *Metal Gear Solid V* but devoid of context, they reveal much about the underlying nature of play as a value-laden (and colonizing) process of game development. They also signal the forceful pursuit of a singular form of (photo)realism, and articulate an ideology (and a corporate philosophy) aligned with technological teleology. In this particular public presentation of the engine, the virtual conference room, often used as a reference model for linear space lighting, includes four figures: two armed soldiers (one from the trailer for *Metal Gear Solid V: The Phantom Pain* and the other from the trailer for *Metal Gear Solid V: Ground Zeroes), The Phantom Pain* protagonist Snake in full combat gear, and a young black male character of uncertain origin produced by 3D scanning. This construct unnecessarily racializes rendered space, and illustrates the ease with which random bodies can be freely associated, staged to interact, and asked to reenact cycles of power and violence. The young man stands shirtless and vulnerable; although he has been conceived as a signpost of the power of advanced 3D rendering technologies, he also stands as a randomly produced, object-oriented visual trope, a universal signifier of subjugation.

Game publisher Konami maintained ownership of the Fox Engine after the company separated from Kojima Productions in 2015, while Hideo Kojima moved on to the Decima engine, developed in collaboration with Amsterdam-based Guerrilla Games (a subsidiary of Sony Interactive Entertainment Europe), for the build of his next project, *Death Stranding* (2019). The partnership with Guerrilla Games was a natural fit for the game designer, as it tracked with a December 2015 agreement between Kojima Productions and Sony Computer Entertainment for the build of what was initially a PlayStation 4 exclusive software title. Kojima collaborated with Guerrilla Games to modify the developer's original engine source code, and shaped the open world engine to match the technical and creative demands of his new game (Renardson 2017). Among other modifications to the engine, the Guerrilla Games team combined a precomputed

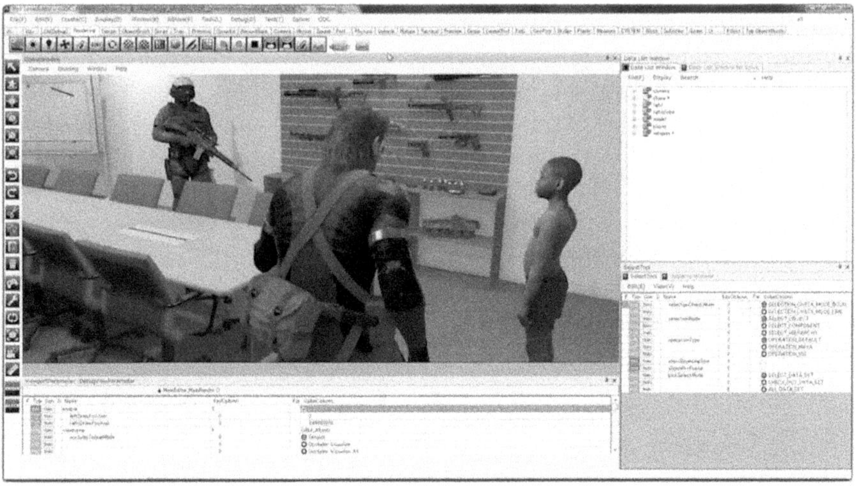

FIGURE 3.6 "Photorealism Through the Eyes of a Fox: The Core of *Metal Gear Solid: Ground Zeroes*." 2013 Game Developers Conference.
Copyright 2013 Konami Digital Entertainment Co., Ltd.

atmospheric scattering model with an analytic height fog model to create expressive atmospheric aerial perspectives (Carpentier and Ishiyama 2017). Moving from the Fox Engine to the Decima engine, Kojima has continued to use source code as a discursive construction of visual excess.

Visual pleasure and informatic code are woven together in the game production pipeline, for identity is a data type—a mathematical variable—that is literally bound to bodily articulation and played potential. The informatic mode of cybernetic typing is made manifest in everything from motion capture, to transcoding, to statistical analysis, to keying attributes and actions to specific numeric variables; the degree of its prominence provides an index for the very dominance of informatic organization, which has recolonized the function of identity. We must not look beyond the representation, we must look underneath it to find its coordinates, seeing the mappable body as a physiognomic system and a mechanical system. There is value in critical game praxis to mobilize (rather than resolve) this tension between surface and substrate, to interrogate realism by calling out both the formal and structural properties of a game text (Galloway 2004). This is not a call for a particular form of realism (narrative realism, representational realism or social realism), but rather a call for attending to how realism in all of its (interactive game-based) forms remains connected to game architectures, and how, while certain game components may be repurposed to more openly expressive ends, engines are driven by rules with limited variables. At the same time, the push toward realism in any of its forms is not linear or unidirectional. Multiple engines are running at any one moment: MT Framework properties are running simultaneously with RE Engine properties, and multiple engines may still be at play within any game development company or community. These overlapping architectures are both a matter of game development timelines but also of the inherent technological needs or aesthetic choices (a game's visual vocabulary and game mechanic are commonly driven by a range of expressive considerations, including genre) being made by developers.

The *Resident Evil 7* development team brought their knowledge of the RE Engine to Capcom's *Devil May Cry 5* (released in 2019), where it was paired with facial scan technology to construct high-fidelity characters, combining high-definition images with high-speed combat without compromising runtime response. Senior Producer Michiteru Okabe outlines part of the production process by noting,

> Actors bearing a close resemblance to the character images were hired overseas, clothed in original costumes and makeup, and incorporated as 3D data via 3D scanning systems. We also employed 3Lateral's techniques to craft characters with a wealth of expressions.
>
> *(Capcom Investor Relations 2018)*

The production pipeline for *Devil May Cry 5* included several forms of image processing and motion capture, and separated body motion from facial animation. The pursuit of graphical realism was driven not only by the RE Engine development environment, but by the importance of the game's protagonists who are part of a larger video game franchise, first launched in 2001 and subsequently adapted for multiple media forms: animated television shows, comic books, novels and pachislo (slot) machines. The RE Engine has also been used for the 2019 release of *Resident Evil 2*, a remake of the 1998 game that incorporates updated game mechanics, revised camera perspectives, a dynamic 3D sound mix and enhanced resolution. Epic Games acquired Serbia-based 3Lateral in January 2019, pulling the technology for crafting digital characters closer to the Unreal Engine, a signpost that the field of fidelitous data simulation (and the proprietary technologies that support it) is increasingly competitive.

The push to move game franchises forward with enhanced graphical supports is aligned with the push to bind computer-generated data to lived experience—to connect graphical effect to sensory-motor affect more seamlessly, and to broader speculative considerations of what is possible beyond the game (the latent potential of the technologies of representation). The seductive pull of the video game ecosystem is grounded in the promise of engine-based work that serves as the lynchpin between data and embodiment. At its most reductive, this is why remade, rebuilt and remastered video games are so popular. They promise deepened engagement with familiar characters and are a welcome return to known narrative pleasures, and game publishers consistently foreground their state-of-the-art development platforms to authenticate these value propositions.

FIGURE 3.7 *Devil May Cry 5* principal 3D photography.
Copyright 2018 Capcom Co., Ltd.

Recycling enhances profitability, but also highlights the power and progress of a developer's core technologies. It is not surprising, then, that Capcom quickly followed its rebuilt *Resident Evil 2* with the RE Engine build of *Resident Evil 3*, a game originally released in 1999 and set to hit stores in its reengineered form in 2020.

Game history is complicated by the intersecting lineages of remastered games; more pointedly, reengineered games erase the industrial dimensions of their original labor (and preceding forms of pleasure and play). Across this history of serialized games and engines, scripting appears to move unidirectionally toward a more transposable (and prescriptive) language. To be truly transformative in our analysis of conflicted playable objects and their architectures, we must consider games as a process and a pipeline, and not simply a sum of intellectual properties, assets and representations.

As with systemic racism and oppression, the historical conditions of the engine are concealed by versioning, as swappable assets become the only knowable and comfortable signs of difference. Therein lies the bind: technological revealing (attending to changes in the technology) circumscribes and cancels historicity, lures us into the myth of technological determinism, and pulls us away from the socioeconomic and ideologically laden conditions that drive the game industry pipeline, and in doing so undoes agency. The Fox Engine, the RE Engine and engine development more generally has begun to privilege artistic simulation (from photographic reference models) over artistic creation. These engines displace the burden of representation to the imaging technologies that are advancing the more seamless correspondences found in datacentric workflows. Notably, these engines align the visual field with the material parameters and presets (such as lighting and textures) and the algorithmic approximations of the environment (such as atmosphere, weather and time of day) that are bound to each development framework, and the game camera parameters that function as digital derivatives of real-world values and that determine how we see the game world.

Games are not simply representational products, they are also layered player-centric simulations of the visual field and the field of view, and while we may not let go of the stereotypical nature of their representations, we must pay attention to the structure of the player's (designed) experience. To connect the game engine to a reading of race, gender, sexuality, and representational politics more broadly, we might suggest that it is ultimately the engine that allows or disallows shifts in the vocabulary of those relations. The game theorist must move beyond the study of representations to consider actions and the worlds in which they transpire, and the deepest ideological critique must attend to a game's underlying informatics (data-driven technical protocols). Rather than looking at and evaluating the representation on screen, we need to explore the cultural dimensions of technology and situate the engine as an industrially bound discursive construct. The questions of identity politics raised by traditional screen studies cannot be satisfactorily mapped onto the material relations embodied by video game play, nor can they be readily synthesized with the various industrial discourses that drive game production. To speak about the industrial logics of program and code we must adopt a radically distinct language of difference. Despite the apparent unidirectional push to establish best practices, software represents merely one set of fixed relations for what is otherwise a context-free set of abstractions. Langdon Winner (1980) suggests that "the things we call 'technologies' are ways of building order in our world" (127). The game engine is a technical system that requires an internal logic, but that logic is defined by external attitudes and approaches—the matter of industry. To what extent does the engine organize labor?

The principles of engine design present a particular difficulty in our effort to understand the impact of an algorithm on the matter of visual representation; ideological analysis is occluded by encapsulation (in object-oriented systems) or by the distributed interaction of bundled data across engine subsystems. By its very nature as a series of layered subsystems each responsible for distinct facets of design, interaction, manipulation and control, game engine architecture makes it difficult to locate the image, as game objects do not exist in isolation—they are articulated as instances, as collections of attributes and behaviors (or data and code) that inform the momentary construction of an object. The game image is better understood as a field of play—of interacting and transformable objects in an environment of varying affordances. It may be overly reductive to consider Barry, Natalia, Claire, Moira, Chris and Sheva as equivalent data-determined objects with associated attributes, behaviors and transformative potentials, but any consideration of what they look like must be coupled to a closer analysis of how they can act and be acted upon (the fundamentals of their respective scripts), connecting art, design, programming and systems. To truly resolve any lingering interpretive difficulty, we need to map their difference onto the sameness of their underlying code, which is a two-fold act of making things visible. My effort to dissect the representational field of gameplay, and to isolate it as a distinct by-product of game engine design, has left me with a pile of data. But that is perhaps a powerful starting point for furthering this inquiry into what I have implied at the outset of this project—that code persists, and that we live in a culture increasingly defined by its automated and efficient (game) engines. By pointing to the critical importance of data as the building block of game architecture, game design and (game) objecthood more generally—by suggesting that subjectivity is not defined by images but by an underlying data set—we can understand how engines can so easily colonize non-game spaces, bringing the same object trouble to bear on other cultural fields. This is the matter of the next chapter, as I broaden the field of play to consider the role of game engine architecture in everyday life.

4

NEW MEDIA ECOSYSTEMS: AMAZON AND THE ADVANCING GAME ECONOMY

The ongoing industrial migrations of game engines (across entertainment forms, 3D imaging, prototyping and manufacturing, scientific visualization, architectural rendering, cross-platform mixed reality, and within the military) suggest they have broad power for organizing the cultural field around the mechanics of play. Game engines have been tethered to other engines—to other program-driven processes. While the study of parallel development frameworks may not be part of the traditional purview of game studies, the widespread deployment of interconnected software architectures is part of the larger horizon of integrated systems of interaction, of structuring the broad contours of commerce, and organizing the rituals of work and play. Moreover, a game engine may be understood as a software package (a framework of integrated libraries) that does non-game-specific work, even though it is commonly associated with game development and execution. The drive toward engine development was a drive toward efficiency in the game industry that eliminated the need for writing a customized piece of software for each game. The movement toward "operating systems," toward the formalization of libraries of functional code, has led to a new economy of labor that both eliminates the centrality of unique coding acts while situating code as a new currency (the ascendant value of proprietary authorship tools).

Amazon is a key player in this new economy, translating any number of interactive acts into engine-based transactions, using an algorithm to distill agency into a linear input with a readily defined outcome, or one that can be refined over time. Amazon software, hardware and data holdings form an elaborate ecosystem that crosses a series of industrial vectors: trade; manufacturing; science; technology; entertainment; news; information; transportation; home automation. The company's array of engines, artificial intelligence and machine learning connects the dots between public and private domains, between bodies and technologies. Alexa (Amazon's intelligent voice recognition and natural language understanding service), for example, bridges the Echo family of smart home devices (the Echo Look, Dot, Spot and Button), the Fire TV and Fire Tablet and the Cloud Cam, as well as devices outside the Amazon family and beyond domestic space (Alexa has been available in all BMW vehicles since the 2018 model year). And all of these vectors further the centrality of Amazon's cloud services platform: from computing power to database storage to networking to content delivery across enterprise and e-commerce. The broad product category of Alexa gadgets seamlessly integrates AI into the spaces of everyday life, and moves parallel information streams, conversational interfaces and deep learning (dependent on feature extraction and dimensional reduction) across work and play, business and home, and the flows of commerce. But what remains invisible are the interconnected nodes across the neural network that make machine learning possible, leaving us to critique only the more obvious signposts of a datacentric culture-industry. Amazon games, for example, bring the potential of in-skill purchases to the Alexa landscape, upselling consumers to Amazon Prime and a digital warehouse of knowledge-based games that include Trivial Pursuit Tap and Jeopardy.

Amazon has taken a broad and deep approach to context-aware products and services, and has squarely situated itself within new paradigms of computing, where ubiquitous computing has bled into spatial computing (blending technology with the physical environment to create meaningful spatial interactions). Moreover, the company continues to further what can be described as an advancing game-based economy. Amazon's Alexa-based gadgets, such as the Echo Button, can be controlled by game engine directives that translate button presses into events; the technical parameters of the Alexa Engine (and its game engine component) govern game design within this particular ecosystem. Alexa game skills are limited by the technical demands of voice recognition and have led most game designers to build mechanics that integrate a limited number of voice design decisions for Alexa-enabled devices. Real-time interactions can be bottlenecked by complex communication chains, and long, non-deterministic inputs can confuse Alexa's automatic speech recognition and natural language processing engines. Game developers need to operate within these particular constraints; complex semantics need to be parsed on the design-side of the interactive circuit.

As part of its nascent investment in game-based technologies, in a multi-million-dollar deal with game developer Crytek, Amazon licensed the CryEngine in 2015 as a codebase for its own proprietary Lumberyard engine, a cross-platform 3D game engine fully integrated with Amazon Web Services (AWS) and Twitch. With this acquisition, Amazon effectively expanded its web services by consolidating a suite of products and services for video game developers (tools for building, hosting and livestreaming) that depend on reliable convergent data

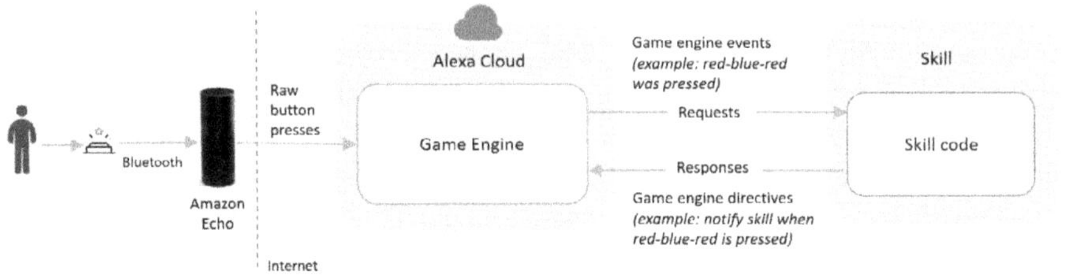

FIGURE 4.1 Alexa Game Engine interaction.
Copyright 2019 Amazon.

flows. Amazon's 2014 acquisition of the game-streaming platform Twitch and its integration with AWS has deepened the company's attachment to an expansive game community, and connected developers to players who can be mined for information. The $970 million that Amazon spent on Twitch was an investment in bolstering AWS, increasing the data holdings and the cross-industrial functionality of its cloud-computing service and making more and more industries dependent on its data warehouses and services. And Twitch briefly expanded Amazon's retail portal; in 2017, the service was opened to video game sales, connecting publishers directly to viewers through its streamers' channels, although the service was discontinued just eighteen months after launch. Despite these starts, stops and pivots, and while Amazon's game engine adoption rate lags behind that of other developers, including Unity Technologies and Epic Games, the company seems to be invested in pushing game-based mechanics into a broad range of Internet-connected devices. By testing out playful engagements with extended reality that will undoubtedly inform the company's cloud-based services and products, and by integrating AWS and Twitch into the Lumberyard engine's scripting tools, Amazon has developed increasing dependencies on its cloud technology while capturing the viewers and game players gathered on Twitch. Amazon is using game space as a testing ground for new technologies, new modes of being, and new forms of interaction. For example, Twitch ChatPlay allows developers to build customized game interactions with the Twitch community. Amazon is using Lumberyard, AWS and Twitch to crowdsource its research (by sharing its codebase and "reading" its communities) in the transactional nature of code, interface and user experience, as the company looks to refine its suite of services, products and devices to secure its role in larger computationally driven media ecologies.

These iterative game-oriented enterprises link research and development in the information technology sector to the more quotidian activities of everyday life, while the imperatives of a common engine-driven codebase remain largely invisible in everyday commercial flows and within domestic space. While the centrality of Lumberyard to the Amazon ecosystem is far less certain than Alexa, Lumberyard developers have continued to expand its functionality. Features such as the text-to-speech pipeline of Amazon Polly widen the field of interaction between game developers and clients by enhancing the development workflow, adding to the production pipeline both dynamic real-time voice creation and modification, and automated facial animation (lip synch) for rapid prototyping. Both enhancements are dependent on the responsive feedback of Amazon's cloud data services, again increasing interdependencies within the company's datacentric ecosystem.

Amazon's technology strategy can be used as a model for understanding the ideological machinations and practiced imperatives of a hermetic codebase and its associated information economy. As game space and lived space continue to converge, bound together by new industrial arrangements in extended reality, the major 3D authoring tools and their respective parent companies will continue to have a significant impact on contemporary visual culture. While I have suggested that code is the new horizon for media studies, we are already living with and through code, and it is already forcefully reshaping the culture at large. This chapter foregrounds Amazon as a case study model of a swiftly iterative new media ecosystem—an industrial arrangement that has emerged to concretize the exchange value of integrated software and hardware mechanisms, with the broader goals of connecting information to e-commerce, and pairing knowledge to technobiographic identity models.

Language, Knowledge and Embodiment

With its 2017 acquisition of Body Labs, a 3D body modeling startup that first leveraged its statistical modeling techniques to aid law enforcement, Amazon expanded its investments in artificial intelligence; in 2019, the company began recruiting human subjects for a body scanning study at its New York City offices (rewarding participants with a twenty-five dollar Amazon gift card). Amazon's interest in avatar-based technologies is part of a wider visual communications and e-commerce strategy that is still in development, but when conjoined with the company's networked communication investments and structures, it forms part of a dense mimetic thicket, ripe with ideological resonances.

Researchers at Bell Labs understood the importance of contextualized messaging and meaning within technical systems as early as 1948, when they began to explore the fundamental problem of communication across circuitry and were faced with the discord between the semantic aspects of communication and the problems of engineering. "A Mathematical Theory of Communication," published by Claude Shannon in the 1948 issue of the *Bell System Technical Journal*, reads potential communiqués in statistical and logarithmic terms—transposing communication into numerical probabilities and signal-to-noise ratios (Shannon, 1948). The birth of computer culture in the 1950s was largely about solving the language problem, and the inroads in computer language development and artificial intelligence made throughout the decade laid the groundwork for subsequent research in human-centered interface design and automatic problem solving (Freedman, 2018b). The language gap between speech, bodies and computation has only continued to close, and natural-language services such as Amazon Polly work to bridge that gap, translating scripted protocols into spoken commands as part of the development process and in service of the (post-production) field of play. Pushing further, the goal of Amazon's Real World Image Study is to collect comprehensive data sets to guide the production of statistically predicated human forms—or knowable bodies.

On the matter of knowledge, in 2016 and 2019 Amazon unveiled a series of online education services for teachers; Amazon Inspire was followed by Amazon Ignite. The company's forays into the educational technology market for primary and secondary schools, and its efforts to expand its platform model, can be understood as consecutive attempts to close the loop on information exchange and seal the two ends of its marketplace of commerce and ideas. With closer attention to Amazon's acquisition and build strategy, and its hermetic information systems and workflows, we can unravel the complex intersections of the company's techno-centric portfolio and more properly consider the impact of Amazon's holdings and approach—as a media company with significant traction in e-commerce, engine-based middleware and related media and communications hardware—on broader game-based economies. Amazon's approach parallels the strategies of other global multimedia conglomerates, including Alphabet (and Google) and Microsoft. Each of these media companies has produced or acquired proprietary engine-based (or engine-compliant) middleware to bind together the broad holdings of their ecosystems and to advance their respective business models, linking technology to culture while expanding corporate value. While Google has not developed its own engine, the company's Stadia cloud gaming platform is strategically built on an open source Linux foundation with Vulkan cross-platform graphics and computing API, and supports the more common developer tools including Unity, Unreal and Havok. And Game Builder, Google's drag-and-drop 3D game development tool, is essentially a programming-free (though JavaScript compatible) entry point for code-averse game developers; the sandbox approach to 3D level building features a card-based visual programming system that compiles rudimentary gameplay objects and mechanics to help build the game. In their respective efforts to capture market share, Amazon, Google and Microsoft are striving for balance as they build proprietary platforms (and custom hardware) for open source developers. Apple continues to pursue game development with its proprietary iOS- and MacOS-compliant tools—frameworks for logic, game architecture and graphics that include GameplayKit, SceneKit and Metal. Apple Arcade, a monthly subscription service, tethers an evolving gameplay catalog to the company's proprietary device chain, and features timed-exclusive launch titles from several high profile developers, including Capcom and Konami. To highlight how, exactly, these elaborate media and information networks interact as (eco)systems, this chapter focuses on Amazon's engine-based technologies, and in particular the interplay of its dual development engines: Alexa and Lumberyard.

Building a Cloud-Based Ecosystem

Amazon's interest in the game industry precedes its formal investments in game technologies and game development; founded as an online marketplace for books in 1994, the company expanded its retail offerings in subsequent years, and has been in the business of selling video games since the late 1990s. Amazon added to its game holdings with the 2014 acquisition of Twitch and its acquisition of California-based Double Helix Games in the same year (acquiring the studio's talent and its intellectual property), and continued to increase its apparent commitment to game development by recruiting a number of leading game designers to build out its own game studio. In parallel, Amazon has continued to refine its tablets and devices to accommodate cloud-based services and address the computer power needed for seamless gaming experiences. The constant in this shifting landscape of strategic investments has been the AWS cloud infrastructure, and a commitment to acquiring larger and larger consumer data sets. The model of building cloud-dependent games has pushed the heavy lifting of the game engine and of computing power away from devices and into the cloud. AWS can execute scene rendering and then push rendered content back to a tablet or device, all the time using the Amazon API Gateway to monitor available bandwidth, enable stateful communication and ensure fluid gameplay. While I have used AWS as a shorthand for referencing Amazon's cloud-based services, the data management products bundled within AWS are much more nuanced, and can support full build, deploy and scaling of cross-platform games. Among its core game backend products (runtime or execution services), the company offers Amazon Simple Notification Service (SNS) for push messaging to subscribers across distributed systems, Cognito for securing, saving and synchronizing user data (such as application preferences and game states), Aurora as a managed relational database for developers, and DynamoDB for the global replication of player data across a network. This list represents just a fraction of the interconnected holdings in the AWS ecosystem.

In November 2017, Amazon announced a suite of new machine learning features for its AWS cloud computing business. Among Amazon's AI announcements are Amazon SageMaker, which lets companies build and train newly developed machine learning algorithms; Amazon Rekognition Video, which uses AI to detect objects and faces in customers' video content; Amazon Transcribe, which turns audio into text; Amazon Translate, which translates text; and Amazon Comprehend, which analyzes text for sentiment and key phrases.

By addressing these information networks, we can reveal how the digital and the material are actually coterminous. While materiality is commonly equated with physicality—the objects of human-computer interaction—we must push back against the notion that the digital is inherently immaterial, only made material through creative design. Digital systems may already be material. Paul

Dourish (2011) notes, "When we focus on information as a material object—either as it is instantiated in information systems of all sorts, or as it manifests itself in the representational systems that contribute to the shape and character of life in information society—then we begin to recognize the historical particularities, cultural specificities, and political consequences of information work" (4). Amazon is clearly invested in material goods—the more obvious signposts of consumer culture—as it sells a broad range of products, stored in and delivered from its warehouses. At the same time, Amazon has built a number of interactive objects to make selling products more habitual, and a number of services (Prime, Prime Now and Key) to make consumption more convenient, and even more pervasive. Delivery services operate across distinct spaces—home, store locker, car—and in some instances literally open up these spaces, granting Amazon physical access borne of a natural-language processing system delivered as a cloud-based query. But behind these products and services is a much more precious commodity—consumer data (and the consumer insights that may be drawn from that data). On the materiality of information, my focus connects the materialities of information goods and their symbolic values to the transformation of space by information (Alexa's listening radius) and changes in organizational practice, and the material conditions of information technology production and the regimes of governance. These are the underlying principles of materiality that undergird the Amazon ecosystem, that structure our practical encounters with the materiality of information, and that shape thought and non-digital material practice. Media studies should engage with the materiality of information beyond representation and metaphor, though reading Amazon's body politic by connecting political and information economies to subject-object relations remains a critical and rather satisfying entry point. This is an obvious inflection point indicating that something is indeed happening within an information network, and within a networked economy that depends on the presence of a technobiographic subject (the negotiation between centering information and centering the subject, and on translating the subject into additional data points as part of the loop of machine learning). Amazon is part of a larger cultural shift that is redefining the limits of effective computability, extending algorithmic influence into the machinery of the information economy (Finn, 2017). Amazon is one of any number of companies and services (Facebook, Google, Hulu, Netflix, Lyft, Uber, GrubHub, and intelligent assistants such as Alexa and Siri) invested in the ongoing formation of new culture machines, made possible through the myriad humanistic attachments of algorithms.

Everyday Engines

The Alexa Engine (the speech recognition engine that performs real-time speech analysis) team moves toward the vision of delivering what Amazon refers to as "the Star Trek computer" to its customers—the world's most adept intelligent personal assistant, accessible via natural voice commands on any connected device. The Alexa Engine integrates Alexa technologies that go into Amazon and third-party devices; it is the underlying component for Alexa that allows other teams to build experiences. The company continues to build and iterate one set of common APIs for Amazon and third-party devices and developers (developers can build Alexa Skills apps to connect Alexa to other devices and services such as Lyft, Hulu and Ring effectively broadening the Amazon ecosystem). The Alexa Engine takes in all Alexa traffic and integrates the different Alexa technology components. The Alexa Language Technologies team works on services that interact with the engine, like Automatic Speech Recognition (ASR), Language Understanding Systems, Text to Speech and Facial Recognition.

Engines have become critical components of most media development pipelines and new information and distribution economies, including mixed reality and artificial intelligence (both may be understood as engine-driven blended environments); they are part of a broader industrial arrangement that may help us understand the impact of code and the production of meaning in games and other engine-driven artifacts by introducing the design process as a rich textual field in which to situate traditional textual analysis. It is only by using a pipeline model (that illuminates the writing and revision of an engine, and the negotiations common within large team development) that we can set the groundwork for intervening with the ideological imperatives of code, as information is more often than not part of a flow, a series of interactions and interventions designed to connect algorithms to material outcomes. Game design is a process and, by attaching the appropriate pipeline model to game studies analysis, we can highlight the discursive tensions that persist as game developers negotiate the publication cycle, the hardware cycle, the evolving mechanics of screen culture, the mediating influence of location and context, and the cultural demands of audiences. In this landscape, engine-based mechanics serve as an industrial shorthand, speeding up the build and release of a broad array of interactive properties. Game engines have evolved into everyday engines, and have colonized a wide range of industrial economies. More pointedly, to understand the underlying mechanics of the new culture industries, the introduction of process into game studies is a critical part of building procedural literacy for media theorists, designers and consumers looking to navigate this terrain.

In this manner, while the Lumberyard engine and in particular the Lumberyard Starter Game may be the most obvious shared asset architecture in the Amazon ecosystem—positioned as an open source framework—we must understand that the other engine, known only by her first name, does much to conceal its framework and to naturalize subject object relations, even as it determines the relative utility of exploration, emits the signals of agency, and regulates the relative impact of our presence on the world we inhabit. The nature of human-centered code work is transparency; contemporary information industries shape artificial intelligence and interface design to foster connection and intimacy, and to nurture transactional bonds without calling out the matter of software. Program code is complex and not obviously meaningful, especially outside the context of its associated libraries that may exist across multiple virtualized spaces and in multiple forms (the script, the database). Program structure does not have a singular correlation with end-user experience. Instead, we need to focus on the transactional nature of code, interface, device, content and user, and the role of software in larger media ecologies.

The Starter Game is a small, third-person game that is built with the Lumberyard component entity system. The game provides a quick entry point for developers to play with the tools, and take apart and reuse elements from the game's pre-built environment. Developers can use Jack, the playable robot character, or any other assets in the Starter Game sample (or the Lumberyard Prefabs Library of internal assets and objects) to prototype their own projects. As a self-contained set of functional assets, the Starter Game and the associated Lumberyard libraries function much like the other pre-built playable demos offered by other engine developers that illustrate engine properties and can be used as basic building blocks or shortcuts to larger builds. Lumberyard also allows the integration of a number of third-party tools and pre-constituted packages of code and assets, known as gems, that add functionality and complement the engine's visual scripting system; gems are modular code and content collections that can be shared across projects. Tools such as SpeedTree for vegetation modeling, and gems such as EMotion FX for creating character animations are indicative of the plug and play nature of the engine.

Amazon has integrated its Lumberyard engine with Twitch (for engaging fan communities through livestreaming) and Amazon Web Services (for building and hosting); while Lumberyard is free and includes full source code, developers pay for the infrastructure resources they use on AWS. And Amazon Game Studios has hired several industry veterans to build out the company's own game properties using its proprietary Lumberyard architecture to showcase what a more aggressive approach to Lumberyard-based development might yield. Yet

FIGURE 4.2 Starter Game promotional image from the Amazon Game Tech Blog. Copyright 2019 Amazon.

FIGURE 4.3 SpeedTree development environment.
Copyright 2019 SpeedTree.

even without having fully realized Lumberyard's value, Twitch has firmly established Amazon's place in cloud streaming services, a move perhaps more critical than the development of a successful engine, as Google and Microsoft are currently exploring parallel cloud-based ventures that will undoubtedly radically transform how games are played and will situate the console and PC gaming market within a larger field of networkable deployments. Google's Stadia game streaming platform is dependent on the Google Cloud and features YouTube integration, while Microsoft is looking to rollout out its XCloud streaming service, backed by the Game Stack development kit that bundles together Microsoft's platforms, tools and services, including Azure (Microsoft's public cloud computing platform), PlayFab (a backend platform acquired by Microsoft in 2018 to support the post-launch operation of cloud-connected games), DirectX, Visual Studio, Xbox Live, App Center and Havok. And as part of securing their robust development ecosystems, each company is also promoting a dependency on its own privately managed data centers. Amazon's strategy in the video game industry proper remains uncertain, in part signaled by an announcement days after the June 2019 Electronic Entertainment Expo convention (E3) in Los Angeles that the company was reorganizing and laying off dozens of employees from its video game division. Amazon Game Studios has seen the departure of top tier talent and the cancellation of multiple planned game titles since the division stepped up its commitments in 2014 (the studio launched in 2012), and its investment in the Crytek engine has not yet proven profitable or impactful for video game development.

Amazon's movement into game production extends beyond the mechanics of its engines. Elsewhere in this manuscript, I suggest that gamification (the build of game-like experiences and reward systems into quotidian rituals, workaday experiences, and a multitude of corporate ventures) is distinct from the movement of engines into public and private sectors, although both actions extend the traditional purview of game studies and game work. As physical spaces and processes are transformed into game-like experiences, they are more commonly gamified without any of the corresponding dependencies on a game engine or other core game technologies. Gamified experiences and operations carry with them the signature traces and the ritual engagements of video games, but are often not supported by the same technological infrastructures, though there may of course be programming parallels and similar data-driven dependencies. However, I believe that the two processes—one of technological migration (the movement of engines into non-game spaces, the influence of engines on non-game industry approaches to the marketplace of goods, services and ideas) and one of procedural migration (the gamification of non-game spaces)—are being leveraged in tandem to produce more significant cultural and ideological shifts and a more pervasive overhaul of the technological imaginary.

Amazon, for example, is using the values and tactics of video game play to increase productivity inside its warehouses. A May 2019 *Washington Post* story reports that since 2017, Amazon has rolled out a gamification experiment to five company warehouses. The Amazon-developed games are optimized for small screens at employee workstations: "With names like *MissionRacer, PicksInSpace, Dragon Duel* and *CastleCrafter*, the games have simple graphics akin to early Nintendo games like *Super Mario Bros*, workers say" (Bensinger, 2019). Employees who connect these playful metrics to the completion of physical tasks, often in team-based or competitive modes, are rewarded for their efforts. Amazon is not alone in these pursuits. Most providers of common goods and services have developed similar exercises, from Starbucks (Star) Rewards program to activity-based reward systems for Lyft and Uber drivers and passengers. Gamification can lead to higher productivity, especially in repetitive low-skill work, but these systems also lead to higher surveillance, facilitating the production of more precise metrics. And like the operations of the engine, the data-layer of these interactions—the algorithm—remains hidden from sight.

While Lumberyard has an uncertain future as Amazon's core game architecture, which some game developers have ascribed to the uniqueness of the CryEngine codebase (it has a steeper learning curve than Unity and Unreal), Amazon's engine-based economy is not collapsing. The same principles that drive game engine design are driving the design of multi-purpose "everyday" engines, and at the same time, the engines of everyday life are adapting to the logics of play. Alexa's status as a datacentric utility is being reframed by an expanding suite of adaptive skills; the engine is home to a new economy of app development driven by sound and data. Amazon's Alexa Skill Builder's Guide outlines the essential rules of engagement for building voice-first games, and details ideal voice-first mechanics, the tactics of acoustic immersion, and the frameworks for in-skill purchasing.

Alexa's voice user interface (VUI) returns us to the essential problem of language, and the prescriptive tendencies of most development environments, as the *Alexa Design Guide* suggests, "To be effective, you must design VUIs to adapt to the many ways customers might express meaning and intent through speech" (Amazon, 2019). This is the matter of probability. Alexa skills are essentially apps for Echo devices; as these communicate through Alexa voice services they must follow particular interaction patterns. The act of translation, of building, "adaptable, personal and relatable" speech is facilitated by the Alexa Presentation Language (APL), which foregrounds the necessary conditional layouts and data binding expressions for purposeful relays between human speech and data-driven Alexa-enabled screen devices, structured by an associated APL document. And for situational voice-design processes, the Automatic Speech Recognition (ASR) and Natural Language Understanding (NLU) engines of Alexa call for simple inputs, to avoid complex semantics and reduce the overall cognitive load necessary for a timely response. The Alexa Skills Kit Developer Console acts as the central environment for building custom skills. The console streamlines the build process; it houses the tools for designing an interaction model, complete with intents (what the skill is tasked to do), utterances (how the user will ask the skill to do them) and custom logic, and assigning an associated endpoint (specifying where the services are hosted and the custom logic resides, and where Alexa will look for relevant data sets). Alexa skills are activated by an invocation name, designed to be part of the natural flow of conversation, as a casual launch point for the voice user interface. Amazon's nascent game economy may be best represented by the adaptive use of natural language processing—crowd-sourced through Alexa development, and tested and played within its ecosystem—where the value of data is being more casually yet forcefully articulated by developers and players.

While Amazon is not the first company to move beyond graphical user interfaces, it has made significant strides in voice-first interaction, playfully expanding the tenets of situational design while using conversation to elicit a largely cooperative disposition toward data (suggesting that data is only meaningful as a process and like the product in a warehouse, its value is derived only through transaction). Voice-first interactions present a unique challenge of affordance. While our engagements with voice-enabled technologies might teach us new forms of interaction, cueing us in to what commands are acceptable to launch or run a process, the language problem, the problem of the unpredictability of speech, is solved by training the natural language understanding engine to adapt to the user. It might conform or simply bend to the initiative of the user, or move to a mixed initiative system of control and response between user and system that guides the interaction within the parameters of a skill.

The Maze, released in 2018, is an immersive Amazon Alexa voice game made in partnership with HBO for the conclusion of the second season of *Westworld*. Built as a choose-your-own adventure style game, the Alexa skill is activated by the command "Alexa, open Westworld." While the game extends the season's central quest in an apparently open-ended, exploratory fashion, the game is still an over-determined object that, as its trailer and press materials suggest, can be approximated not simply by its narrative, but by a series of interrelated data sets that reveal the boundaries of a system comprised of "11,000 lines of script, sixty player-generated paths and thirty-two ways to die." The game also pushes Alexa's native voice to the margins, opening the device up as a container for other media-driven imaginaries (led by other voice actors). Television is not the only expanded frame for Alexa-enabled devices. Video game space is also an arena for voice-enabled experimentation. The *Destiny 2* (2017) Ghost skill, created by game developer Bungie, adds hands-free real-time Alexa voice commands to the game. Connecting two AI bodies, and linking the Alexa Engine to Bungie's proprietary game engine, the skill allows players to speak through Alexa to Ghost, the in-game companion. In a more ad hoc approach to game expansion, Jamie Grossman, a UK-based *Fortnite* (2017) player, combined a custom Alexa skill with an Alexa-enabled device (a motorized fan, a multi-color smart light bulb and a smart plug) to extend his sensory experience of the game. As an uncertified custom skill, Grossman's experiment is not a game modification *per se*, but simply a code-based workaround that reads the game state and communicates that state to Alexa; Epic's game and engine (*Fortnite* is built on the developer's Unreal Engine 4) operate independently of the do-it-yourself Alexa skill and its home-brewed codebase.

In Amazon's case, the purposeful cross-industrial work of the engine has been more fully realized through Alexa rather than Lumberyard. Yet Amazon is not alone in re-orienting the field of gaming and pivoting with its associated technologies. Soon after its release in 2010, Kinect hackers began appropriating Microsoft's Xbox 360 motion-sensor add-on to explore new forms of 3D building, exploiting the device's RGB camera, microphone array and depth sensor. The Kinect enabled voice and gesture control for video games, and was initially designed to enhance more traditional gameplay; under the guise of Project Natal (the initial codename for the Kinect), it seeded future forms of interactive entertainment. Microsoft responded in kind to these random acts of hacking with a beta release of a Kinect software development kit to drive experimentation with the device more formally. While the technology dead-ended as a gaming peripheral, it is experiencing new life as part of Azure Kinect DK, a development environment that includes the Azure Kinect camera (a new iteration of the Kinect camera that features depth and orientation sensors, and a spatial microphone array) and a number of software development kits for Azure-based speech and vision services, as well as body tracking. The HoloLens mixed-reality headset also features depth-camera technology that evolved from Kinect hardware. Both technologies, unveiled in early 2019, are positioned to cross multiple industrial vectors—health, science, manufacturing, retail, entertainment. Through the Azure Kinect DK and the HoloLens, Microsoft is looking to build a robust ecosystem of sound, vision, object-oriented, sensing and cloud-based computing that connects camera-based technology to Microsoft's cloud services, and serves the needs of a diverse base of enterprise clients in the expanded field of the Internet of Things.

The Ecosystem Problem

For developers that take an ecosystem approach to software, hardware and infrastructure, much of the clutter and unpredictability of upstart experiments with code can be cleared away to shore up a language, a logic model and an ideology. The Echo Dot Kids Edition encases Alexa in a colorful bumper and includes a one-year subscription to Amazon's FreeTime Unlimited that provides access to age appropriate entertainment and activities developed or published by some of the largest media companies. The device has come under scrutiny by a coalition of consumer advocacy groups in a combined complaint that alleges the smart speaker violates the Children's Online Privacy Protection Act (COPPA), a 1998 law that sharply delimits what data companies can collect from minors without parental consent. The complaint, "Request for Investigation of Amazon, Inc.'s Echo Dot Kids Edition for Violating the Children's Online Privacy Protection Act," submitted on May 9, 2019 to the Federal Trade Commission by the Campaign for a Commercial-Free Childhood, the Center for Digital Democracy and seventeen additional complainants, points to the vagaries and potential illegalities of Amazon's data collection, and the company's failure to consistently solicit and verify parental consent. The request outlines the types of voice recordings that are captured by the Echo Dot and detailed in its voice history, and speculates in a footnote that "some children will likely speak to the Echo a few hundred times in a day, especially if playing interactive games that ask for answers" (Campbell and Barrett, 2019, 31).

Alexa-based gameplay is a rich repository of public and private data, a network of information made even richer by developer-designed queries and transactional user engagements. The Echo Dot Kids Edition is bound to its unrestricted counterparts by a common codebase that is designed to remember over time so as to provide ever more seamless learned engagements. Amazon's holdings are saturated with the data residue of each unique consumer; the customer profile acts as a root persona of sorts for Alexa's machine learning. Alexa's endless improvement cycles are designed to reduce friction, and to carry over context from one query to the next as the voice assistant becomes more conversational, the exchanges more natural, and the attachments more familiar. Amazon continues to refine its machine learning models, to reduce error rates by allowing the system to automatically make corrections based on contextual cues. Through

FIGURE 4.4 Echo Dot Kids Edition.
Copyright 2019 Amazon.

everywhere Echo devices, Alexa is always within listening distance, and with myriad attachments to screen-based technologies, Alexa's algorithms are given permission to shape our sense of self. A promotional spot for the Echo Look codifies Alexa's value while promising an even higher return on investment from the all-too-familiar virtual assistant: "Alexa helps with thousands of things, and now she can help you look your best." The Echo Look, marketed as a wardrobe consultant, features a hands-free camera that responds to voice commands; its vertical orientation allows users to take full-length portrait-mode photos and to capture full 360-degree views. The device interacts with Style Check, a virtual consulting service for those needing a second opinion on their clothing choices. The app solicits feedback from fashion specialists and deploys a machine learning algorithm to refine the client's "look book" over time.

Taken together, the Echo Look and the Echo Dot Kids Edition illustrate the ecosystem problem that operates across Amazon's holdings. Echo Buttons may be the most overt solicitation to play with Alexa; sold in pairs, when linked to a compatible Echo device the gadgets function much like traditional game show buzzers. They can be pressed to play games from the Alexa Skills library or synched to activate an Alexa smart home routine. Dots and buttons litter the landscape; they stand as individual points, but they form a densely clustered neural

FIGURE 4.5 Echo Look.
Copyright 2019 Amazon.

network. As an ecosystem of data, devices and software-related events, what we can see most immediately across this terrain are interrelated impacts on the economy, technoscientific knowledge, communication, news and information, education, health and well-being, and governance. But more broadly we can see the specter of mutability, of the state changes inherent to software, play, and the neatly aligned principles of engine-based physics, logics and mechanics. Adrian Mackenzie (2006) suggests that if we follow the evolutionary movements of code, we will see "many objects, practices, environments and behaviors are becoming more software-like" (3). Mackenzie goes further to propose that software has become more like a neighborhood; it is something familiar, interwoven with the fabric of our lives, and perhaps almost sentient, that has lost the quality of abstraction that governed its early life (3). Neural networks help us cluster and classify. They interpret data. They group unlabeled data according to common attributes, and they classify data when they are trained on a cleanly circumscribed data set. We have to ask about our place in this ecosystem, about the problems we want to solve, the questions we need to ask, the availability of the necessary data, and the relative correlation between that data and our inquiry. We have to teach the algorithm; we have to understand how deep learning maps inputs to outputs. The ecosystem problem is not simply one of transparency; it is also one of literacy, made all the more complex as our virtual assistants are trained to be literate. This is a deeper problem than that of the game engine, of developing the requisite computational literacies to understand the underlying algorithmic drives of an engine. Game engines do not speak to us; they are not particularly seductive structures. Yet they produce a set of visual knowledges that can be openly read. If the true organizing power of code lies in its mutability, we need to be mindful of play as it migrates into new terrain and as a distributed code object, constantly modified and prone to "exacerbating slippages in agency" (Mackenzie, 2006, 71). The ecosystem problem is a problem of agency that requires we understand the organizational function of code work as both technical and social. Moving on to consider code "out there" in the world, the next chapter necessarily sets the question of self aside for a moment (though I will pick up this topic later) to unmask the environmental impact of engines. By privileging the visual imprint of game engines, my aim is to move us through any difficulty we may have with reading code, to develop a method for deciphering a broader range of opaque code-dependent intellectual properties.

5

INDUSTRIES AT PLAY: MATERIALITY, MIXED REALITY AND MEDIATED ENVIRONMENTS

The location-based game *Pokémon GO* has significantly raised the profile of augmented reality and context-dependent play. Since the game's launch in summer 2016, mobile devices have been making over the public sphere, creating new vectors that cut across otherwise stable and well-trodden maps. By purposefully folding in commonly under-explored landmarks, these mobile pursuits have, to a large extent, thoughtfully re-activated public space. The game, made by the Silicon Valley firm Niantic, Inc., uses augmented reality (AR) to layer virtual objects (cute, cartoonish Pokémon creatures) onto an actual city map. Knight Foundation, with its investments in civic engagement, took note of *Pokémon GO*'s ability to bring residents into public spaces and launched a partnership with Niantic to explore how *Pokémon GO* might enhance or augment existing efforts to support public life. The partnership launched in Charlotte, North Carolina, in May 2017 at an open-streets festival and continued in three additional Knight communities: Akron, Philadelphia and San Jose. Working with American University, Knight Foundation tracked the impact of this partnership in an effort to discern lessons that others might apply to the role of ubiquitous computing in civic development—playful strategies to create more engaged communities. The report, "Cities Remix a Playful Platform: Experiments to Embed *Pokémon GO*" (Stokes et al., 2018) suggests that if (developed and) placed in the right hands, AR games can be one of several constructive tools for cities to strengthen civic engagement and build stronger communities.

Pokémon GO is built on the Unity game engine, while its mobile backend relies on a number of Google Cloud services, as it draws from real-world maps. The game is both an application and a scalable database system. The Google App Engine environment supports the retail-oriented, transactional nature of the game, with App Engine microservices managing such elements as user profiles and records. Google Cloud Datastore serves as the game's primary database for capturing the game world, supporting data analytics and enabling machine learning. And the Google Kubernetes Engine runs the game's container-based application logic, orchestrates the various applications and processes, and allocates and tracks resources in the cloud—to dynamically grow parts of the application in response to the volume of user requests. This infrastructure design can readily support concurrent access by millions of players across a network, solving one of the primary problems for connected game development by providing the resources necessary for connected single-player, real-time multiplayer, and real-time massive-multiplayer experiences (with the necessary technological affordances for game, world and data persistence). Container-based applications are fairly isolated from underlying infrastructure, since the required operating system, libraries, frameworks and dependencies can be packaged as a distinct unit running on the same global network.

A series of partnerships between Unity and Google were announced throughout 2018; far from a simple data share, both companies articulated a relationship that includes shared infrastructure. The collaboration is part of the wider migration of Unity's platform to Google Cloud, and it followed an existing partnership between Unity and Google that opened up the latter's ubiquitous mapping platform to Unity, providing an option for developers to build games and AR experiences on Google Maps. To understand the sum of these efforts, developers can now build games in the Unity engine and utilize Google for infrastructure management, situating development, testing, hosting and play in the same environment (Murnane, 2018).

The technical alliance between Unity and Google also includes the integration of Google's AdMob platform into Unity's game engine (through the Google Mobile Ads Unity plugin) and the parallel migration of Google's Universal App Campaigns (designed to generate ads on the fly from prebuilt asset inventories and use machine learning to monitor ad performance rates over time), building what Google has intended as a seamless developer experience inside the Unity editor. Google advertisers have access to Unity's mobile gaming network, and developers have access to a wider range of advertisers within a common ecosystem. In this landscape of connected games, players are connected to other players; and players are also connected to developers and marketers. Connected games depend on the reliability and global availability of an enterprise-grade infrastructure. Google has promoted its tight integration with Unity as a considerable step toward "democratizing" connected games (Dutta, 2018), aptly identifying robust monetization opportunities as a lynchpin for success and an undeniable performance metric for developers. The virtues of connected games are often associated with a baseline ethical ideal that attempts to reconcile the transformation of the world into a sandbox for digital assets with ideas of community betterment. However, the baseline ideal is compromised by an opposing entrepreneurial impulse that literally hosts play within a continuum of experiences and data sets that monitor and monetize engagement—a tendency made all too obvious by Niantic's addition of sponsored locations to its mobile map-based properties. Both *Pokémon GO* and the developer's more recent *Harry Potter: Wizards Unite* (a partnership between Niantic and Warner Bros. Interactive Entertainment) incorporate ad-based territories; the former has featured PokéStops at McDonalds and Starbucks, while the latter has added magical inns and fortresses sponsored by AT&T (which owns Warner Bros.) and Simon (mall and outlet) properties.

The interrelated dependencies between Niantic and Google are not surprising, given Niantic's origin as a Google startup in 2010 and Niantic CEO John Hanke's earlier role in the design of Google Maps, Google Earth and other geo-based Google properties. The insights that drive Google Earth can be traced back as far as 1996 in *From Space to Your Face*, a visual demo produced by Silicon Graphics (SGI) to showcase the company's 3D graphics hardware architecture (the RealityEngine and InfiniteReality). After cycling through a series of 3D images, the demo zooms ever-downward from an aerial view of the Earth to a terrain view, then it closes in on an animated 3D image of a Nintendo 64 game console perched on a mountain peak, and, finally, it tracks inward to reveal the console's MIPS R4300i microprocessor (Jennings, 2011). In 1999, a group of former SGI engineers formed Intrinsic Graphics to expand on the technical conceits of the SGI demo and focus on developing high-performance, cross-platform game middleware. The following year, the team launched Intrinsic Alchemy, a game development environment with supports for PC and console builds. In 2001, Intrinsic Graphics spun off Keyhole, a software development company focused on geospatial data visualization. John Hanke was brought on as CEO of Keyhole and led the development of EarthViewer, a consumer-facing, game-like system with access to extensive databases of network-hosted geographic information that included satellite imagery and aerial photography. EarthViewer pulled together these data sets to produce interactive 3D models of the Earth. In-Q-Tel, the venture capital arm of the Central Intelligence Agency, invested in Keyhole in 2003 to further the development of EarthViewer (the first prototype of the application was built in 2001) on behalf of the National Imagery and Mapping Agency, which understood the value of Keyhole's technology for the national security community and recognized an opportunity to use EarthViewer to support US missions in Iraq. The application was acquired by Google in 2004 and became the foundation for Google Earth.

Hanke joined Google as part of Keyhole's acquisition. After it was formed as an internal Google startup in 2010, Niantic pursued the development of two mobile location-based applications: *Field Trip*, which launched in 2012, and *Ingress*, which launched the following year. Both are based on points of interest and the collection of third-party data; where *Ingress* has an interrelated science fiction backstory, *Field Trip* functions as a real-time personal tour guide. Together these pursuits bring knowledge and play to a similarly coded architecture—one that has direct ties to the wider US intelligence community while being wrapped in the legacies of related game technologies.

Niantic became an independent entity in 2015 with investments from Google, The Pokémon Company and Nintendo. Niantic's desire to "transform the Earth into the new game board" (About Niantic, 2015–2020) is dependent on a pipeline of integrated partnerships. With the build of the standalone Niantic Real World Platform (NRWP), the company actively pursued the development of its own tech ecosystem, partly by taking ownership of existing knowledge capital (selectively assimilating additional research assets). In 2018, the company acquired the Boston startup Escher Reality and the London startup Matrix Mill to consolidate a suite of holdings in computer vision, machine learning, mapping and object recognition—core supports of Niantic's platform. The acquisition accelerated its work in spatial computing for augmented reality and added occlusion to its core architecture to allow greater interaction of digital content with the physical world by continuously mapping the environment. Niantic's Real World Platform is perhaps the company's greatest asset, and like a traditional game engine, it is a reusable, proprietary framework open to third-party licensing. Designed from a fundamental shift in perspective, Niantic's operating system was developed to support more seamless interactions between AR objects and real-world 3D space: "The Niantic Real World Platform advances the way computers see the world, moving from a model centered around roads and cars to a world centered around people" (Niantic Blog, 2018). This people-centric model uses the principles and techniques of machine learning and computer vision to interpret and understand the visual field, accurately identify and classify objects, detect and react to visual inputs, quickly shape the augmented environment around the player's movements, and support large-scale, interactive experiences wedded to shared geospatial objects and supported by a common infrastructure. Consumer data is central to scaling this experience, as Niantic continues to collect and curate a comprehensive dataset of user-generated places. To this end, *Pokémon GO* players can nominate PokéStops from within their own communities, although these must meet one of several human-interest criteria (cultural, educational or historical value; or a public gathering point, such as a park, library or transportation hub). Though self-contained, Niantic's AR system has multiple dependencies and requires a scalable infrastructure to support seamless data flows from the client-side game application (structured through a Unity API), to the runtime server, to players and sponsors. People are, indeed, central to this exchange. Players interact with the game client and provide critical action data that is passed to the server runtime layer and used to direct a series of connected services. Niantic views its platform as the technological embodiment of the company's core ideals of "exercise, exploration and social interaction" (Niantic Blog, 2019), though these ideals place heavy demands on consumer data plans, a concern raised by Democratic legislators shortly after the game's release, alongside other concerns for public safety following a series of play-related injuries. Niantic frames its work as the grander project of building a global operating system. From this perspective, we might falsely equate technical networks with organizational and individual networks—or assume that these three frameworks can be neatly aligned. There are virtuous goals attached to grand-scale world building, which maps our intimate worlds and visualizes the network of public spaces whose details form our sense of self. This larger mapping process is moving details, which may have eluded the broad image captures of Google Maps, to the AR cloud, where, full circle, technology can finally classify and make sense of them. And we have embraced this invitation, willfully bringing technology along with us into the places where we work, recreate and restore. Our games and programs are constantly running and recording—they have become an accepted (computational) base layer, always turned on, always accessible, always networked and always interacting with each other.

A wave of location-based mobile games followed the release of *Pokémon GO*. Many are dependent on the Google ecosystem and make common use of Google Maps. The Google Maps Platform for games allows developers to access real-time Google Maps data. Google also launched a Unity software development kit (SDK) to simplify the incorporation of mapping data into game environments, and an API for developers to create gameplay experiences around real-world locations. Taken together, these three integrated parts allow developers to realize the Google directive to transform the world into a playground. Unity integration allows developers to build detailed worlds using Maps data as a base to paint over or transform, creating unique game environments that still feel connected to the real world. It is a more nuanced form of augmentation that melds machine layers and naturalizes the imperatives of engine-based algorithmic manipulation—combining augmented reality and location-based gameplay. Google encourages developers to transform the natural world using Unity, turning topographic features into customizable game assets filtered through Unity's physics, lighting, AI and post-processing effects. It leverages its API to drive players into specified real-world locations. The central premise of *The Walking Dead: Our World* (published by Next Games, 2018) is to "fight walkers in the real world," and the game's narrative drive is to "explore and defend your neighborhood" (Next Games, 2020). The game attempts to monetize the experience through in-game purchases, building in a number of preset paywalls that restrict exploration (the game's energy-based system is a time gating mechanic). Other 2018 mobile releases include *Ghostbusters World* (published by FourThirtyThree) and *Jurassic World Alive* (Ludia), both built in Unity with Google Maps integration. As is the case with Niantic's platform, in the hands of each developer, the Unity build environment is leveraged for its reusability—as a foundation for iterative intellectual properties that, like any sustainable genre, feature a repeatable set of characteristics. Rather than teasing apart the representational attributes (the assets) of each of these location-based games, or even their variations on a user interface, we need to pay closer attention to how human-centric "user events" interact with the computer-mediated layer of the same communication structures (Chun, 2006, 249). As engine-driven environments become a norm of engagement, the threat to the known user is not about how much data is recorded with each interaction, but how familiar those interactions become, and how readily they are mapped onto what seem to be rather divergent pathways.

If we understand space as the practice of place (Certeau, 1984), and the result of the labors and rituals of individuals who negotiate its orderliness, we can situate our study of game engines as one additional layer of complexity that helps us probe beneath any theory of representation to see code and engine as interconnected discursive and material strategies that seek to conform, to present "proper" models of space (Kitchin and Dodge, 2011, 70). Scrutinizing the algorithmic nature of the engine (a feature common to its many subsystems, including AI), we can see how code transforms space and how engine-based operations are increasingly leveraged to produce automated solutions to relational problems (Kitchin and Dodge, 2011, 73). Adrian Mackenzie (2003) suggests that as technical objects evolve over time, they develop their own teleology—they become more concrete (17). Even though it is context-dependent, the common work that engines are asked to do across multiple social, cultural and economic vectors can bind together these diverse realities and, in doing so, level both individual agency and collective life.

Mapping and Engine-Driven Environments

The series of technological insights used in mobile game development have been fully integrated into other commercial enterprises. The client base for the Google Maps Platform includes insurers, financial service providers and real estate agencies (Allstate, Allianz, Redfin). The platform builds a certain dependency that parallels the dependency on the versioning of the underlying engine. Working with Google Maps, developers have access to all of the current cloud-based mapping information, and the AR-based experience can stay updated as Google continuously adds more buildings, roads, parks and other topographic assets. Allstate uses the Google Maps Platform for its GoodHome app to create an exploratory map that visualizes customers' homes with location-specific information about common and costly claims. The app binds together geolocation, real-time weather animation, city population statistics and localized tips to help people protect their homes. It pulls data from nine APIs, including Google Maps, Onboard Informatics, Weather Underground, Berkeley Lab's Home Energy Saver and Allstate's Common & Costly Claims. While Allstate claims it is helping people live a good life (through the company's good hands), and invests in their protection through risk assessment and abatement, these interrelated data sets reduce individuals and families to fluid fiduciary subjects whose assets can be continuously reassessed and valuated.

Foregrounding process, this knowledge of the subject is useful for drawing out an analytical distinction regarding code. Code is a textual and social practice, actively written, tested, distributed and enacted; it is instantiated, but also concretized, as software—engineered and bound to a commercial product, where it becomes functional, purposeful and prescriptive (Berry, Philosophy, 2011, 31–32). Code is continuously transcribed as software and, as a result, appropriated as an ongoing cultural practice (Fuller, 2003, 173). And while Unity, Unreal and other engines may be publicly knowable, as part of the landscape of open source development, what stands between the open source tool, the private company and the end user is always a proprietary API. The API is the cornerstone of the political economy of software development, boosting the performance of a company's own products and queries, and setting it apart from its competitors (Berry, Philosophy, 2011, 70).

Game engines and the associated software libraries are sites of aggressive entrepreneurship. Viewed collectively, they are an arena of research and development that is changing the landscape of contemporary visual culture, knowledge production, object orientation and engagement; and they are broadening the strategic investments of already integrated media industries (deepening the foundations of the culture-industry). Engines take years to develop and are becoming increasingly complex in their code. The Unreal Engine, created by Epic Games, has been in production since 1994 and contains over 2.5 million lines of code. Epic co-founder and technical director Tim Sweeney has pointed out that the code work of the Unreal Engine is comparable to the complexity of whole operating systems from just a decade ago (Stuart, 2009). David Berry (Philosophy, 2011) notes: "Understanding computer code and software is difficult enough, but when they are built into complicated assemblages that can be geographically dispersed and operating in highly complex inter-dependent ways, it is no surprise that we are still struggling to comprehend these systems and technologies as running code" (99). As a runtime operation, as an executable structure that exceeds its textual form, code collapses space and time, binds together diverse actors and mediates human experience; it may seem to run autonomously, but it is also bound to these operations that it must turn into a linear flow. Engines, APIs and databases, as parts of software structures, must produce readable results; together, they function as invented code objects that, as Bruno Latour (1986) suggests, "must have the properties of being mobile but also immutable, presentable, readable and combinable with one another" (7). Individual circuits of articulation can be commingled and interwoven with each other to produce deeper cultural logics. In Allstate's hands, discrete software objects have been bundled together to create a detailed family portrait founded on algorithmic models of authority that treat social realities as fundamentally technical problems (Pasquale, 2015, 8).

Engine-driven environments are becoming increasingly commonplace across the mediated reality ecosystem—the umbrella of extended reality (XR) and the descriptive forms of augmented (AR), virtual (VR) and mixed reality (MR)—and, as they do so, they are deepening the associated technical and ideological complexities of algorithmic processes. In a climate of increasingly dense technological assemblages, algorithmic processes are accumulating greater social, cultural and economic capital. Frank Pasquale (2015) notes that, across systems of governance, "critical decisions are made not on the basis of the data *per se*, but on the basis of data analyzed algorithmically" (21). These projects and systems are interconnected through the common deployment of proprietary engines, such as Unity and Unreal, that depend on the mutual brokerage of data. Game engines have stimulated applied innovation across convergent media fields (film and television, journalism, game and interaction design) and across genres (from news to entertainment), and they are central to the technological and content-driven variations on the common theme of immersion. Game engine technologies highlight developing synergies across fields, the changing landscape of what were once distinct media industries, and the blurred boundaries between media and content forms (and perhaps the colonization of critical media industries by techno-fetishistic entrepreneurial drives). We can read this quite literally in the fluid transmedia intertextuality fostered by *The Walking Dead, Ghostbusters, Jurassic World, Harry Potter* and other entertainment properties that have been made over into location-based mobile experiences, each inserting the physical world into a pre-existing and familiar genre-laden supersystem of blended assets.

Though engaged with the production of code, engine developers have been consistently attentive to the business of desire (and its relative freedom as a commodity). This desire has coalesced around three organizing fantasies—post-traumatic integration, embodiment and cultural production—that are shaped by code and uniquely tethered together by an engine. And the fantasies of integration and embodiment have been speedily advanced by the principles and mechanics of XR.

Game developers, mobile app developers and programmers are leading the expanded deployment of engines in extended reality applications, where engines drive asset creation and execution, even as most industry analysis remains focused on hardware (rather than software and middleware). Predictions about which device or platform will conquer the marketplace are too numerous to inventory. The study of human-machine interaction in real-and-virtual combined environments has landed squarely on commodity production—a choice of wearables or handheld devices in a broad range of industrial and cultural enterprises. Bracketing out the disparate ideological work performed by each of these experiments or fully developed enterprise efforts, these investigations are largely about tools. When they break out to become more productive, they stand as critical and practical negotiations of various data layers. That is to suggest that many of the larger questions about build, asset development and engine deployment remain unasked. Whether the world is remapped or simply renegotiated along a coded continuum, or whether it is more radically aligned according to the industrial logic of geopolitical territorialization seem to be matters that are too unwieldy, or they are simply obscured by the more immediate gratifications of knowledge production and acquisition, mastering one's domain, or the pursuit of the real through simulation.

As I have indicated elsewhere, we must remember that code carries power relations and distributes agency. Code organizes everyday life and contours personhood, yet it readily disappears behind functional surfaces and the onward push toward efficiency (in work and leisure). The push toward virtual mobility (or rather, mobilized virtuality) is indicative of an ongoing pursuit of mastery—controlling the game world and, by extension, the world at large. For commercial developers, this is about harnessing, transforming and delivering data; it is about reproducing the world and patterning human behavior along a particular and productive axis of desire (for example, writing a quest with quantifiable outcomes). For players or consumers, there is the promise of fulfillment, of organizing the world; these experiences are less about liberating the body from its normal limitations and more about fixing perception (knowing the world as a series of discrete object lessons). While the pleasure of immersion is commonly formulated around the body without limits, mobilized virtuality associates pleasure with the pursuit of knowledge and the creation of order. These mobile experiences should not be associated with what has often been understood in discussions of immersion as the development of cyborg consciousness (Friedman, 1999), of internalizing computational logic; for the body and the world are aligned with computation as part of the development pipeline and in gameplay at the level of the engine. The moment of possibility when the player might be understood as an extension of a computer process is undone by the disciplinary logic of map-based games.

Mapping and the Visual Record

Maps are commonplace tools for understanding the world; the act of transcription is self-evident. As a visual record, maps present a primary concretization of travel; their subjugation to the logic of a game engine brings with it a secondary order of fixity. And game architecture, the grammar of the engine, holds onto that duality—the affective dimension of the game depends on a heightened awareness of spectacle that, at the same time, requires the seamless operation of the engine, its libraries, and its associated cloud-based supports. Location-based gameplay and adjacent map-based systems move us closer to understanding computation as a representational medium, although what remains hidden are the constraints of specific tools. The realization of a "frictionless ideal," of interweaving a quantitative data layer with a qualitative graphical overlay, conceals the matter of process, of work, of the complex systems that undergird cause and effect (Mateas, "Procedural Literacy," 2005, 105) and bind data to experience. Our attention is drawn outward here, to focus on the sociopolitical dimensions of data and attend to the geopolitics of spatialized knowledge, rather than inward toward the body.

In October 2007, the architectural firm HKS announced a licensing deal with Epic Games to bring the Unreal Engine 3 into the company's development process in order to produce detailed interactive models and environments for future projects and allow clients to see proposed new structures in more intimate detail through real-time 3D visualizations. HKS modeled the W Hotel and the surrounding landscape in downtown Dallas using Unreal technology, and the firm deployed the engine in the pre-visualization work associated with the new Dallas Cowboys stadium, as well as stadiums for the Indianapolis Colts and the Liverpool, England, football club.

HKS is not alone in applying game engine architecture to architectural work writ large. London-based PLP Architecture has been experimenting with both Unity and Unreal to create virtual versions of building proposals, working with both game engines to create real-time, immersive and interactive visualizations. Similarly, Vancouver firm AES Engineering has used game engine technologies to illustrate architectural lighting concepts and effects for the firm's clients, and to create interactive visualizations (rather than static prebuilt renderings) to clarify the agency's design intent in its site plans. Map-based systems are being integrated into interactive visualizations to study the terrain, open source and editorialize the terrain, and ultimately build over it. We might see this latter activity as akin to level design in the engine-based 3D renders produced by a number of architectural firms.

FIGURE 5.1 HKS interactive ray-traced stadium design with Unreal Engine. Copyright 2019 HKS.

The Unreal Engine has expanded to find its own niche in commercial VR systems. In 2015, BMW adopted the Unreal Engine for a mixed-reality development process to advance its vehicle prototyping and, in doing so, effectively transformed its production methods and its labor force. Coupling VR hardware (the HTC Vive headset and developer kit) with the Unreal Engine, BMW has become more agile in its approach to design and engineering; the company's development engineers are able to harness data from simulated environmental driver testing to inform both vehicle form and function. At the 2016 Game Developers Conference, British automaker McLaren announced a similar partnership with Epic Games to license the Unreal Engine for its own proprietary model designs.

What marries these various industrial enterprises is their mutual dependence on a stable data-driven architecture (a game engine) that seems, paradoxically, malleable and context-dependent. The unilateral deployment of game engines as a foundation for data visualization illustrates the possible integration of distinct experiential impulses within a common codebase and the value of engine-based mechanics in commercial non-game applications. Enterprise users of the Unreal Engine will likely overtake game users by the end of 2019. The Unreal Engine is to Epic Games what AWS is to Amazon; both companies monetize the proprietary infrastructure used to support their core businesses. Over time, these infrastructure offerings have become core businesses of their own. The game engine is a corporately held communication infrastructure, perhaps even more powerful in that it can be scaled or localized without losing its integrity. This ability to scale has logically situated building and modeling within a common pattern language. Each engine fulfills an organizational fantasy, opens up an automated and repeatable process, and drives problems toward contextually aware solutions; each engine is an object-oriented software solution designed to be reused. Well-designed systems have clearly defined and efficient code structures that make them accessible, open to evaluation, and readily deployed; and while they are built to solve particular problems that occur over and over again in the built environment, their true value lies in their ability to address future problems and adapt to new requirements (Gamma et al., 1995, 2).

The HKS ARCHengine, built on the Unreal codebase, aligns architectural design with the processes and discourses of other industries. Touting the prescient nature of its engine-based work, the firm's promotional literature notes: "Architects are scrambling to provide the best possible presentation using techniques from Hollywood, Madison Avenue, NASA, and Nintendo to translate and transcend their designs" (Foresiepi, 2004, 35). Only an uneasy equivalence can be drawn across these industrial vectors, where clients do not have a particularly heightened level of agency—where perspectival relations are drawn for them and, perhaps, contoured around them as a purely technical function of algorithmically determined procedural animation. In these terms, advanced previsualization techniques simply extend the horizon of visual spectacle or lead to certain regulating efficiencies that shape the means of production. Once again, profit-driven methods push social realities to the margins, as these values are not readily drawn into the encoded rules of localized proprietary engines.

Next Generation Engines

Pushing further to consider emerging application space, we can understand the increasing dependency on engines and the increasing cultural capital of game developers within vertically integrated culture industries as having a significant impact on labor itself. The evolution of embodiment and the requisite build of engine-driven blended environments is about more than aligning game space with lived space; play is not the only imperative. Mixed reality efforts have been supported by next generation game engines that can meet the relatively high data demands—for scene detail, framerate and resolution—associated with immersive experiences. Unity provides support for Microsoft's HoloLens (a self-contained holographic computer), while Unreal supports a broad range of VR and AR hardware, including the Oculus Rift and Quest, HTC Vive and Google VR.

The future of blended reality and its enterprise applications depends on the progress of its engines, which continue to be extended in the singular pursuit of realism. The study of engines moves us well beyond the paradigms of both ludology and narratology, and further into a "critical political analysis of the medium" (Dyer-Witheford, 2009, xxvi). It allows us to pull back the game layer, the playable interface, to more forcefully consider the economic and political conditions of game development and deployment and the associated labors of production. I am trying to avoid the representational trap that Lev Manovich (2001) lays out in *The Language of New Media*, in which he suggests digitization has ushered in a change in media culture writ large by fundamentally changing the nature of its artifacts. Instead, my focus is on the software structures that undergird digital manipulation of old media and form the foundation of contemporary fabrication. Such an analysis requires holding onto material structures while giving heightened attention to the functional structures of computational media (Bogost, 2006, 27).

The horizontal movement of engines into distinct vertically integrated market sectors should not be confused with the crude dynamics of gamification—with appropriating (and capitalizing on) the incidental mechanics, properties, rewards and behaviors of gameplay. Nor should we assume the movement of engines into other market sectors is a signpost of the persistence of play as a broad cultural attitude. In fact, game engines are quite often used as closed systems for the build of new assets—assets that can be mobilized, but not played; assets that are conceived, outsourced and developed remotely (in isolation), and then later deployed in deeply saturated and socialized semantic contexts. That is to suggest that these assets become fully articulated, fully meaningful, only when they enter the public domain. The engine has become a primary unit of both play and non-play; in the latter state, as part of its dominant enterprise application, game engines are not being used to gamify. Indeed, they are breaking the magic circle. Game engines are commonly being used to build experiences that do not have the inherent properties of games; they are being used for radical efficiency. Game engines have not been adequately considered for their role in establishing the field of play, setting rules, and reframing the magic circle, as Jesper Juul (2008) suggests, as a negotiated boundary—one being crossed not simply by players, but by developers.

Working with The Future Group, a company that specializes in immersive mixed reality and real-time photorealistic visual effects, in 2018 The Weather Channel began building out the various elements it would need to make extreme weather events feel like they were happening in-studio, as part of a live, multi-camera production environment. Using Unreal, The Future Group translated real-time water levels and events into graphic effects, mapping the storm surge caused by Hurricane Florence across the eastern seaboard in September 2018 (Figure 5.2). In June of the same year, The Weather Channel aired a similar real-time, in-studio demonstration of the lifecycle of a tornado, dropping virtual debris around network meteorologist Jim Cantore.

Bringing extreme weather to life is not an entirely altruistic pursuit; it makes for compelling television. By shaping weather into spectacle, the tactics of immersion also work to make meteorology more knowable. Datacentric metrics (windspeed, storm surge) and live storm data are transformed into more readily recognizable and quantifiable assets. Large-scale objects mapped in relation to the

FIGURE 5.2 The Weather Group and The Future Group bring mixed reality to The Weather Channel with Unreal Engine.

Copyright 2019 The Weather Channel.

human body quantify their size and potential impact, as a loose corollary to a heads-up display. Visualizations help residents understand the localized impact of environmental events through a perverse aesthetics of disaster. Channeled through the code-based mechanics of engine-driven extended reality, the studio, the landscape of television, and the world at large are tethered together as machine-readable sites. This new (media) economy of oversaturated effects is recontouring technoscientific knowledge and binding algorithmic culture to the logic of visual spectacle.

In the private sector, more companies are using engine-based VR to transform the way they train and develop their employees, filtering real-world experiences through technologically mediated environments. Most of these efforts are outsourced to independent developers with the talent and technology to focus on nascent forms of professional development. Strivr, one such company, has been working with a broad range of vendors, including Walmart, as it continues to expand its VR training portfolio by building virtual environments for the company's employee training academies. The primary build environment for Strivr is the Oculus Rift, with the majority of its experiences driven by the Unity engine. Strivr markets its investment in immersive learning experiences as "a new approach to human capital" (Strivr, 2019, 3) that can drive real-world behavioral change. The data and analytics available through Unity provide feedback to both developers and clients. Industry applications cull usage data to answer a number of mission critical questions. Who uses the product and for how long? What are the common user errors? At the same time, these applications form a holistic profile of the user—head and eye movements can be mapped to return-on-investment metrics. Walmart's VR-enhanced training experiences are focused on active store scenarios—managing spills and accidents, resolving customer service situations, stocking the produce wet wall, handling new technologies (such as in-store pickup towers)—that test the performance of its sales associates and assess compliance.

In 2017, UPS announced the integration of VR simulations into the company's own training curriculum. UPS developed its experiences in-house, building for the HTC Vive headset with a Unity framework to fabricate workplace-related assets, such as hyper-realistic streetscapes. These simulators, designed to help drivers spot road hazards, have been deployed for training at the company's Integrad instructional facilities (developed in collaboration with MIT and Virginia Tech). At its training facilities, UPS uses a hands-on approach to teach its workforce the fundamentals of driving delivery vehicles and delivering packages. Trainees practice driving UPS delivery trucks in a replica outdoor city that has real streets and sidewalks with simulated delivery and pickup sites.

These interactive studies of the environment are designed to elicit new knowledges or enhance human performance, and they all employ a scientific approach to draw civilized geographies. They draw maps based on common coded principles of projection, working across inscription (the domain of engines) and cognition (the domain of human subjects), and they insist on optical consistency (Latour, 1986, 8). The engines that drive these experiences are inherently prescriptive for both social and scientific reasons; they are framed by the incessant demands of pattern recognition, both in understanding the behaviors of human subjects and in establishing the architectural patterns of clean code that drive the development of engine-based experiences. Architectural patterns promote clean organization and simplify unit testing. In the context of Unity and Unreal applications, such patterning ties together the disparate scripts that would otherwise be scattered throughout the program hierarchy and formalizes the communication between components that might otherwise develop inconsistencies. The most common software design patterns bifurcate concerns, separating the main business logic of the program from its presentation (the user interface). Game engines consistently follow this organizational logic, as their parts are defined by their functionality—for example, rendering, animation, physics, networking and scripting. They inherently separate logic, render and input. For example, the Unreal architecture uses modules to separate concerns; the engine is implemented as a large collection of modules (that encapsulate a set of functionalities) that are augmented by game-specific modules.

The worldview proposed by Walmart, UPS, The Weather Channel and, indeed, many open-world game developers is driven by a scientific method that traverses technology and culture—binding together how the engine sees the world with how the developer agent as a cultural subject sees the world. Both work together to make the world visible, and both are governed by the same overarching economic infrastructure. Here I am following Latour's (1986) logic on the power of inscription:

> What is so important in the images and in the inscriptions scientists and engineers are busy obtaining, drawing, inspecting, calculating and discussing? It is, first of all, the unique advantage they give in the rhetorical or polemical situation. "You doubt of what I say? I'll show you."
>
> *(p. 14)*

These broad-ranging optical pursuits are designed to promote a consistent perspective; indeed, the mechanics of immersion depend on optical consistency. Each ideological imperative is bound to its technical corollary.

The Knight Foundation/Niantic report from the Playful Cities Group is grounded on a straightforward question: "How can cities position large platforms—including those managed by game companies—for local goals?" (Stokes et al., 2018, 1). The assumption is that game engine architectures and assets can readily bridge industrial and municipal vectors, a practice that is now commonplace—as engine source code continues to bind together industry-specific software environments and holdings (Unreal to architectural drafting, Unity to mapping). The push toward software integration across multiple economic sectors is, in fact, key to the valuation of companies such as Epic Games.

One of the primary obstacles to the localization of *Pokémon GO* was a set of conflicting priorities—the desire for a responsive application that could meet unique public needs and aptly describe local neighborhoods (augmented micro-regionalism) was in opposition to the company's (Niantic) ongoing attention to operational stability and growth. This tension was most obvious at the data layer, and it was tied to the relational value of city data that might otherwise be used as a lever for community engagement, a site for storytelling, an active repository of a community's history and a touchpoint for agency. The developmental emphasis on architectural patterns and the "passion for clean code" are signposts of smart application development that may simplify the transactions between designers and programmers in the game development pipeline. However, these best practices—these universal calls to order—are a form of governance that calls out a series of structured interactions and sets the terms for participation. While our critique readily reveals the degree to which the public sphere can be colonized or whitewashed by the logic of algorithmic certainty, we need to work harder to unravel the complex economies of data and the processes of aggregation and integration, teasing out the design pattern to understand the structured relations between the model (game logic), the view (user interface), the controller (device) and the user (citizen player). In the case of extreme weather, aggregation and integration have forged a new pornography of disaster.

The Role of Alternative Languages

There have been a number of distinct efforts to bend otherwise rigid engine architectures to meet the "unruliness" of cultural complexity. The Torque 3D engine, developed by GarageGames and released through a permissive MIT open source license in 2012, is written in (and can be added to, altered or optimized with) C++. As the release documentation assures, "Using TorqueScript and the collection of tools that are included with Torque 3D, you can build complete games (of many different genres) without ever touching a single line of C++ code" (GarageGames, 2017, 3). With further words of encouragement, the developer states quite frankly, "Do not be intimated. This documentation will show you how to create games without touching the source code at all" (GarageGames, 2017, 3). Torque 3D has its roots in the Torque Game Engine, which was built from technology developed by Dynamix and subsequently licensed by GarageGames, a studio formed by departing Dynamix personnel. In 2001, pursuing a collaborative shareware model (with publishing restrictions attached to revenue caps), GarageGames offered the Torque Game Engine and its full source code to independent developers through a $100 indie license, making it significantly more affordable than competing frameworks. At the opposite end of the price spectrum, id Software's *Quake III Arena* engine (id Tech 3) carried a hefty price tag of $250,000 for a single title license (Pedersen, 2003, 189). GarageGames discontinued sales of the Torque Game Engine in 2009, with the release of Torque 3D.

The prospect of deploying an engine without touching the source code is a promising one, but most game development projects require some degree of customization. Torque 3D is one of several tools that make such a promise, alongside GameMaker, RPG Maker, GameSalad and Adventure Game Studio. More robust engines such as Unity and Unreal make similar claims. The Unreal Engine offers Blueprints visual scripting, a node-based interface that allows non-programmers to work with a broad range of common gameplay elements; the Unity editor supports dragging pre-built scripts onto in-game objects; and the online Unity community offers a large supply of publicly sourced code and assets. But fast prototyping in Unity and Unreal still requires that non-programmers know how to navigate the engine interface and understand fundamental programming concepts, such as components and nodes. At the same time, prototyping with pre-built assets is, in itself, a limiting gesture, setting additional parameters on gameplay and content that may be counterproductive or counter-intuitive to a more expressive vocabulary of game design and experience, interfere with a developer's efforts to create more open and direct communication with players, and close down the dialogue between artist and audience. Those engines that foster a dependency on a visual programming interface do very little to advance computational literacy and to unmask the imperatives of code. At the same time, most entry-level engines, such as GameMaker and GameSalad, foster a particular approach to game development that is driven by their operational simplicity, where a dragging-and-dropping development environment pushes interactive storytellers in a particular direction, and where the operational imperatives of, for example, RPG Maker are aligned with a particular storytelling mode or genre (such as the role-playing game). Tools such as GameSalad are celebrated for their ability to teach the fundamentals of game design, and visual programming languages such as Scratch have been expressly developed to introduce younger students to programming basics; but the codification of particular fundamentals can also lead to a certain stagnation, to the normativizing of a style or approach, and to the supremacy of visual coding (a graphical rather than textual approach to programming). While these tools do not actively conceal the operational imperatives of more complex engines, they do little to familiarize students and instructors with the labors of those industries that write the governing conditions of code, and they subtly reify a new digital divide grounded in computational literacy.

In a study of the build of a game engine toolkit to support indigenous Australian Aboriginal storytelling, the ACID (Australasian CRC for Interaction Design) research cohort (a collaboration of university and industry partners) confronted the challenge of building an immersive narrative that could respond to the nuanced knowledges of indigenous peoples—intimate understandings of (and engagements with) rural lands built around communal experiences that might escape the logic of computational exactitude. Acknowledging this tension, the authors of the study note one of the central challenges of traditional game engines is the persistence of orthogonal built environments—a routine parameter that subjects the natural landscape to the logic of computation, rather than designing the subsystem architecture to meet the logic of the lived environment (Wyeld et al., 2007, 262). The study raises the critical question of "how technology can assist in the empowering of cultural identity in an increasingly homogenous world mediated by Western cultural values advanced by the same technology" (Wyeld et al., 2007, 267). In the case of ACID, the solution was to build a localized, licensed toolkit that contained regional assets built in consultation with represented communities, and that could be readily accessed across a networked structure.

The more dominant trend in topographic documentation and simulation, as predicated by the work of large-scale software developers, sharply diverges from the aforementioned model of community-driven asset creation and withholds the most advanced prospects of reciprocal empowerment. The challenge is not that game developers do not know how to use their tools. Many independent developers are selecting an appropriate platform; deftly creating, building and sharing assets; and crafting relatively open experiences to uniquely expressive ends (a subject I take up more forcefully in a subsequent chapter). Rather, the challenge is in the toolsets themselves and the governing parameters attached to physical objects, procedural animations and environmental interactions. This is, perhaps, the inherent limit of computing systems, of mapping computational descriptions onto physical descriptions—situating objects within a coordinate system of vector operations—and more problematically, onto causal relations (Piccinini, 2009). But mapping has become a widely accepted industrial practice, aligned with efficiency, certainty and security.

Data Visualization and Geographic Capital

Geographically based game tools can readily transform landscape into a playable interface, and as they do so, they inherently guide us against entropy to produce knowable space; algorithmic certainty is a functional imperative of game engines.

Mourning the loss of the traveler, Michel de Certeau (1984) suggests that the map in its current flattened geographical form is disengaged from the dimensional itineraries that were the condition of its possibility. Mapping marks a movement from description (and the actual experience of the terrain) to prescription; the mechanics of drafting produce a stagnant concretization of travel—not even a souvenir, but simply a grid. The representation of movement fosters inertia, allowing us to move without warranting any dialogue about the process. Even as these grids become three-dimensional, as we move from two-dimensional software design to spatial computing, the reinvented user experience depends on control (responsive mechanisms for eye-tracking, head-positioning, hand gestures and voice).

De Certeau's concern is made manifest in contemporary navigation programs, such as Google Maps or the grander Google Earth, as well as new forms of meaningful spatial interaction; these are all variations on a database, commonly used only as mechanisms for getting somewhere or for securely navigating new and uncertain terrain. Travel and movement have become politicized only in their very depoliticization, in the reduction of temporally and spatially bound experiences to a series of coordinates. An engine, in one broad sweep, is capable of enacting (in parallel fashion) buildings, neighborhoods, communities, homes and workplaces. This may seem an inherently practical exercise of (computing) power, but it is nevertheless a value-laden transcription.

As we are presented with new imaging technologies, we are also offered new ways of organizing the visual field. But such new patterns, structures and forms of organization may find opposition in the cultures and traditions (the social contexts) that ground them. The digital age, as with any significant evolutionary period, necessitates looking forward and backward; it warrants a dual attention, an understanding of both continuities and discontinuities. *Pokémon GO* may be of value to revitalizing Western forms of engagement, but the game's release in China has been hindered by a number of cloud conflicts, which include limited access to Google services; these obstacles highlight the lasting power of the state apparatus, illustrate radically distinct (though potentially aligned) logics of territorial control that hinge on how data are allowed to flow (and how data are mined), and remind us of the lingering materiality of digital culture (as it remains bound to formal structures and policies).

Herbert Marcuse (1964) warns, "In advanced capitalism, technical rationality is embodied, in spite of its irrational use, in the productive apparatus" (22). Marcuse cautions us about the loss of viable space for transcending historical practice. Freeing up computation and freeing up culture requires a cooperative interaction that makes sense of the complexity of everyday life without necessitating reductionism or inflexible dependence on predetermined courses of action, understandings, laws of engagement or programs. Code and data, and software and hardware, interact as a discursive construct (and each is a discursive construction in its own right) shaped by history, culture, industry and technology that may encourage certain forms of engagement (Freedman, 2011). But the outcomes of their applied uses may provide some useful lessons in understanding to what degree individuality is compromised by the general computational codes and filters of industrially sanctioned technological forms, or to what degree these codes can be massaged.

In an age of pervasive computing, we must read ourselves against the dominant forms of technological projection and consider how technology, too, is practiced. My goal in the next chapter is to highlight several key pressure points between personal agency and industrial design, as autobiography, collectivity, community and civic life are dynamic processes that are all too commonly channeled through static sign systems—engineered by a series of interrelated organizing technologies that orient us to the world, shape our social movements and influence our developmental pathways.

6

GAME ENGINE ARCHITECTURE: VISUALIZING SPACE AND PLACE

Throughout this book, one of the underlying assumptions has been that closed design and deployment systems inevitably push human agency in particular directions; and my goal in discussing the mechanics of software has been to reveal how technologies function as causal influences in the social trajectories of individuals and, by extension, their communities. To gain greater access to this critical vantage point that situates individuals in more communal frameworks, this chapter moves outside the bounds of game engines *per se* to reflect on other forms of engines and conversely to consider the influence of engine-based games in the absence of their mechanics. These additional paths of analysis will productively expand our perspective, and allow us to more fully consider the influence of software and its associated engine components on everyday life, on public space, and more narrowly on the civic axis of the open data movement (a particular form of software practice) that is being used to aggregate, analyze and develop the open world.

In *A Pattern Language* (Alexander, 1977), architect Christopher Alexander suggests that a shared pattern language is central to the vitality of city planning and construction; a systematized yet human-centered design language can be used to reference common problems and solutions in the built environment, as well as the interrelatedness of these causal chains, where larger patterns inform smaller ones, and where smaller patterns are dependent on deliberate large-scale practices:

> This is a fundamental view of the world. It says that when you build a thing you cannot merely build that thing in isolation, but must also repair the world around it, and within it, so that the larger world at that one place becomes more coherent, and more whole; and the thing which you make takes its place in the web of nature, as you make it.

This is the matter of responsive worldbuilding, or connecting higher and lower level orders of design; and it suggests a careful attention to situated practices, to reciprocal engagements, and to re-establishing the natural order of things—to allowing physical design to respond to human relationships. Alexander is, in part, arguing against the narrowing frame of computer-assisted architectural visualization, and suggesting that coding can make design systems more nuanced and complex, that algorithms can reveal formerly unseen possibilities, and that in practiced application, planned physical structures can allow room for accidental discoveries, nuanced and unplanned adjacencies—what Alexander (1965) terms a "semilattice" structure found in the complex network of overlaps, redundancies and unanticipated interactions that make the city more dynamic and discoverable.

The emphasis on coherence and on constant repair might remind us of the operational imperatives of engine-based logic; revisions to the software layer (to the codebase) need to be constantly sealed over to produce stability in a game's runtime components and consistency in its animated assets and environments. And patterns, in their modularity and in their ability to be purposefully redeployed, bear a marked similarity to the determining logic of game engines and their principle *raison d'être*. And engines, broadly (and perhaps too deterministically) speaking, have consequences; they are built to regulate, interpret, organize, emulate, automate, render and visualize. As we build, we should not simply look for patterns or browse through a catalog of pattern maps that can be laid over new problems; instead patterns must be derived through process. That is to suggest they must unfold as part of the design process. Game engine development, in the hands of independent developers, is an effort to actively build new patterns; the engine is a site where code coalesces (forms a pattern) and becomes a unique solution that aligns with a novel problem. That discovery, that new coded connection point between problem and solution, may of course then be repeated—it becomes an organic pattern language, and a focused environmental solution. Yet it also becomes a pathway that equates data and agency, and concretizes, normalizes and conceals its procedural imperatives. And in the hands of larger developers, the movement from discovery to stasis is much swifter and more pervasive, as it leverages the flows of global capital and leads to more rigidly determined models of industrial labor (and marketplace dependencies) that interfere with ongoing and perhaps more radical forms of revision.

Synthetic Environments and Engine-Based Entertainment

Game engines are tools that are shaping our engagement with real, virtual and blended environments, and as I have hopefully made clear, engines are shaping how we engage with a world of everyday objects that have been made over to conform to the conditions of a machine-readable economy. Game engines are increasingly at the center of diverse forms of media spectacle—film, television, theme parks (which draw from the references of film, television, games and other aspects of visual culture)—and are part of the fabric of industrial entertainment, as well as news and information. Engines and their algorithms are a part of integrated data processing systems (controlled ecosystems for digital content creation and digital asset management) and have become a natural part of optical and auditory experience. Game engines are at the heart of an ever-expanding visual effects industry. They are shaping the perceptions of audiences and the workflows of content creators, fostering certain dependencies within localized development pipelines on algorithmic design and translation. We can understand this, perhaps too simply, as a layered approach to the construction of environmentally bound visual culture—assembling 2D and 3D art and assets into scenes with defined coordinate maps, added lighting, audio, special effects, physics and animation, and in the case of games and other interactive media forms, scripted interactivity, artificial intelligence, gameplay logic and an overlaid graphical user interface—realized through several distinct yet synthesized engine-based operations.

Film and television directors often turn to engine-driven storyboard animatics and stunt visualizations as part of the production process; while visual effects teams depend on game engines as part of previsualization and post-production asset building, environmental effects and compositing, and a number of real-time render constructs that have significantly broadened the field of in-camera visual effects. Engines are also an increasingly common previsualization tool for a number of non-media industries. A number of major Hollywood studios have expanded their programming teams to leverage data-oriented approaches to image production and address complex design challenges; several have built proprietary engine-based tools or framework layers to feed third-party engines or complement well-established design tools. In 2017, DreamWorks Animation introduced MoonRay, a high-speed rendering architecture designed to accelerate image generation while supporting collaborative workflows. As with most proprietary software systems, MoonRay integrates a wide variety of third-party toolsets for 3D visualization, including Autodesk Maya and MotionBuilder—taking advantage of large-scale distributed rendering as part of a modern system architecture that utilizes open source components and differentiated APIs to produce a more intuitive workflow (Lee et al., 2017), while still honoring the industry-standard development environments that are familiar to most artists and the scripting languages and patterns that are familiar to most programmers. This blended approach to design, both algorithmic and visual, is modeled after the dually informed methodology of the games industry, which depends heavily on data-oriented design at the systems layer and in visual processing, while drawing from object-oriented approaches for asset creation. MoonRay uses a particular subset of computational algorithms—image-based Monte Carlo rendering algorithms—for modeling complex visual systems. The unique requirements of an image synthesis algorithm depend on the application (Lafortune, 1996, 3); as film and media producers pursue higher degrees of realism (accurate scene geometry, illumination effects and physics) they create stronger dependencies between modeling (inputs) and rendering (outputs). Lighting, textures, materials and other object-oriented and elemental attributes and effects are translated into rule-based operations with readily managed parameters and inheritance-based properties. Software-driven synthetic imagery is commonly tied to an established object orientation and scene grammar that binds objects to their environments and adheres to familiar markers of fidelity. Physically based rendering is noticeably advancing the field of cinematography (using physics informed by natural environmental mechanics as a base for creative expression). Industrial Light & Magic (ILM) has integrated the Unreal Engine into StageCraft VR, the company's virtual production system, to allow its creative teams to work with real-time assets as part of a more robust and collaborative approach to cinematic previsualization, production design and performance capture. The Lucasfilm production of *Solo: A Star Wars Story* (2018) blended engine-based visualizations with traditional filmmaking techniques to streamline the workflow and build of complex visual effects sequences and virtual sets; similarly, *The Mandalorian* (2019) draws from a suite of virtual production tools made available through the Unreal Engine and follows an emerging trend that weds engine-based rendering to live-action filmmaking (shooting in a responsive blended environment and seamlessly matching physical sets to virtual environmental assets that can be modified in real time).

In 2019, both Unity Technologies and Epic Games were recognized by the Advanced Imaging Society for their respective contributions to the entertainment industry—for building integrated software systems that have transformed the creative processes of the industry by driving data-intensive, real-time collaborative production methods across game and non-game media forms. DreamWorks Animation was recognized as well, as part of an ever-expanding list of software-driven approaches to the design of visual content.

Epic's Unreal Engine has become part of an evolving industrial entertainment complex. As with Unity, the company has leveraged its engine to push beyond video games into television, film and virtual reality, and meet the emerging visualization needs of multiple media and information industries; and the company has continued to diversify its portfolio by building out its core technologies well beyond its own intellectual properties, balancing the company's reputation on both its games and its engine. For both Unity and Epic, the engine acts as a stabilizing economic force, as the key to building out lucrative partnership agreements that also illustrate the synergies between developing games and developing technologies (Crecente, 2016), and that bind together diverse industry segments in a wide-reaching software service model (in the same way that Autodesk software services architecture, construction, engineering, manufacturing, media, entertainment and education, and Adobe has its own enterprise market share).

At the March 2016 Game Developers Conference, Epic introduced Sequencer, a multi-track non-linear editor that can be used to power visual effects across content forms (film, television, video games), and forecasted the tool's use in live broadcasts. The Weather Channel's extreme weather assets are evidence of Epic's vision. In 2017, the Nickelodeon group launched its Entertainment Lab, an initiative that has broadened the company's youth-centered media portfolio by reaching into alternative authoring pipelines. Since its formation, the Entertainment Lab has relied on the Unreal Engine for several of its VR projects and is currently exploring how game engines might shift the studio's approach to animation—a move toward real-time rendering that can also facilitate cross-platform development, to reach kids across screens and to seamlessly integrate other media-rich experiences. Describing the in-development animated project *Meet the Voxels* (working title), Senior Vice President Chris Young has suggested,

> Our vision is to take the real-time technology we've been exploring in the Lab and marry it with a creative concept that connects with kids and their passion for video games. We designed this next-gen animation workflow and filled it with characters who can exist naturally across multiple platforms from day one.
>
> *(Nickelodeon, 2018)*

The cross-platform expansion of the Nickelodeon brand is being intentionally driven to reach young audiences across platforms and devices, and extends beyond new intellectual properties to parallel ventures that have deepened the engagement with existing brands; the *SpongeBob Challenge*, for example, is an Alexa skill that expands the single-screen experience to capitalize on the game-based potential of the smart speaker's voice-interaction. Nickelodeon is not the only major media brand using engine-based technologies to transform its approach to content creation and its governing attention to storytelling and worldbuilding. A custom implementation of the Unreal Engine is a critical run-time component of the Millennium Falcon attraction in Galaxy's Edge, a physical expansion of the *Star Wars* universe that opened at Disney parks in 2019 (Champagne, 2018). Game-based technologies are driving the next generation of transmedia storytelling. Game engines are at the center of a series of ubiquitous entertainment supersystems, and are being used to construct an expanded field of (platform agnostic) stories, assets and environments.

Unity Technologies is more properly understood as a software development company. Unlike Epic Games, Unity is not a game developer, although the company is firmly positioned to take on an expansive suite of similar business clients—architecture, design, construction, engineering, manufacturing, film, television, and other industries dependent on customizable visualization engines often hybridized with other development tools. The Unity engine was fused with live-action filmmaking techniques to create the 2019 release of *The Lion King*, in what the production team has described as a virtual production process that required a Unity-compatible asset management system and a method for translating and refining 3D scene files shot in Unity. Taken together, these non-game sectors form a significant part of Unity's revenue base. Like Epic, Unity is also investing in building the foundation layers for augmented and virtual reality content creation, and focused on enhancing data performance and developing automated AI solutions to speed the development process for media-dependent industrial applications. Both companies are invested in the algorithmic underpinnings of visual communication, and building the requisite communication infrastructure; and both companies are exploiting the graphical capabilities of game engine technologies to drive interaction, animation, previsualization, visualization and simulation across distinct creative economies.

Variations on a Theme Park: The Horrors of Game Engine Architecture

Game engines are transforming the media production pipeline and at the same time pushing the technological thresholds of mediated experience. Theme park designers have abandoned "flat rides" in favor of immersive experiences, to create blended environments that seamlessly integrate video and visual effects (VFX) and depend on the rendering power of game engines both in action and as part of the design process (advanced computer graphics drive previsualization); theme park owners have shifted their attention from hardware to media-driven experiences—immersive location-based entertainment that can be readily modified over time (McGowan, 2018). Nonetheless, as a theme park is still a physical space and a geographically bound experience, a tourist destination with active thoroughfares, market places and food courts, and a site of organized pedestrian flows, digital immersion happens hand-in-hand with its analog components and corollaries. Engines have not simply transformed the physical experience of the theme park, they have also shaped the psychosocial dimensions of engagement to produce what we might identify as the lingering trace of gamified spatial interaction. As a foundational architecture, the game engine is a system of control. It can function like the panopticon. As a universal agent of visualization, it can induce a persistent state of potential renderability and transformed visibility—intimating routine algorithmic manipulation. Game engines have become a stalwart component of ritualized storytelling and knowledge production; this is perhaps most obvious in a particular form of reflexive video game architecture—the game house or maze.

In 2012, Universal Studios introduced the first of its video game houses at its US parks as part of Halloween Horror Nights, an annual Halloween-themed special event that premiered at Universal Studios theme parks in the early 1990s. As part of its 2012 line-up of haunted houses and scare zones populated by live actors, Universal collaborated with game developer Konami to build a life-size walkthrough of *Silent Hill*, one of the company's primary survival horror game franchises. The teaser promoting the 2012 event mixes gameplay footage with hidden camera footage of park patrons, and plays on the fluid status of this intellectual property: "This is not a game. This is not a movie. This is real."

Following the success of this first foray into game space, in September 2013 Universal partnered with game developer Capcom to build an environment based on the *Resident Evil* franchise for its Orlando, Florida park. Universal Studios Japan had already developed the same intellectual property for its Osaka park—as a street environment for its September 2012 theme park makeover, and as a limited-run live-action shooting attraction that opened in July 2013. The latter build, *Biohazard: The Real* equipped visitors with a model gun loaded with 30 virtual bullets, and set them off on a quest to eradicate a viral contagion while navigating the theme park maze of in-game characters and set pieces, traveling the corridors of the Raccoon City Police Department and the Umbrella Research Center. Universal Studios Japan has also collaborated with Capcom on builds of the *Monster Hunter* franchise and is collaborating with Nintendo on Super Nintendo World, an upcoming theme park expansion that broke ground in 2017 with the promise of unparalleled game-based immersion.

The life-size set pieces of Halloween Horror Nights prioritize the realness of their environments and characters, foregrounding these assets, these signposts over narrative or agency—showcasing live actors as central game protagonists, creatures and bosses in readily identifiable game level designs, replete with the pleasures of their narrative associations and their ideological trappings. Those visiting the *Silent Hill* house encounter the game's monstrous nurses and the menacing Pyramid Head as they roam the streets of the titular town, while

FIGURE 6.1 *Resident Evil* theme park attraction at Halloween Horror Nights, Universal Studios Japan.

Copyright 2012 Universal Studios and Capcom Co., Ltd. All rights reserved.

those visiting the *Resident Evil* house enter a soundstage transformed into Raccoon City, where Leon Kennedy and Jill Valentine battle an assortment of bio-organic weapons and zombified creatures culled from several installments in the video game franchise. Within these built soundstage environments, our bodies are not simply at play. We are also projected, read by the industry and asked to engage in specific ways with its commodities; in these instances, theme park visitors are moved through choreographed "on-rails" experiences, along predetermined pathways that allow each level to be quickly reset for the next wave of participants. As we move through the darkly lit maze-like structure, we are not only passively read and acted upon, we are also projecting, caught in the act of revealing our fears and desires as we activate the fright night experience; and we are completing a circuit of relations that situates video games as one fragment of a grander enterprise of transmedia (moving between media) storytelling in a transmedia economy.

Theorists such as Janet Murray (1997) argue that a game is not simply a text to be read, but an experience to be had; such analyses offer context, point to narrative, history and interaction, and foreground the performative nature of gameplay and emphasize the value of individual agency. We must push further to consider how performance is contoured, as game architectures begin to migrate. Video game studies brings to the forefront the degree to which the rules that govern more historically grounded machines of production and projection can be tethered to a series of peripherals, and inversely the degree to which, in contemporary media space, computation informs most machines of projection within quite diverse institutional settings. Games extend our understanding of play and its centrality in the culture at large, and in the more focused case of video games, they remind us of embodiment even in the face of total immersion. Seeing the body under duress and feeling the body under duress, games often crystallize a complex relationship between corporeal experience (the body) and subjectivity. Studies of interactive media emphasize that consumers do not simply read images, they occupy and play through (or with) them; and the narrative space is often conflicted, the contextual elements and plot details never fully sewn up. Game narratives are often purposefully messy, and the discussions about images and stories are an important aspect of framing any consideration of the representational practices of particular media economies; in the case of the theme park attraction, our experience with the house or maze is continuously reflexive, measured against our experience with a paired intellectual property. As the two experiences have decidedly different interactive mechanics, we are left to measure the psychosocial dimensions of these respective engagements as well as the relative parity of their assets. The question is not whether the experience is real, but whether the analog characters and settings of the house match their digital counterparts; this reflexive distance suggests a studied engagement akin to a walkthrough, a method of play that asks us to openly consider the work (and strategies) of a game, and interrupts the conditions of immersion.

While video games are often connected to other entertainment forms and are part of grander culture-industry supersystems, as a theme park attraction the serialized game property is literally flattened out as one of many icons on a street map guide, and its narrative economy is reduced to a series of familiar signifiers that channel participants along a pre-determined traffic pattern through the soundstage and around the park (to use a parallel game mechanic metaphor—the open world becomes an on-rails experience). Visitors approach the park itself as a larger game-like structure; navigating the park requires a strategy built on the efficient use of time and location, as the wait times for each house get longer as the evening progresses. Embodiment and agency, even as they may be linked to a specific narrative proposition, give way to more generalized spatio-temporal conceits, as tourists navigate the terrain of the theme park and develop strategy guides for maximizing their time while circumventing crowds. Like the game universe, Universal's theme park environments have limits, beyond which the mesh is no longer rendered (the backstage beyond the backlot). But the discursive limits of the studio's playable space do not speak productively to the constitutive limits of game architecture. Rather, they echo the benign machinations of the corporate enclave. This attempt to approximate game architecture undoes the traces of agency that may be found in more authentic states of play.

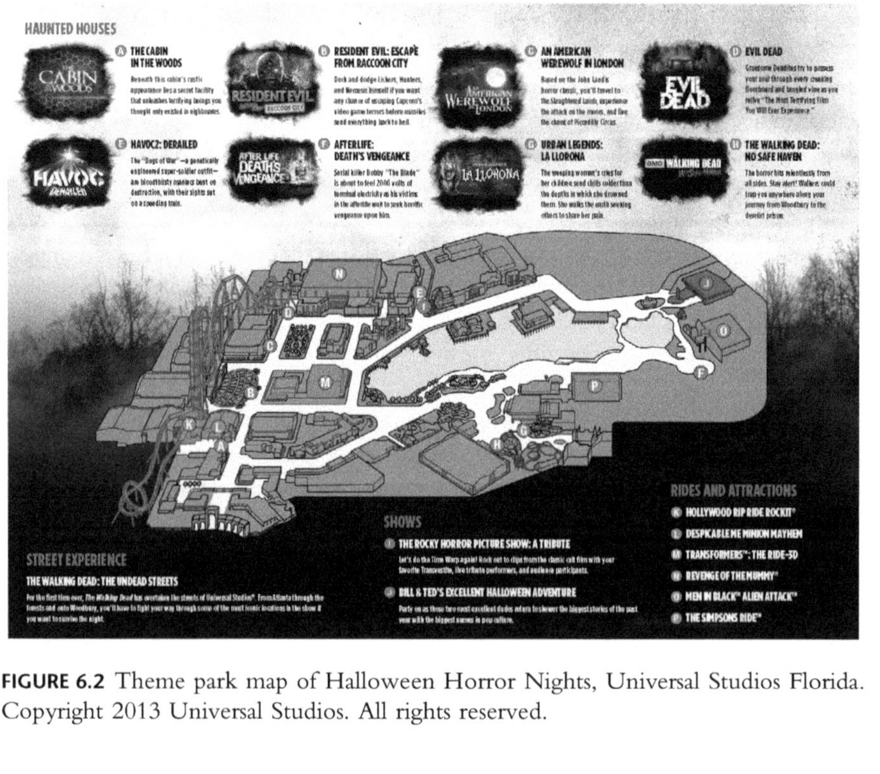

FIGURE 6.2 Theme park map of Halloween Horror Nights, Universal Studios Florida. Copyright 2013 Universal Studios. All rights reserved.

While the maze is not a game *per se*, it nonetheless mimics several game-based attributes; it is a rule-based formal system with variable outcomes, dependent on player exertion and influence. The formal properties of the maze are a well-structured design problem, to conceal scare actors, to delimit flow and regulate traffic, and to evoke a heightened emotional response. These are dominant structuring tendencies that form an architecture—a physics engine of sorts (contouring body dynamics and collision response)—that is consistently redeployed across new game-specific assets and intellectual properties as the theme park houses change each year, but the rules and mechanics of engagement remain largely unaltered.

The cognitive mapping required of participants navigating maze space as game space does not yield transparency, nor does it yield any insight into more totalizing forms of algorithmic control. For maze space is itself embedded inside the machination of the theme park, and like most theme parks, its lessons are left behind through a complex array of exits that slowly return the player to a state of relative freedom, as the mediating signs of the studio fade from view. In this manner, the maze state is much like a game state—a planned pattern of information (in this case analog rather than digital) that can nonetheless be influenced by the player's interaction. While a guest's pattern of engagement is not entirely predictable, there are rules. But one would have to stop short of suggesting there is precise algorithmic manipulation, response and control in a maze state. There are limits on the efficacy of the maze—call it human/actor error. And the general rules of irrelevance that govern gameplay (ignoring many aspects of context) are often undone by larger environmental cues (the theme park is, after all, a geographically situated property subject to real-world weather conditions).

The uneasy alliance between game space and maze space is perhaps mitigated by generic convention; survival horror is appropriate fodder for Halloween, not only for its thematic affinity, but also for the stylistic principles that guide the genre—for interactivity in survival horror is not about changing the game world, but about changing the player's mental state. And survival horror is readily mapped and demarcated, for its primary subject-object relations situate and condition the player to be victimized by scripted events, to be willfully acted upon. In its purest form, survival horror has been praised for privileging atmosphere over action (thus the critical assaults on more recent installments in the *Resident Evil* series, which has skirted survival horror in favor of modern warfare). The environmental landscape of survival horror, populated by darkened passageways and derelict structures, lends itself to a material transcription that is the hallmark of theme park architecture; survival horror games and their theme park corollaries capitalize on the uncertain qualities of the maze. Yet many of the essential attributes of survival horror games, the threat of failure, the threat of bodily harm, the threat posed by limited resources, are psychically discharged by this rezoned version of material embodiment. Although the HUD-inscribed avatar remediates the player's body in game space, it offers more potent affordances for bodily harm, and as such is a more powerful signifier of the body under duress than the body bound by maze space, embedded in soundstage architecture, circumscribed by theme park design, each layer with its own rule-based systems.

The theme park is and is not an allegory of control; it successfully monetizes the intellectual property even as it effaces the fundamental mechanisms of the property and the instrumentality of its code by substituting in its place other forms of flow and regulated behavior and mutual involvement. In parallel fashion, critical studies of game space and the popular reception of maze space commonly place more focused attention on visual analysis, ignore certain material relations and pattern structures, and perpetuate a particular absence in game studies that can be overcome by software and console studies and their attempts to make computation real. There are of course more expansive theme park experiences that engage with interactivity in more tech-saturated ways than the scare maze, but my focus here is the persistence of a certain regulatory tendency that governs every attraction, and the ever-present interplay of analog and digital artifacts—the principles, structures and mechanics that form the built environment.

Lessons from the Theme Park: City Planning

Themed spaces are built from multiple architectural, material, performative and technological supports, and have a narrative and symbolic complexity that governs their environs (Lukas, 2016). Engine-based tools facilitate the steady flow of ideation, the formulation of serial problem statements, and the rapid-fire prototyping of uniquely built solutions; and they offer the trope of seamless transformation, of change without transition, of resistance-free development. They speak to the durability and elasticity of data, and the ease of volumetric erasure, revision and substitution. It is not surprising that the transformations rendered by game engines are most powerful when they are applied to fantastic spaces, and that architectural firms such as HKS and PLP welcome the challenge of developing monumental showcase locales, such as hotels and stadiums—separate spaces that are relatively unhindered by the organizational and aesthetic logics of their surroundings. Spaces of entertainment and leisure present a dual challenge; they invite more expressive approaches to data, yet they must be functional and aligned with already established modes of inquiry, exploration and spectatorship. Themed spaces, and those re-developed to align with any given set of ideological and practical imperatives, are borne from a web of associations, from existing semiotic exchanges (the language of city officials, urban planners and entertainment executives); while they complicate agency by folding it into any number of narrative entanglements, publicly and privately commoditized spaces are not divorced from these larger signifying practices.

We have to consider to what extent our stories matter as objects of exchange, as digital assets, as components in systems that include other procedurally generated artifacts—as non-hierarchical agents in actor-networks readily recontoured by algorithmic manipulation. Probing the structural power of technical objects, Michel Callon (1991) asks, "What is the strange alchemy that allows us to transmute groups of non-humans into networks that define and link heterogeneous actors?" (136). Outlining the affinities between engineering and the social sciences, Callon reminds us that the programs embodied in technical objects are inherently social in nature; they "communicate, issue orders, interrupt one another and follow protocols" (136). Engines are textual agents; they are explicitly defined as such, and tasked with performing a number of assignments and displacements.

Smart cities are saturated with and mobilized by data, and the rhetorical invocation of the smart city is aligned with the new urbanist principle of neighborliness (Reisenleitner, 2016, 286), and the progressive democratic principle of citizenship (with the necessary attention to equity, inclusion and opportunity). From a somewhat distant and generalized perspective, smart cities are a collection of heterogeneous neighborhoods, engineered as a collective, networked for seamless data flows, transformed for the better into non-hierarchical actors. At their best, they are designed with and not for their inhabitants, and the urban technology embedded in them (the infrastructure of fiber optic networks, pervasive Wi-Fi and municipal sensors) leads to community health and well-being, greater quality of life, and sustained economic opportunity and growth. At their best, the urban technology deployments that define smart cities are planned inclusively and aligned with the public interest. Smart cities are networks; as such they do not privilege their residents, although they are designed to do so. Humans and technical objects have the same value in a digitally responsive actor-network, an organism composed of interdependent social and technical parts. Once configured, the smart city becomes semi-autonomous, embodying the tenets of (and requisite components for) machine learning. It is a self-regulating city engine.

We need to be guarded in our valuation of smart city solutions. The complexities of urban living, the legacies of injustice, inequity and failed urban planning cannot be undone by technology; red lines cannot simply be erased. The effects of longstanding discriminatory practices are deep and wide, echoed throughout infrastructure, economic development, housing, healthcare, food access, transportation, business development and other public and private sector services. Ben Green (2019) cautions against the build of a city that is "superficially smart" (4), where technology is conceived as just one more layer, when the network (of social services) itself may have already failed.

Robert Sampson (2012) argues that neighborhoods have durable properties that are interwoven with a broad range of social phenomena; even the pedestrian experience of disorder, of occasional street level chaos or incongruence, is undergirded by discrete forms of social organization, as neighborhoods themselves are embedded in larger relational networks: "Contrary to the common assumption of independence of social units, the animating idea is that neighborhoods are interdependent and characterized by a functional relationship between what happens at one point in space and what happens elsewhere" (239). Sampson suggests that the dual processes of diffusion and exposure (which are both physical and social) highlight the very real spatial interdependence between neighborhoods (239) as well as the lasting impact of place, even against the persistent pull of national crises and the changing directives associated with regulating the quality of life across a city. This spatial interdependence has led to unidimensional smart city solutions; data collection allows us to see city residents in the aggregate, and visualize biophysical, environmental and social trends as layerable quality of life indicators. There is a circular argument at work here that reflects an all too common techno-deterministic logic—using data-informed decision making to drive datacentric smart city solutions, while sidestepping the necessary institutional reforms. Green (2019) counters, "Technology does not take an inevitable path, however. We shape technology by embedding values in its design and developing it to achieve particular outcomes" (6). The value propositions attached to smart city technologies are often normative, perhaps socially optimal, but conceived within limited frames of reference, or within limited models of social agency that obscure existing inequities and willfully erase hyper-local systems of interaction.

In the broadest terms, the open world is always a contested space. And not surprisingly, we can view its variably proffered in-game corollary through a similar lens. Cities, both fictive and real, are a common feature of game space. Street maps (and their quadrants) provide known signs of navigation, readily identifiable zones of action, and easy heads-up metrics of progression; they give structure to an open world environment, they situate any number of executable missions, and they localize narrative conflict. The *Grand Theft Auto* series (published by Rockstar Games) has introduced us to Vice City and Liberty City (among others); the *Dead Rising* franchise (published by Capcom) has, in two installments, introduced us to Fortune City and Los Perdidos (though the former is a resort and not a municipality); and the long-running *SimCity* series popularized open-ended city building, urban simulation and infrastructure management. Imagined from the ground up, yet forged from the urban imaginary of game studios, these fictional places have slippery identity politics. *Grand Theft Auto: San Andreas* was at the center of a 2005 debate over video game content; and while the debate focused largely on the explicit sexual content associated with a *Hot Coffee* modification to the game (a mod that opened up otherwise unenterable game space), it also rekindled the all too familiar talking points that draw a straight line of causation from video game violence to sweeping moral decline. Most of these urban cityscapes invite engagement by featuring destructible environments—a particular function of the game engine that allows the game's polygonal models to change in response to any number of in-game events, effectively modifying the shape of data after altering standard collision detection and response. While the primary pleasure of *Dead Rising* is, fundamentally, technical (an engine-based operation), it is also visual and narrative. The game attaches an experimental ethos to the mechanics of killing, as it encourages players to disassemble and reassemble environmental assets to build increasingly inventive combination weapons—weapons that have their own destructive physics.

Avalanche Studios employed algorithmically dependent procedural generation to lay the foundation for the open world of *Just Cause* (2006), a process driven by the first iteration of the studio's proprietary engine. The Avalanche Engine was built from the ground up for sandbox gameplay in open worlds with large render distances (a measurement from the player to the environmental horizon), and capable of rendering a terrain system heavily dependent on efficient resource management and relatively high visual fidelity. The world of *Just Cause* is produced from a landscape system built from a pattern language of hierarchical patch maps; patch maps are two-dimensional spatial containers of data that specify the geographic type and physical features of the terrain. Following similar principles of procedural generation (while using the Lightweight Java Game Library), terrain creation in the sandbox game *Minecraft* (released by Mojang in 2011 and acquired by Microsoft in 2014) is governed by algorithmically-dependent map seeds that generate terrain on the fly, following a consistent world logic, as the player explores the editable game world. Procedurally generated game systems produce seemingly infinite variety in the world and in the gameplay experience. Whether it is a unique world attached to an original intellectual property, a world adapted from another media form, a world mapped onto existing cities and societies, or a rule-bound world that is (at least partially) player-generated, what matters as we consider game design as a process is both the content of the game world and its mechanics (how it is architected), as material techniques (the underlying matter of programming) and environmental assets instrumentally shape our engagement.

Open world games tend to balance the directives of exploration and campaign-based play, the concomitant mechanics of movement and combat, and the various signposts of progression (skill building, new mechanics, upgrades, and other forms of "leveling up" that often serve as keys to unlock new areas of exploration) that are all respectively grown from a base design of the game world at large—a set of organizing principles. They invite us to play in and with the city's properties and exploit or manage its resources. These systems are all tied back to the engine, and the terms of algorithmic possibility set within its parallel subsystems. And these systems all invite a colonizing perspective borne from a certain projection of perspective—from particular mapping principles unique to each property (or more properly, tied to the overarching visualizing power of the engine) that describe the relationships between locations and contour the player's engagement, hybridizing digital mapping with digital tourism (seeing the world through the eyes of an engine that determines what is possible, laid out through both worldbuilding and mission scripting tools). The city is always tied to an engine that renders it visible, makes it sustainable, and draws the player's itinerary; the engine guarantees continuity in the game state, and engine AI manages the complex tasks and interactions of each large game world. Ecosystem AI and accurate rendering and physics are fundamental conditions of these cities, consistent across Rockstar's adoption of Criterion Software's RenderWare engine and its development of the proprietary RAGE (Rockstar Advanced Game Engine); as well as Blue Castle Games' proprietary engine and Capcom Vancouver's Forge engine (used to define Fortune City and Los Perdidos for *Dead Rising 2* and *Dead Rising 3*, respectively). And the movement from one engine to the next often marks a basic pursuit of the real—of improvements in the visual field that can be connected to improvements in processing power and the speed and reliability of streaming services, and the overarching problem of large-scale data management. In Vice City, Liberty City, Fortune City and Los Perdidos, urban grit is tied to a materiality driven by an engine—an attention to graphical texture, particle effects, depth of field and other visual flourishes. While *SimCity* is essentially an open container that has not always been governed by an engine (the 2013 release utilizes the GlassBox engine for dynamic simulation, tying buildings, structures and resource agents to integrated simulation rules), as players expand their cities they must parse increasingly interlinked game-based decision trees and foresee the cumulative socio-economic impact of ongoing urban development. Lead designer Stone Librande describes his creative process for the 2013 *SimCity* release as a form of bookending:

> I came up with two extreme cases—around the office we call them "Berkeley" and "Pittsburgh," or "Green City" and "Dirty City." We said, if you are the kind of player who wants to make utopia—a city with wind power, solar power, lots of education and culture, and everything's beautiful and green and low density—then this would be the path you would take in our game. But then we made a parallel path for a really greedy player who just wants to make as much money as possible, and is just exploiting or even torturing their Sims. In that scenario, you're not educating them; you're just using them as slave labor to make money for your city. You put coal power plants in, you put dumps everywhere, and you don't care about their health.
> *(Manaugh and Twilley, 2013)*

Using these loose predictive analytics, the *SimCity* developers set what they perceived as practical boundaries on the game's design; in doing so, Librande and his team grounded the art, build and gameplay experience on an unsettling and reductive binary—reading the end results to determine the game's logic models and systems, and circumscribing urbanity in the process. The lesson here, from theme park to open world to neighborhood networks and cities, is in the relative equivalencies that we can draw between the forms of control that guide each framework, the relative dimensions of their respective maps, the processes by which their itineraries are drawn, versioned and made material, the interconnectedness (both mechanical and ideological) of vision and technology, and the relative value attached to play (whether it be free or rule-based expression).

The counterpoint to the emphasis in smart city development on function and utility has been a concomitant attention to community-driven needs (grounded in individual experiences) as part of civic user testing, prototyping and measured deployment (data collection and assessment). Often the community conversations are front-loaded as isolated points of engagement, and lead to tentative and underdeveloped exploration, rather than ongoing and responsive modification and iteration; dialogic development can be protracted and messy. The concept of playable cities, while formulated in opposition to early technology-driven approaches to smart city design, has often been willfully delegated to the private sector (the case of Niantic). Most commercial and municipal uses of city space give limited attention to local and regional inflections of space—inflections that can be stubbornly resistant to the wholesale transformations driven by urban planning and development. Most commercial and municipal developers envision the playable city as one without disruption, and rarely allow community-driven play to commingle with citywide systems and infrastructure (although a number of public interest groups are working to invert this hierarchy). City builders and worldbuilders share a limited number of approaches to composition and engagement; they share a limited number of attitudes and approaches to how they render the terrain, and how they situate social actors in relation to the terrain. 3D visualization is always accompanied by a fixed (or pre-determined, though movable, engine-based) perspective that governs how we see and understand the

FIGURE 6.3 *SimCity* Insider's Look at the GlassBox Game Engine. Copyright 2012 Electronic Arts Inc.

(game) world. This perspective, drawn from a virtual camera, carries with it an often-unspoken disciplinary power. It is not surprising that game engines have been mapped onto cities. There are clear structural and operational parallels between core game technologies and modern societal infrastructures; engines and cities are networks of complexly layered subsystems, of interdependent private and public works, each of which operates within its own regulatory regime (Austin et al., 2015).

Esri CityEngine is a 3D visualization tool (developed by the Zurich team of the Environmental Systems Research Institute) that has become central to urban planning, architecture and design in cities around the world. CityEngine allows municipal planners and developers to see the relationships of projects, assess their feasibility, visualize the impact of zoning laws, share proposals with public interest groups and decision makers, and plan their implementation; as an all-purpose visualization engine, Esri's 3D modeling software supports the creation of cities based on real-world geographic information system (GIS) data, but also allows developers to model fictional geographies and move assets between Esri and more popular game-based toolsets such as Unity and Unreal (to capitalize on the render power of game-based technologies). Esri developers have positioned CityEngine as a tool for building city models for cross-platform deployment within other software development environments. CityEngine files can be exported in various formats for import into both Unity and Unreal, where additional support for VR control can be added with the Oculus Rift or HTC Vive SDK; the CityEngine VR Experience combines Esri's backend work in geo-referencing, data integration, 3D modeling and scenario development with the work of game developers such as Epic in real-time rendering and VR control. The Unreal Studio, an enterprise suite released by Epic in 2017, introduced the ability to directly export 3D data (via Datasmith, a CAD transfer tool) from CityEngine into the Unreal Engine 4 workflow, to take advantage of the additional functionality of the game engine. Moving from a GIS-based model of spatial relationships to a game-based model of data-driven visualizations, Esri has altered the urban planning workflow and changed the relative value of geographical weighting to privilege more fantastic forms of spatial interaction; this is CityEngine at its most basic, as the engine weds procedural modeling (using rule-based object design to build large environments from repeatable geometries) to urban analysis (Mitropoulou et al., 2019). CityEngine works through Computer Generated Architecture (CGA) rules that can be easily varied to replicate the structural diversity of a typical urban environment. Beyond the unique grammar of this computationally bound building process, the forms of visualization native to VR alter our experience of the terrain, and expand the visual language of traditional 3D games; for example, teleport locomotion is a common substitute for continuous travel in VR landscapes, as it allows users to readily move between distant locations within a scene (following a number of developer-determined prefabs). For broad city visualizations, teleportation expedites our analysis, leads to a more efficient survey of the land, and selectively skips across interstitial terrain, blocking out those corridors that have limited semantic connection to the work at hand.

CityEngine follows a rule-based system of 3D geometries (a procedural approach to modeling) that allows developers to accurately visualize buildings, streets and municipal infrastructure networks, and create dynamic 3D models of large-scale urban environments. New software ecosystems, and their correlative data flows and cloud-based services have led to new ways of imaging and imagining the city. These systems must demonstrate a remarkable degree of coherence to support the interoperability of a GIS engine and a game engine, the relatively fluid transcription of geolocative data into correlative application file formats (including Autodesk FBX, AutoCAD DXF), and the build of a composite city model using multiple software suites (for example, using a shared data set to model infrastructure design in InfraWorks and architectural design in AutoCAD).

These new patterns of organization have been attached to the values associated with transparency, and with the virtues of engaging citizens in the design of smart cities; in its promotional literature, Esri proposes its CityEngine can bring a community vision to life. This is the language of the technological imaginary, and it leaves us to wonder whether this ability to transform space, to subject it to the algorithmic manipulation of a game-like system, can ultimately undo the otherwise durable quality of place. We need to rigorously assess the physical, social and economic impacts of driving urban renewal and civic design through software,

FIGURE 6.4 Unreal Engine and CityEngine: The Future of Urban Design Visualization. Content is the intellectual property of Esri and is used herein with permission. Copyright 2019 Esri and its licensors. All rights reserved.

even when the end goals seem to be aligned with community betterment and a commitment to environmentally responsible design.

This conundrum highlights the need for a shared commitment to digital and media literacy and algorithmic accountability (among city officials and city residents) in a municipal landscape increasingly governed and developed using code-based datacentric decision-making and visualization strategies—where the information gathered from smart devices, social platforms and public sensors and surveys (or, from a network perspective, interlinked GIS-dependent systems) is fueling the engine-based mechanics of speculative infrastructure design and localized approaches to urban planning and problem solving. Geographic information systems, borne in part from the development of computational geography in the 1960s, have followed the logic of computer culture, of automated and integrated database systems, and of data-informed decision making—building solutions, discovering meaning through data. This is not simply a matter of data visualization, but again, as I continue to focus on the data layer, on the matter of engines, the emphasis here is on the persistence of code—spatial analysis and visualization trade in the currency of a common computational language, a language of representation and analysis that has aligned geographers, city planners, governance bodies, architects, designers and game developers. To re-politicize the algorithmic dynamics of urban development, and build a new urban mechanics, we need to link studies of visual culture (of seeing geographic displacement) to situated studies of code. To see code as habitus is to recognize it as the architectural condition for the all too consequential embodiment of cultural capital (Bourdieu, 1986), and to fully understand its impact on city residents, neighborhoods and communities.

As part of the expanded visual vocabulary of city planning, CityEngine supports the side-by-side comparison of distinct redevelopment scenarios, and the juxtaposition and ready substitution of existing building sites with proposed (and alternate) designs. The engine accommodates rapid architectural adjustments, modifications to building footprints, and alterations to surrounding streetscapes; and the engine allows developers to fuse satellite imagery and 3D terrain with street and building data from OpenStreetMap. Moreover, by connecting CityEngine and game engine workflows, Esri-based designs can be enhanced with game-based assets; and the level designs of open source games can be remapped with Esri's engine. In 2018, Houseal Lavigne Associates, an urban design and development firm based in Chicago, built a new localized *Counter-Strike* map by modeling and rendering the company's offices and several surrounding city blocks using SketchUp, CityEngine and Valve's Source engine (Fabricius, 2018). The playable game map merges the firm's work space with game space, and draws the city into a series of genre-driven game exploits; the hyper-realistic 3D environment frames Chicago as a reimagined combat zone that can be dropped into any Source engine game.

FIGURE 6.5 Making game maps with CityEngine: Google Street View. Copyright 2019 Google.

FIGURE 6.6 Making game maps with CityEngine: Game Level View. Copyright 2018 Houseal Lavigne Associates.

CityEngine and Unreal have been combined for robust architectural visualization and large-scale urban planning projects by global design firms including HOK, which uses Epic's game engine as a tool to aggregate CAD data sets and files from several standalone 3D modeling software packages (including Rhino, Revit and SketchUp), rapidly render scenes and assets, and dynamically modify integrated building plans across a project life cycle (Pimentel, 2019). Unreal has allowed HOK and other architectural firms to develop more responsive client-centered communication models using real-time 3D environments to bring to life still renderings, technical drawings and other static visualization methods. Using Unreal as part of the development workflow, and Datasmith to ingest data from complex 3D models, design firms can realize a high degree of flexible visual fidelity in a shortened period of time.

This synthesis of tools by Esri and Epic Games aligns the workflows, ideations and communication patterns of geographic mapping, urban design and visualization, shoring up spatial data and analytics to anchor the urban imaginary. Design firms that draw from SmartCode, a model transect-based planning and zoning document first published in 2003, can quickly recalibrate local ordinances and conditions using CityEngine, and visualize redefined transects—rapidly transforming the terrain and dynamically transitioning from natural, rural, suburban and urban land uses. These acts lay the foundation for (and foster dynamic connections between) environmental, municipal and building layers as part of a quickly editable geographic projection that can readily elide the initial proposition of the transect model. Following the human-centered design principles of new urbanism, the SmartCode was drafted to promote specific quality of life outcomes such as civically oriented placemaking, walkability and ecological sustainability.

These data flows between CityEngine, Unreal and other real-time visualization tools fuse the city as we know it with a projection of what is possible; yet both of these poles are limited and speculative. Our knowledge of the city is always partial, comprised only of those maps we have unlocked (to use a game metaphor), and inherently framed by our position and status. It may be stating the obvious, but where we live determines what we know, and merits a careful attention to the privilege (or marginalization) associated with location. An all too common benchmark of causality is the finding that where you live affects how long you live, with life expectancy varying widely from zip code to zip code in most urban areas. Economic disparities and health disparities go hand in hand, and certain demographic qualities—high rates of unemployment, low household income, low education rates, racial and ethnic densities—negatively impact life expectancy in most neighborhoods. These decidedly non-visual data points are not part of building geometries.

One of the goals of Esri's ArcGIS mapping and analytics platform—a software tool that translates data into location-based insights—is to counter this form of radical erasure. The company tackles this proposition with a simplified formula: "Translate problems into spatial answers." ArcGIS geospatial vector data can be imported into Esri's CityEngine, to align quality of life indices with the contours of the technological imaginary and its geographic futures; but the goals of connecting seemingly disconnected data points are to produce clean data and to build visually compelling maps, charts and spatial analyses—

to reveal relationships and correlations, to visualize distributions. There is value to mapping events and visualizing the terrain, and to situating these activities in a historical context. But we need to understand the motivations behind each scenario. How is geographic data aggregated and shared? What are the mechanics of engine-based mapping? Esri's Community Maps Program has been built out with contributed user data that is reviewed by Esri staff before being added to the company's basemaps. But these crowdsourced components only serve to make the Esri ecosystem more robust and attractive—more data rich and application dependent—as the company continues to introduce new proprietary tools (such as the Sweet web editor) to place data in context and drive localized problem solving. Like an engine, these rule-based applications are self-regulating data frameworks; they automate tasks and guide interaction while maintaining the integrity of the overall system.

Engines have tremendous prescriptive power in a machine-readable experience economy, as they drastically change the way we understand and plan our future. New imaging technologies offer new methods for conceptualizing and arranging the visual field and present us with new perspectives on our environment (and perhaps new approaches to sustainability). If code and data, and software and hardware, are discursively and contractually bound to each other, their applications and outcomes may provide some useful lessons in understanding to what degree space and place, engagement and subjectivity can be contoured by the disciplinary logics of computerization and algorithmic manipulation.

As we engage in spatial thinking, we use the properties of space to structure and solve problems. The real-time translation of lived space into data (the input process) and back again (the output process) carries with it signposts of both memory and agency, even as this circle of translation is tethered to an engine that lacks the same geographic fixity. Stated more simply, the same engine can be used to render any environment, yet the general utility of the engine does not undo the localized social and political significance of its application. Engines have consequences, and as with their corresponding assets and objects, they foster new forms of movement, action and social relations.

The question I am raising is whether the engine-based mechanics of urban development and renewal—the use of Esri's rich data maps to survey the land, and the use of Unity and Unreal (and CityEngine) to visualize structural change—are aligned with the purposeful application of smart city technologies. The question is not whether these technologies can be integrated, whether the same data can be seamlessly imported and exported into the appropriate development environments, but whether the ideological drivers are in alignment. And in this admixture of proprietary software environments, publicly held data is often blended with privately held assets. Open data does not inevitably yield transparent designs and transparent acts of governance. The seamless flow of data can belie fundamental and complex situational problems; the effortless representation of community, perfected through rich data sets, can seal over conflict. Esri's city planning tools are not simply designed for data visualization, they are built for storytelling; basemaps are fundamentally story maps, an aggregate of signs that can be used to visually document problems and strengthen the case for proposed municipal projects. This is not to suggest that the city-as-platform model is bankrupt; as Stephen Goldsmith and Susan Crawford (2014) note, many city governments are using data to more actively engage with their constituents, and asset sharing can strengthen the communication between city offices. By moving data across city departments, city leaders can start to see relationships among their constituents, across districts and services, and between problems and events that may otherwise seem unrelated; city leaders and their residents can start to know the city differently (Goldsmith and Crawford, 2014, 82). In the right hands and with the right motives, community mapping can strengthen community engagement. And although maps can be empowering, they can also be prescriptive, producing focused forms of knowledge that privilege certain forms of vision, shape data in discrete ways, and require agile technological literacy. Proprietary engine-based visualization is grounded in licensed authorship.

Beyond the Civic Sector

In 2009, NASA launched *Eyes on the Earth*. Developed using Unity's browser-based visualization technology, the application displays the location of all of NASA's currently operating Earth-observing missions in real time. These missions constantly monitor our planet's vital signs, such as sea-level height, the concentration of carbon dioxide in our atmosphere, global temperatures, and the state of sea ice in the Arctic. Widening its scope, in 2011, NASA launched *Eyes on the Solar System*, an interactive web-based tool that allows users to experience missions in real time (and to travel through time); the tool is populated with NASA data dating back to 1950 and projected to 2050. In 2019, the application development team at the Jet Propulsion Laboratory of the California Institute of Technology released a mobile-friendly web-based version of its digital orrery, built with Three.js (a lightweight JavaScript 3D library) rather than Unity.

NASA has also developed a series of game-based properties that focus on the agency's labor. The agency released its first mission simulator game *Moonbase Alpha* in 2010 as part of its Learning Technologies Project, a project designed to support the delivery of NASA content through a number of interactive applications. NASA's game has a kindred spirit in *Moonbase: Lunar Colony Simulator*, a habitation and infrastructure game developed by Wesson International in 1990. NASA's *Moonbase Alpha*, built on the Unreal Engine 3, has single and multiplayer options that allow participants to step into the role of an exploration team member in a futuristic 3D lunar settlement. Players must work to restore critical systems and oxygen flow after a meteor strike damages a solar array and the

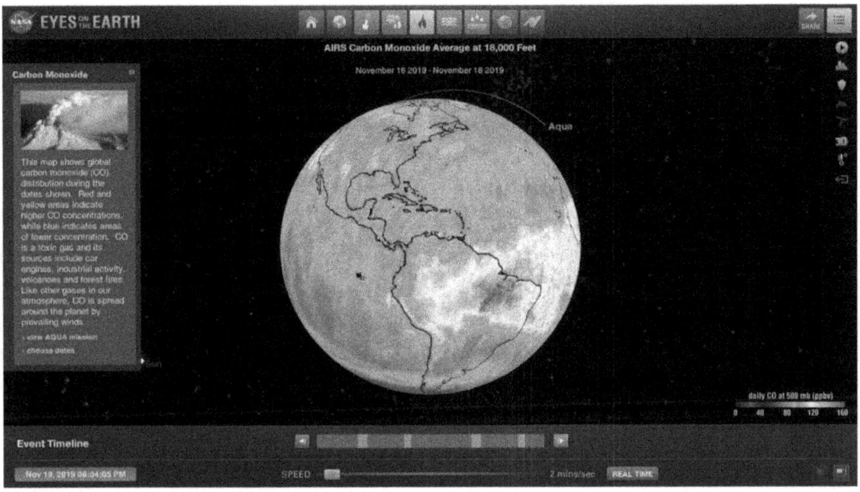

FIGURE 6.7 NASA *Eyes on the Earth.*
Courtesy NASA/JPL-Caltech.

team's life support equipment. *Moonbase Alpha* is designed to require players to gain and demonstrate STEM (science, technology, engineering and math) knowledge to succeed. While the game was developed as an educational tool, it became popular in YouTube circles due to the openness of its text to speech engine, which allowed less goal-oriented players to create and record their own nonsensical and non-goal-oriented gameplay videos.

NASA released its second game title, *NetworKing*, in 2011, building with the Unity Web Player. The game allows players to take on the role of a network manager (paralleling the work of the information technology division at the Ames Research Center, the game's developer) and puts them in charge of building up a communications network to support a series of scientific missions. Players are tasked with setting up worldwide command stations, acquiring clients and resources, and building and upgrading network systems: "As you develop your network, you'll receive increasingly lucrative contracts from satellites. You can win the game by working your way through the upgrade tree to unlock the Integrated Network" (NASA, 2019).

Both educational games illustrate NASA's commitment to foster reform in STEM teaching and learning, and signal the currency of software as a tool to shape human knowledge and experience. NASA's geographically based applications and games transform each landscape into a playable interface, drawn from a database into a nexus of several complex interactions that are foundational for the production of embodied space in locative and map-based media. As graphically oriented displays of space, NASA's Unity and Unreal projects are merely single permutations of distinct data sets; and the sum of interface and database cannot be separated from its cultural layer, its contextual markers, and its historical and psychosocial dimensions (Freedman, 2018b). Sites evolve and their evolution—their adaptive dynamism—is consistent with an understanding of technologies as transformative tools. The NASA project (a sum total of its serialized intellectual properties) is accompanied by its own discursive regime that promotes and makes commonsense its message.

NASA is not the only agency actively mapping the terrain, and aligning engine-based imperatives with federally sponsored research. A project undertaken in 2005 by the Institute for Creative Technologies (ICT) at the University of Southern California (USC) in collaboration with the Office of Naval Research and Virtually Better, Inc. extends the industrial applications of immersive technology and amplifies the foundational principles of game-based logic. The collaborative designed an immersive interactive system from the game components of *Full Spectrum Warrior* (a real-time tactics video game first sold to the home console and PC market in 2004, and later released in 2008 as a free download sponsored by the United States Army) and the Unreal Engine for the treatment of combat-related PTSD. As a real-time simulator, itself based on a digital combat simulator, the clinical tool known as *Virtual Iraq* reproduces the sights, sounds and tactile cues of a war zone, and effectively closes the cycle of military service from training (initiated with *Full Spectrum Warrior*) to treatment (Dyer-Witheford and de Peuter, 2009, 98).

This particular marriage between the game industry and the military complex can be traced back to the late 1990s when the Army created a $45 million research program to tap into the growing video game industry. The funding established the ICT at USC, which conducted research and hired game companies and movie studios to collaborate. While the game companies were trying to build more realistic war simulations for next generation consoles, the Army had a convergent interest in realism to develop high-tech immersive teaching aids. Tracing the origins of the term "full spectrum," Nick Dyer-Witheford and Greig de Peuter (2009) note that it was first attached to US military doctrine by the Joint Chiefs of Staff in 2000, in a report that proposed "full spectrum dominance," designating the ability of US forces "to conduct prompt, sustained, and synchronized operations with combinations of forces tailored to specific situations and with access to and freedom to operate in all domains—space, sea, land, air, and information" (Joint Chiefs of Staff, 2000, 6).

The military-entertainment-industrial complex has a long history, and is attached to the rise of networked communication and computation. Early game developers were similarly simultaneously engaged in military research and the purposeful application of new technologies—and states of experimentation and play. In fact, play informs research, much in the same way that play can inform the culture at large (and move it forward). Experimentation is part of the scientific process, and science is part of the creative process. When physicist William Higinbotham introduced the electronic computer game *Tennis for Two* at Brookhaven National Laboratory in 1958, he effectively brought the matter of playful interaction to scientific measurement, translation and visualization.

Circuits of Meaning

What do these game-based and game-adjacent experiences teach end users about interaction and data visualization, and the interplay between information, space and place? These engine-driven works are not designed as social commentaries, but as enterprise solutions, although the mental models they propose or operationalize, the management practices they embody, the flawlessness of their technological remediation as they mitigate between various states, may impact our understanding of the real world and our expectations of process and progression. These experiences effectively close the gap between subjectivity and what Ian Bogost refers to as "unit-operational rules" (Bogost, 2006, 120). But this is the logical endpoint of a networked subject in an engine-driven environment where algorithms uniformly impact both human and non-human actors; and the available catalog of engine-based practices only continues to expand.

Since its work on *Virtual Iraq*, Virtually Better has continued its efforts in the build of evidence-based virtual reality exposure therapy systems in behavioral healthcare environments with Unity, developing virtual reality experiences to treat a wide spectrum of mental health disorders. And since 2011, Unity has had an active partnership with the US military. The company's initial press release promotes the broad potential and comprehensive benefit of its proprietary engine: "Today's announcement means that Unity can be used to create and deploy task management trainers, virtual worlds, situational awareness trainers, cultural awareness trainers, medical trainers and various other serious game applications for the US Army and Air Force" (Unity Technologies, 2011).

When it is most opaque, information technology fosters a factory logic of subjectivity and engagement; spatial computing can be mobilized as a colonizing force. If we look at a grander scale, beyond the role of an engine in a particular object or as part of a limited workflow, we will see that engines are agents for organizing the world and for worldbuilding; they serve both fictive and nonfictive space, and often tie together these two realms. And as they do so, individuals and communities are inevitably rendered as figural and geographic assets, subject to algorithmic manipulation and treatment. We need to consider the relative bounded nature of these practices, and the possibility for building truly responsive and open frameworks.

I opened this chapter with a consideration of a particular theme park attraction, where the familiar is made unfamiliar—a house transformed from a safe space into one that needs to be approached with caution. Soundstages are large, open containers; they are designed to be flexible, to accommodate almost any narrative fantasy. Yet they are still bounded and governed, technically constrained and privately owned. Finding our way in the dark, and engulfed by visceral attractions, we may forget that we are in an enclosure. By pausing to understand how engines work, we can become more acutely aware of the ideological weight of systematized navigation and, more broadly, the values proffered in distinct procedural uses of data. Engine-based practices are a sum of the contradictory impulses of freedom and control; they represent the net force of technical and social conceits, and the promise and peril of speculative projection.

7

THE LITTLE ENGINE THAT COULD: INDEPENDENT DEVELOPERS AND THE GLOBAL GAMES MARKET

Game technologies are connected to the political and economic impacts of globalization and the outsourcing of labor within various national industrial economies of game design and development—a process that leads to rather complicated and conflicted representational codes as intellectual properties move across (and are consumed across) cultural borders. Game technologies are often found at the center of cultural exchange as part of larger software ecosystems that may still have localized cultural influence. The transformation of the game industry from the mid-1990s onward is inherently tied to the ongoing social and economic changes associated with the rise of networked capital (Kirkpatrick, 2013, 99). The embedded software frameworks of the game industry are dependent on the more generalized advancements in information and communication technologies that have occurred within a global marketplace (of investment, trade, production and consumption). The game economy is part of the information economy, and those individuals, organizations and basic activities of the game industry are part of the broad operations of information capitalism. Developers, publishers and console manufacturers are bound together by common professional and technical standards; and game designers and artists are left to react to the articulations of a global market. Graeme Kirkpatrick (2013) delineates this thread of causation by suggesting:

> The core technologies of game manufacture serve particular interests, intruding on concept development and product differentiation in ways that are determinate for the quality of the resulting products. This has particular consequences for those who work in the industry, who are largely drawn to games by their own status as gamers, but who find themselves subject to new, more intrusive forms of exploitation.
>
> *(100)*

Game engine technologies are part of a larger shift in the game industry, following and indeed enabling the flow of networked capital, and changing the nature of game production labor—global development networks make local networks less stable as they do not contribute to the supports that are fundamental to the growth of a regional (or even national) workforce. The contours of the video game business are complicated by the diversification of the industry across what are often discrete areas of production with distinct production pipelines, software frameworks and hardware specifications—a network that includes triple-A titles, casual, mobile, handheld and independent games.

In looking to understand the negotiations of independent game developers with larger commercial and industrial imperatives, my research extends into several international development communities in Germany. My goal here is to tease out the particularities of creative labor against what might otherwise be read as the inescapable disciplinary logic of global capital—to understand the tradeoffs between creativity and efficiency, between thoughtfully and uniquely inflected design and development and the unilateral demands of the marketplace. The games industry is a site of creativity and innovation, and in studying the work of independent developers, I have found spaces where these concepts are bound together in praxis—where independent artists and studios have realized new modes of expression by tackling specific design problems. Innovation, in these cases, should not be confused with critical acclaim, but rather I use the term to describe the efforts of independent developers to push against the limits of existing software products, or to create change within their regional industries. Running against the grain of innovation, game workers are part of a global games industry, bound to "transnational production networks" that serve varied cultural and business interests (Deuze et al., 2007, 336), and are tied to and challenged by technological parameters that continuously re-direct game development. Mark Deuze et al. (2007) note, "As the global hardware manufacturing industry continually renews and replaces its technologies, the creative work of game developers (including, but not limited to, the technicians) must be understood as taking place in a context of permanent change" (338). Game workers must negotiate the ongoing governmentality of computation as well as the very real influence of local and national governments and businesses looking to simultaneously draw in and align the creative industries with regional economic interests.

While there are many more expansive examinations of the global games industry, among them influential market and policy research by Aphra Kerr (2006, 2017) and Giuditta De Prato et al. (2010), my attention remains on the core technology of the game engine—the software layer that allows the higher-level application (game content) to readily interact with a number of lower layers (subsystems, drivers, operating systems) and, by extension, system hardware. The engine is, effectively, the development environment. While technology plays a significant role in the development of game works, my conversations with individual game developers and within unique production communities is in part an attempt to shift the focus away from the technicity of games (a consideration of the constitutive nature of game technology, in this case, in relation to both game producers and game players, and more broadly, in relation to humans and culture) by considering the nuances of equally influential regional, national and organizational forces and structures. In their study of the Japanese video game industry, Yuko Aoyama and Hiro Izushi (2003) connect Japan's particular industrial formations to the social and historical foundations of the nation's creative imaginary, and the highly skilled talent emerging from the consumer electronics industry (426). Following this pursuit, I am purposefully shifting the weight of my argument away from any assumption about ubiquitous technology standards and toward particular cultural economies of production and the creative labors of individual artists. This is a situated analysis of both game technologies and game workers that considers the social, cultural, economic and vocational supports for video game production. Software is central to this field of activity; yet game developers have varied impressions of their tools. For small development teams, a common licensed game engine (with a plug-and-play functionality that accepts shareable pre-built assets) can be empowering and fundamentally democratizing; but for those developers with a creative problem that pushes the limits of a ready-built software architecture, even the most user-friendly engine can seem oppressive and homogenizing (Nicoll and Keogh, 2019, 8), absent a deeper understanding of text-based programming logic and syntax. Every production workflow inevitably yields to a form of self-governance, a turn toward efficiency, to meet the practical demands of entrepreneurship.

I began this work in Hamburg, a site of state-supported game development and the locus of the collaborative game industry incubator Gamecity:Hamburg, to consider the sustainability of localized industrial game economies in ever-more interlocked and corporatized global media flows, and the role of state funding in regional game development. My first round of interviews was with independent game studios, as I began to survey Germany's support of its regional game economy. My work consisted of two studies: one conducted in 2011 and a follow-up conducted in 2017. The first study focused on a select number of independent development studios in Hamburg supported by the Gamecity brand; the second study included follow up site visits with those studios still operating in Hamburg (some had closed, while others had been acquired by larger companies), but also broadened my scope to include studios in Berlin and Frankfurt, in an effort to consider game development more broadly across Germany. These studies in Germany are focused on the work of emerging game developers who are responding to industry trends in innovative ways and developing proprietary tools that match specific technical or artistic demands that are not otherwise being met by industry standards; these studies bring to the foreground the unique challenges that face independent studios in their regional yet nationally linked economies, and in part highlight how German financing of tech entrepreneurship has impacted the national video game economy.

Broadly, this project highlights international game development communities to consider the relative vitality of local game economies, and serves to regionally inflect my examination of the negotiations that independent studios have to make with multinational hardware, software and middleware developers. My focus here is to understand the conditions for sustainable regional and national game economies within global flows, and in particular the technologies that organize this work.

In my conversations with independent game studios (and developers), my main line of inquiry has been focused on engine choice—understanding the decisions driving engine choice, adoption and development per studio and per project, and the distinct impact of engine choice and versioning on programmers and artists. These teams may have decidedly different mindsets, skill sets and workflows, but they must work with complementary toolsets (and vocabularies) as part of the game development pipeline, and they must ultimately negotiate with hardware developers to gain needed entry to international mobile and console markets. In every case, those who labor in independent studios struggle with economies of scale, as access to talent, technology, viable middleware, proprietary hardware development kits and multiplatform deployment all require early stage investment. And those who work as part of the development pipeline of global media flows are limited in their engagement with regional culture and memory. The difficulty with studying game engines in a global context is a difficulty associated with the study of any large-scale technical system that cuts across multiple geographies and industrial sectors and does not uniformly impact its user groups—some are served by the engine, while others are actively building with the engine. Engines are meaningful only in context, and beyond understanding their generalized contours and their unique features, uncovering the random acts of customization within any given development studio is a difficult task that requires studying the signature traces of individual coders in relation to discrete acts of problem solving. Moreover, these modifications are not simply solutions to design problems, they are barriers to access. On the surface, changes to an information infrastructure, to a game engine, may seem to be simple variations in practice; but they also represent the inscription of new design norms embedded in a particular production culture, and they contribute to the momentum of a large-scale system that is both technical and social (Winner, 1980, 123).

Aphra Kerr (2017) suggests that there are a number of discernible production logics or institutional relationships that drive game development—some are determined by the more generalized forces that drive the commodification of cultural production, others are drawn from related cultural industries and are partly re-determined by native game technologies, while still others are driven by emerging business models, including the incremental impact of a nascent cloud-based economy (15). Kerr suggests that by first understanding the organizational structures of production, we can more readily identify the corporations and trace the networks and projects that stretch across industries (16). Broadly speaking, we can suggest that different industries approach engines through different paradigms, and with different perspectives on their affordances. While I have articulated earlier that engines seal over the latent potential of code, engines are industrial products that are often utilized as middleware in the service of other industries; for example, they are central to the nascent platform-specific build of immersive experiences that are driving innovation across a number of key market sectors.

At least four factors contribute to the sustained development of regional game production: the availability of state funding, access to talent, access to traditional distribution mechanisms (established trade shows and conventions), and the existence of a fully articulated pipeline to connect independent studios to larger global developers (as global networks are central to the infusion of capital into the regional economy—to support tech entrepreneurship, and to recruit and develop talent). Most of these factors are inextricably linked to state support; and while tax incentives are a critical component of stimulating investment by larger international studios looking to establish new headquarters, equally important is government support of the educational enterprise—investment in training programs, in STEM and arts education, and in the development of certificate and degree programs in programming and game development. The access to state funding in combination with access to talent and technology are critical stimuli for the development of independent game studios, investments by larger game production companies, and the emergence of a regional game economy.

The most vibrant national game economies are grounded in four interconnected industrial vectors (and within these vectors are, of course, the valued labors of individuals): the global subsidiary, the entrepreneurial technologist or startup, the client-centered independent studio, and the indie developer and collective. These are permeable arrangements, and significantly, talent often flows across them; moreover, this industrial framework is not simply determined by shifts in the technology, which have indeed been significant over the lifespan of the digital games industry. The process of innovation and stabilization is also driven by economic, political and cultural forces, and dependent on other regional institutional supports—including education, government and finance. Technology is only one circuit in the circulation of capital in the global games industry in what Stephen Kline et al. (2003) refer to as a "mediatized global marketplace" (50). Reading more deeply, Kline suggests that within this technological circuit, "the subject of the interactive experience is now positioned not only as a player but also, and simultaneously, as a 'user' of computers and consoles that are increasingly linked to a networked telecommunications environment" (2003, 55). To this end, to fully unpack the interactive experience we must account for technological innovation, experimentation, diffusion and consolidation, which is about more than the simple passage of new technologies into popular use, but also the economic, legislative and cultural conditions that shape this movement—the emerging global business models. Even as we acknowledge the design and adoption process may occasionally escape this commercial logic (Kline et al., 2003, 56), we need to be precise in our assessment of the degree of such departures. As I have indicated already, the game industry should be understood as more than a sum total of its playable products, of its serialized intellectual properties; it is also an arena for establishing the foundational architectures of the field of play. The development environment, the software system, is an equally critical serialized intellectual property. The game industry, as an information industry, is grounded in a number of subsystem architectures, all of which are immensely profitable commodities. Despite any changes in the overall organization of the digital games industry—the push toward vertical integration (in production, publishing and distribution) has been matched by the pull toward diversification in the PC, online and mobile markets (Kerr and Cawley, 2012)—and among the roster of top companies, the underlying technologies have continued to become increasingly standardized. Those companies building and iterating their own engines do so with a keen attention to return on investment that limits the redevelopment cycle, while those companies utilizing third-party engines do so with an understanding of how far they can customize an existing codebase before interfering with their profit margins (for modding requires maintenance, and the labor costs associated with expanding the size of an in-house programming or development team). Companies with the largest revenues have openly acknowledged the importance of third-party software development, both to fuel cross-platform title builds with other studios and to respond more effectively to the governing industry and education standards that have shaped the talent pool (with most young game artists, programmers and developers being trained in one of several modern game engines and programming languages). Nintendo creative director Shigeru Miyamoto has suggested that the company's own development teams have rapidly gained ground on their Western competitors, largely because the Nintendo Switch, released in 2017, features integration with third-party engines (Hall, 2017). Nintendo in partnership with Epic Games provides fully featured native support for Unreal, an environment being used by many of Nintendo's own programmers; and the company has extended an already existing licensing agreement with Unity Technologies to continue support for the Unity engine on its latest console (building on a worldwide licensing agreement established in September 2012 to provide Unity support for Wii U deployments). It is not surprising that most regional video game studios have selected Unity or Unreal as their primary development environment, as both engines sit squarely within the marketplace and are the training ground for the overwhelming majority of the work force (in part because they both draw from the more dominant programming languages). But the localized conversations about game development are much richer and more nuanced than the decisions driving the selection of a programming language and a software build.

There are a number of game development and publishing hubs in Germany, most of which are gathered around the country's major cities (among them, Berlin, Frankfurt, Hamburg, Hanover and Munich), situated in close proximity to related university programs in game design, engineering and computer science, and operating alongside other established media production communities; and development studios across Germany benefit from Cologne-based Gamescom, Europe's prominent interactive trade show. Frankfurt, Germany's financial center, is home to the regional offices of a number of international media companies, including Nintendo, Sony Interactive Entertainment and Bandai Namco Entertainment; while other major game publishers have sales offices in Germany, or have strategically expanded their global operations by acquiring local development studios. For example, Electronic Arts acquired Phenomic Game Development in 2006 to expand its catalog of real-time strategy games (but shuttered the Ingelheim studio in 2013).

The expansion, contraction and re-allocation of development resources is not unique to the German game economy. German game development (as with development in other national markets) is, in part, being driven by larger studios invested in regionalizing their global operations—to diversify their talent base and to develop marketing hubs that can respond to localized cultural trends. As Kline et al. (2003) have noted, information capitalism is dependent on research, advertising and branding practices (51)—marketing teams gather data about their customers that can be used to refine the corporate messaging connected to particular commodities. But information capitalism is also a matter of turning a profit on regional labor.

In 2017, Electronic Arts closed Visceral Games, its Redwood Shores, California studio, and moved the studio's projects to EA Vancouver; and in 2018 Capcom closed its Vancouver studio to shift resources to its Osaka headquarters. These are just two recent flashpoints in a development landscape where closures and layoffs are commonplace, even as mega-publishers continue to realize record profits. The largest studios consistently run multiple projects, and position their employees as a contingent workforce that can be increased, decreased and released altogether over the various stages of an individual build cycle; in big-budget game development, a development studio will often over hire at the front end to meet a hard release date, only to drastically downsize (or "shift resources") once the title goes to market.

The sheer volume of independent game development companies (for a diversified market across console, PC and mobile platforms) in Germany provides some stability for its national workforce; and investors remain committed to the nation's game economy, which offers highly competitive corporate tax rates, relatively stable labor costs, and a wealth of associated intellectual, technical and creative capital. These elements partly inform the industrial context for game engine development in Germany; a context in which game development and publishing are driven in tandem with broader approaches to systems analysis and design. Yet regionally developed game technologies must still navigate globally held media interests; the German games industry is not immune to the challenges of a marketplace that is increasingly dependent on global capital and governed by strict (corporate) licensing agreements that tie software to hardware. Most game developers will note there is much to be learned from engine failure; that sensitivity is reflected in the large number of articulate postmortems that speak openly to the developer community about those games that have moved successfully through the development cycle, as well as those titles and technologies that never make it to market or have relatively short lifespans.

Gamecity: Hamburg

The Gamecity:Hamburg project was launched in 2003 as a multipronged effort to support the local gaming industry and promote new investment. Gamecity provides a network for those already working in the industry, and by increasing the visibility of the community, the organization has promoted job growth, fueled game development, and encouraged other game companies and game-adjacent investors and developers to set up shop in Hamburg. As an enterprise, the Gamecity collaborative has also developed a cohesive set of measures to promote Hamburg's gaming industry. As a comprehensive value chain for the local games industry, the network includes developers and publishers, technology service providers, advertising and public relations agencies, production houses and consultants, and is open to game studios of varying size.

In Hamburg, my initial research focused on four game companies: Exit Games, Fishlabs, MobileBits and Periscope Studio. These studios present a range of approaches—diverse products and platforms—and more significantly each has developed a proprietary engine. Exit Games built the Photon engine; Fishlabs developed the Abyss engine; MobileBits developed the Delta engine; and Periscope developed the Psai engine.

"Creative city" models such as the one forged in Hamburg depend on the co-location of software and hardware resources and parallel tracks in research and development; these are integral parts of a regionally sustainable circuit of technologically inflected cultural production (Pratt, 1997). The video game industry depends on regular interactions between hardware manufacturing and software publishing, and the underdevelopment or absence of one or both of these industrial components—a lack of co-location—can make it more difficult for a national games economy to gain traction (Aoyama and Izushi, 2003, 426). While the Gamecity network is comprised largely of companies with ten or fewer employees, Hamburg is a robust development ecosystem with a diversified economic infrastructure, supported by the co-location of a large number of affiliated research institutes, schools and universities, and ready access to a skilled workforce. Several of the tech giants have offices in Hamburg; Google opened its German headquarters there in 2001, and Facebook followed suit in 2010 (both companies also have offices in Berlin).

Against the backdrop of multinational corporate expansion, government funding is a key element in building a sustainable framework for German game production, and while state support has lagged, regional funding and institutional research funding have assisted some sectors of the local games industry with early stage investment. In 2008, Periscope Studio received startup funds from the German Federal Ministry of Economics and Technology (BMWi—now known as the Federal Ministry for Economic Affairs and Energy) to develop its Psai engine. A number of venture capital firms have also stepped up to support the nation's technology sector. In 2007, Fishlabs received Series A financing from Neuhaus Partners (based in Hamburg); while Exit Games received Series B financing from Bertelsmann Digital Media Investments (BDMI), Neuhaus Partners and smac partners (formerly Siemens Mobile Acceleration in Communications), following first round investments in 2004. In 2009, MobileBits received seed funds from High-Tech Gründerfonds (a public-private partnership) and MAZ level one (Hamburg); and iVentureCapital (Hamburg) acquired a share of the company in 2012. With a persistent commitment to systems development (the matter of engines), the regional games economy has attracted private investors focused on emerging media, communication and information technologies. The distributed nature of financing across national boundaries and between firms and corporations is a common structural principle of the contemporary games industry, an industry in which distributed and flexible cultural labor has also become the norm (Deuze et al., 2007, 342). Code, data and the intellectual capital of programmers cross national boundaries, establish new flows within "transnational virtual space" (Aneesh, 2006), even as the workforce itself remains in place. Exit Games, for example, has adopted a distributed production strategy, meeting the IT talent where it is, and expanded its team beyond Hamburg by reaching out to Brazil, North Africa, Russia, Sweden and the United States; collaborative tools such as Asana, Slack, Google Apps and Dropbox, have nullified many of the benefits of co-location by facilitating communication and improving workflow management. While large-scale publishers and developers have turned to globalize their operations, often to the detriment of longstanding independent studios that have been transformed overnight into precarious work spaces, many small studios have internationalized their teams in order to compete—to find and keep place-bound creatives, and reduce their overhead costs.

Creative city models are rooted in the net-positive impacts of their associated creative industries—industries intended to bolster regional economic development and, ideally, equitably and inclusively distributed quality of life. They are also grounded in expanding and reframing culture as an industry and as an economic driver within the context of evolving public policy debates that subsume the arts within broader definitional frameworks that include media, information and technology. The creative city model relies significantly on the development of a localized yet globally valued knowledge economy that includes labor (and the associated costs of education, training, recruitment and retention) in any economic valuation, and foregrounds the development of intellectual property (Galloway and Dunlop, 2006). Regional cities need to attend to the economic benefits that come from attaching their cultural products to international markets—demonstrating the creative weight of (and intellectual capital associated with) localized production and, indirectly, highlighting the native supports that make it possible. By successfully promoting cultural enterprise and building a robust portfolio of intellectual properties, creative city leaders can convert an expanding knowledge economy into other forms of economic gain, including urban development. Creative cities are increasingly ranked by their rates of innovation, measured by employment growth and sector-based profitability. While game companies are often bound to local entrepreneurial technology sectors, dependent on adjacent media industries, and attached to regional economic and cultural goals, they remain tied to global technology forecasts. My focus in the case studies that follow is not the cultivation of knowledge workers, nor the environmental conditions of the creative city, but rather on the intellectual capital of regional game developers working within global technology networks, characterized by aggressive entrepreneurship and rapid industrial shifts.

In 2019, the Federal Ministry of Transport and Digital Infrastructure prepared to launch a German games fund, following through with a provision made by the German parliament in November 2018 that allocated 50 million euros to support the regional games industry (although as of September 2019 the fund was absent from the 2020 federal budget draft, and the details of the funding process remained unclear). The number of people employed in Germany's core game sector of developers and publishers dropped by 5.9% from 2018 to 2019, while the number of game companies rose by over 17%—a trend driven largely by small startup studios (German Games Industry Association, August 2019). Although most national game markets continue to grow their audience share and spend rate, the economies that support local production fail to match those trends; this holds true in Germany, where the marketplace is dominated by games produced elsewhere. German-developed games account for only 5.4% of domestic market sales (German Games Industry Association, August 2019). Given these conditional supports, a number of German game studios have built broad portfolios—developing proprietary technologies and establishing themselves as hubs for research and development, while producing independent game titles, subcontracting with larger publishers, or providing game-related client services.

The Abyss Engine: Deep Silver Fishlabs

Fishlabs was founded in 2004 by Michael Schade and Christian Lohr as a mobile games development studio, and acquired by the Koch Media group in 2013, with its assets incorporated into Deep Silver Fishlabs, a new game publishing division of the parent company. Fishlabs found its first successes developing mobile games for Sony Ericsson and Nokia, and with promotional games for clients that included Volkswagen and Barclaycard. Sony Ericsson was one of the first companies to advance mobile 3D gaming through its Java-supported phones, with the 2004 release of the K700. Meeting the software and hardware limitations of the mobile phone market, early mobile games relied on a Java-based API and utilized software rendering rather than hardware-assisted rendering (software rendering is not dependent on graphics hardware, but instead draws from a central processor). The Abyss engine, which was built in 2005 and iterated to version 4.0 through 2016, was developed to meet the processing-intensive demands of 3D graphics across the mobile market, providing support for multiple operating systems; the engine was designed to provide speed, scale and system interoperability while placing minimal demands on the limited memory and power of mobile devices. The Abyss engine provided programmers at Fishlabs with a consistent build process—a cross-platform approach that could target any device.

The same history of PC and console gaming—the movement from software to hardware rendering—has driven the mobile phone market, where game developers have experienced a similar but even faster evolution, as the lifecycle of devices is much shorter, and there are constant changes in graphics processing. Development of the Abyss engine moved from Java to C++ (with OpenGL ES, Open Graphics Library for Embedded Systems, a cross-platform API for rendering 2D and 3D graphics on mobile and embedded systems—systems of integrated hardware and software functions) tailored specifically for mobile devices. The engine and even the studio's Java-based game titles have been adapted to native platforms (including Android and iOS) and redesigned to meet the rapidly evolving specifications of mobile processors and APIs. The engine consists of one source code tree, with a unique but rapid build process for each native platform. The Abyss engine is also a development environment that includes the essential systems for rendering and resource management (Kuhlmann, 2016). Leveraging the graphics power of its engine (and the multiplayer middleware technology of Exit Games), Fishlabs secured a distribution deal with Sony Ericsson in 2005 to place a number of pre-installed demo games on the company's fleet of mobile phones; the deal effectively demonstrated the platform-independence of the Abyss engine, and the company's ability to write an engine that could proficiently extract the hardware specifications of each handset and be adapted to maximize game performance (resolution, framerate, polygon reduction) across devices without changing the look of the game.

Fishlabs remained committed to its own engine (paired with Firelight Technologies FMOD audio middleware) after evaluating both Unity and Unreal, both of which have been subsequently downscaled by their respective parent companies to meet the mobile market. Developers at Fishlabs found that Unity was better suited for casual games that did not require elaborate frame detail; and decided that Unreal, with its finely tuned attention to first-person shooters, did not meet the creative needs of the company's 2005 release, *Galaxy on Fire* (built in Java and subsequently versioned for iOS, Android and other platforms). Moreover, the executable elements of Unity and Unreal are still much larger in size than those of Abyss, placing higher demands on mobile data processing. With its own in-house development team, Fishlabs could properly version and test its engine and closely match the parameters of the engine to the gameplay experience.

Fishlabs effectively leveraged and showcased the technical and creative assets of the company through its own intellectual properties. Moreover, by building with its own engine, Fishlabs guarded the company against the unnecessary risk associated with adopting third-party middleware—a fear that was not unwarranted. When Electronic Arts bought Criterion Software Group from Canon Europe in 2004, the company took control of Criterion's RenderWare engine (as well as Criterion's UK-based development studio); the acquisition traumatized a large segment of the game industry that had depended on the proprietary off-the-shelf 3D engine and would now have to license their core technology from a rival publisher.

With the reorganization under Koch Media, development of the Abyss engine was eventually shelved in favor of adopting an industry-standard framework. While Deep Silver Fishlabs has chosen to focus on building games in Unreal as it moves into the console and PC markets, in its job postings the company highlights experience with other engines including Unity, CryEngine and Frostbite as a bonus for prospective level designers, and foregrounds a number of engine-agnostic level design fundamentals (understanding player direction and player learning curves, gameplay difficulty, pacing, motivation and reward cycles) as key literacies of the field.

Following Andy Pratt et al.'s (2007) call for a more spatially and socially grounded account of the all too commonly abstracted flows of the information society (924), any meaningful consideration of regional development within the global games industry cannot ignore the labor of cultural workers; while they are part of global information networks, they are also key to how those networks of production get territorialized, negotiated and shaped (Kerr and Cawley, 2012, 399)—how despatialized information flows are fixed in place and how the distinctions between corporations, independent studios and freelance developers are superseded by the ability of a network to cut across these sectors and geographies, and across economic units of varying size and stability (Castells, 1996, 471). However abstracted from location it may seem, labor always remains local (Castells, 1996, 476), although the object of production, the cultural expression itself and, as is the case for game engine architectures, the systems of production are almost always abstracted from that same history and geography. While my focus here has been on one particular informatic through line, the game engine, because of its value in setting particular knowledge hierarchies and defining the field of play (the engine governs the labors of production and sets the affordances of player engagement), technology does not erase geography. Game industry workers may be more dispersed than those employed in other entrepreneurial tech sectors that are more tightly bound to regional economic centers, but they depend on training hubs often associated with clustered educational institutions.

While I began my work in Germany with a question about the relative value and lifespan of an engine as a property inside an independent game studio, that question needs to be put into a much more critical frame that asks about the relative value and lifespan of developers tasked with maintaining a proprietary in-house engine. At Deep Silver Fishlabs, the departure from Abyss resulted in downsizing a team that had included a lead engine developer, two supporting engine developers, two tools developers and one graphics developer. Fishlabs built its original engine for Java-supported phones prior to Unity's entrance into the mobile market; had the company remained centrally committed to mobile gaming, Abyss development would have likely shifted to another standard as the studio assumed its role within a larger publishing network. Abyss entered the mobile marketplace at a time when the landscape of mobile operating systems was more diverse and smartphones were limited in use; the in-house engine allowed Fishlabs to quickly adapt games for multiple operating systems to serve any number of handsets, including those manufactured by Nokia and Sony Ericsson. Nokia supported the now discontinued Symbian operating system (and briefly considered MeeGo), which had a sizable market share that was eventually overtaken by iOS and Android. The iPhone operating system gained its current iOS nomenclature in 2010, after the first iPhone was released in 2007, while the first Android native development kit (NDK) was offered in 2009, providing developers with the opportunity to program in C or C++ for Android devices and efficiently reuse their code libraries for other handsets (the effect was to encourage cross-platform game deployments). Within a narrowed field, the uniqueness of the Fishlabs approach yielded to other developers, as Unity, for example, became more invested in the mobile market and gained wider adoption at studios looking to produce mobile games.

When a game development studio uses an in-house engine, its artists can dictate the workflow and features of the development environment; the same does not hold true when a studio adopts an existing third-party engine. In the latter case, artists, animators, level designers and programmers have to negotiate the engines they are asked to work with, and adopt their craft and their processes to the workflow of its editor and its underlying software architecture. For Fishlabs, this was a critical make or buy decision. While the core of the Abyss engine, as with most game engines, is not game driven, the final 5% of the build can be readily adapted to match the form of play; at the same time, the consistent strength of the Abyss engine is its focus on 3D geometry (it is not a 2D engine). In small team development, the work of an engine can come to life around a dedicated program (although even larger studios, including id Software, build game titles that showcase the capabilities of their engines, even as the core technology is built in advance).

In his blog notes on the Abyss engine, Johannes Kuhlmann, Head of Core Technologies at Deep Silver Fishlabs draws particular attention to the human side of software creation noting, "The human side to it—the developers writing, architecting, fixing and using the code—is infinitely more complex than the programs we write" (Kuhlmann, 2017). Algorithmic design is a technical, creative and communicative process that binds the development team together; engine development and versioning is fundamentally a high-touch activity often glossed over by the necessary push toward selective workflow automation (and the common reliance on a build server). In a span of six years, from 2011 to 2017, I have documented a significant shift within Fishlabs, fueled in 2013 by a bankruptcy proceeding, an acquisition, and the company's subsequent attachment to a suite of intellectual properties owned by Deep Silver. This shift has happened as the mobile, console and PC markets continue to converge, as more devices go mobile, as mobile devices garner more processing power, and as graphics-intensive content is more readily streamed across any number of platforms. The home console and PC markets have a more complicated history of divergence and convergence, bound to their relative associations with television, computing and gaming—and the perceived and practiced centrality of hardware to the broad range of affiliated media industries (Finn, 2002). The advancement of mobile communications technologies has only complicated this history. Yet if we focus solely on the industrial and technical dimensions of convergence, we lose sight of the simple fact that the history of Fishlabs, and a development team that found value in the labors of its engine, is bound to that of many other independent studios that have either closed their doors or been acquired by larger stakeholders.

The Delta Engine: MobileBits

MobileBits was founded in 2009 as the parent company of the game development studio exDream, and was acquired by Goodgame Studios in 2015 (which was in turn acquired by the Stillfront Group in 2017). MobileBits focused on developing and publishing mobile games, and built the proprietary Delta engine utilizing Microsoft's .NET software framework. The open source engine supports mobile deployments across iOS, Android and Windows Phone 7 and solves the complexities of cross-platform compatibility and performance. Delta was designed to limit the amount of predetermination built into the engine, to allow game developers to use their existing tools (Autodesk 3ds Max and Maya, Microsoft Visual Studio) within their existing ecosystems while targeting multiple platforms; the Delta engine fits into these workflows and processes (unlike Unity, which requires that developers operate within the common architecture of the Unity editor) and is targeted to developers who are already familiar with PC and console-based development but want their games to run on mobile devices (without the associated costs of rebuilding for each new platform). The Delta engine was built as an alternative to black box engines with closed core architectures such as

Unity, more robust and code-intensive engines such as Unreal, and simpler graphic frameworks such as DirectX, XNA and OpenGL that are better suited for writing lightweight games.

Cross-platform compatibility is a common issue for game developers, who base their game builds on a particular programming language. With the 2010 release of the iOS 4.0 SDK, Apple changed the terms of service of its iPhone licensing agreement to restrict programs originally written in non-Apple approved languages; by restricting the use of middleware and forcing game developers to choose its native iPhone build, Apple limited the ability of developers to work across platforms. The company appeared to be locked in a battle for proprietary content against other handset developers, particularly those using Google's Android operating system, and was also targeting Adobe by restricting the use of Flash on its phones; but the move also impacted Unity developers working with C#. For MobileBits, this meant potentially backtracking with the Delta engine (built with .NET managed code), as Apple looked to tie down its own platform, elevate its Xcode developer tools, and eliminate cross-platform compilers capable of translating foreign platforms into iPhone binaries:

> Applications must be originally written in Objective-C, C, C++, or JavaScript as executed by the iPhone OS WebKit engine, and only code written in C, C++, and Objective-C may compile and directly link against the Documented APIs (e.g., Applications that link to Documented APIs through an intermediary translation or compatibility layer or tool are prohibited).
>
> *(iPhone Developer Program License Agreement, Section 3.3.1, April 2010)*

Those restrictions were effectively lifted after the Federal Trade Commission and the Department of Justice threatened to launch an antitrust inquiry in May 2010. As a relatively small development studio with 20+ employees, MobileBits would not have had the resources to pivot and repeatedly rebuild its central intellectual properties, which include *SoulCraft* (an action role-playing game first released in 2012 for iOS, Android and Windows mobile) and its sequels. Despite the return to more open language supports, the future of the Delta engine is uncertain; as MobileBits is now a subsidiary of a larger holding group, the proprietary technology is no longer a critical resource. The last Delta engine release was in 2014. This is the fate of many in-house engines. They are largely dependent on the stability of their studios and their personnel; if they are not regularly tested, versioned, supported and documented, they inevitably fail to be compatible and fall out of use as governing technologies move forward.

The Photon Engine: Exit Games

Exit Games was founded in 2003 by Chris Wegmann. The company's Photon engine is a cross-platform engine that supports multiplayer game development;

the engine provides a turnkey networking solution for other commercial development suites, including Unity, and allows developers to readily implement a number of real-time multiplayer features, including chat, across mobile, PC and console environments. The Photon engine is part of a suite of products that includes the Photon Cloud, Server and SDK; the cloud services simplify multiplayer cross-platform communication protocols and provide automatic scalability to respond in real-time to the volume of concurrent game players. The base layer product, as a foundation for networked communication, sends packages as fast as possible between players or peers.

The Photon engine is a network engine and cloud service for building cross-platform real-time multiplayer games; the engine handles client and server communications and is designed to manage matchmaking, real-time gameplay (and player inputs), and related scalable multiplayer features (such as maintaining a network-aware game state and syncing changes in the game environment). Photon is equipped with SDKs that include libraries for various platforms, including Unity, iOS, Android and Windows, and support cross-platform interactions (for communication across the possible variants of a game application running on distinct platforms—for example between Android and iOS).

With its focus on Photon rather than game development *per se*, Exit Games has followed a software-as-a-service (SaaS) model for multiplayer game development and hosting; and with its consistent attention to advancing its proprietary engine, followed by widespread cross-platform integration, the company has become a critical middleware provider for networked game development, serving both independent and enterprise clients by offering scalable volume licensing plans, with enterprise customers being the company's major revenue source. The SaaS model allows Exit Games to make its middleware accessible for independents and startups as well as larger studios (including Disney, Square Enix, Ubisoft and Warner Brothers), giving them access to the same tools. Across its development history, Exit Games has addressed the very real matter of isolating platform-dependent code to support real-time multiplayer applications in networked environments. The company has entered into expanded partnerships or developed internal builds with Marmalade (which abandoned its engine in 2018, citing competition in the mobile market from Unity and Unreal, and an unyielding Apple iOS policy), Unity, HTC (with Viveport app store support for connected VR applications) and other interactive systems developers, including Unreal; in turn, these integrations have provided the company with a foothold in the evolving mobile games market. Exit Games has remained focused on tackling the unique problem of handling sizable concurrent player interactions in networked game space, while licensing its integrated middleware solution to other software developers and studios.

While Exit Games has focused on one part of the game development pipeline—one well-architected middleware solution to solve the recurring problem of building scalable networked communication—other software developers have tried to include networking solutions as part of their ever-expanding ecosystems, to diversify their portfolios and shore up their revenue models. Unity, for example, is replacing its legacy UNet multiplayer tools and services with a new networking stack as part of a phased connected games initiative that began in 2018. In the same year, Amazon acquired UK and Ireland-based cloud gaming platform GameSparks to offer a comprehensive suite of backend tools (server-side management of multiplayer data, communication and analytics) to its developer community, while Microsoft acquired Seattle-based PlayFab to integrate parallel game-related networking services into its Azure cloud platform. As Exit Games continues to pursue the matter of real-time communication and data synchronization in networked space, it is addressing the emerging demands of information exchange in augmented and virtual reality, and expanding its portfolio to help companies build reliable interactive applications that have little to do with gaming.

The Psai Engine: Periscope Studio

Periscope Studio has pursued a similar software-as-a-service model in developing its Psai (Periscope Studio Audio Intelligence) engine, but as a client-centered agency has also purposefully diversified its business; Periscope is both a software developer and a full-fledged audio service provider. Periscope was founded in 2007 as a dedicated game audio studio, producing music and interactive scores. The company positioned itself as a one-stop shop for game audio, providing services in music, localization and sound design. Periscope's first composition project was *The Whispered World*, a point-and-click adventure game released in 2009. The game, developed by Daedelic Entertainment and published by Deep Silver, features hand-drawn 2D graphics and was built on a modified version of Visionaire Studio, a cross-platform 2D (and 2.5D) adventure game engine. After working with the Visionaire engine, and experiencing the engine's fixed parameters for music integration, the Periscope production team began to develop a dedicated middleware solution for game music.

The Psai engine was designed to change the production workflow and give composers a tool to more fully engage with the creative process. The Periscope team designed the engine around the complexities of interactive music and the build of music assets that can more intimately react to gameplay events; the engine gives greater control of soundtrack behaviors to the composer or audio studio, and provides game developers with a readily accessible intelligent music system for post-composition audio integration.

Using the Psai tool suite, the composer creates a soundtrack that contains both musical data and a series of related interactive behaviors; following suit, the developer imports these composer-built elements into the game. As part of the development process, the musical score is divided into a number of game-related themes (basic mood, action, and so forth) and segments; these themes and their intensities are then attached to locations, objects and events using the drag and drop functionality of the engine's editor. During runtime, the engine effectively composes music playback on the fly by evaluating player input and recombining state-related musical segments; during gameplay, the interactive soundtrack is controlled by simple trigger scripts that contain two pieces of information—theme and intensity. The goal of truly adaptive music is to further the experience of immersion in part by avoiding repetition or looping; by adapting the intensity of the music and generating an evolving and varied soundtrack, the engine effectively responds to the gameplay experience.

Periscope achieved its first Psai integration with the 2011 release of *Black Mirror III*, a point-and-click adventure game developed by Cranberry Production. Periscope released a Unity port of the Psai engine in 2014 that was followed by the release of several royalty-free music libraries in the Unity Asset Store. By releasing its engine to the public and providing ready-to-go content, Periscope effectively promoted the adoption of its engine. Working alongside the Unity game engine (and written in C# to comply with all of Unity's target platforms), the Psai engine functions as an integrated subsystem that does not affect a game's code.

Periscope Studio remains focused on audio for video games and its audio middleware, although it has expanded to provide audio services to other non-game media industries. In 2012, the studio consolidated its interests in video game localization (translation and voice recording) under Synthesis Germany (part of Synthesis International). Periscope's commitment to the Psai engine is an outgrowth of the studio's origin as a client-centered agency engaged in collaborative problem solving, and its dual expertise in audio production and software development. The studio has found its niche by solving one of the central problems associated with composing music for video games—the difficulty of purposefully aligning audio with real-time adaptive play mechanics. Periscope Studio's composer-first approach has led to a fairly well-defined division of labor (the team includes composers, sound designers, software developers and product managers) that reflects the game development pipeline more broadly—where artists and programmers work side by side, and where the best development tools are shaped by the creative process.

Berlin and Frankfurt

My research in Germany is not a comprehensive analysis of the nation's game industry; rather it is intentionally focused on studios that have built their own software frameworks. The entrepreneurial spirit driving engine-based work is undoubtedly a condition of stable cultural and industrial supports. Over the six-year span of my research, mobile games (both smartphone and tablet games) have gained significant market share, and now account for the largest segment of the global games market, with mobile games at 45%, console games at 32%, and PC games at 23% of total 2019 revenues (Newzoo, 2019).

Small development studios often build their own cross-platform games while also providing game solutions for clients looking to enter the mobile games market. This provides a balanced revenue model for those independent developers looking for creative control over their own intellectual properties, while understanding the value associated with client-centered work. Within these dual revenue streams, small studios adopt a broad range of technologies—maintaining their own game engines for internal projects, marrying those engines with third-party middleware to expand the functionality of their engines, and adopting tools such as Unity to meet the rapid prototyping needs of their clients. Most small studios do not have the resources to pursue the console market, but with a market that is increasingly diversified and mobile, they are building to match an ecosystem of operating environments that includes PC, Mac, iOS, Android, Linux and browser-based games.

When I returned to Germany in 2017, I expanded my study to include game studios in Berlin and Frankfurt, as both cities have thriving media economies and relatively large game communities. As a point of contrast, I am limiting my attention here to two illustrative case studies: Black Pants Studio, a small studio with offices in Berlin and Kassel, and Crytek, one of the industry's largest stakeholders, with headquarters in Frankfurt.

The Scape Engine: Black Pants Studio

Black Pants Studio is an independent developer and publisher with a core team of four staff: two programmers, one animator and one comic artist. The studio was officially founded in 2012, but several of its original members began development on the proprietary Scape engine in 2002 to support a particular type of interactive play, folding dynamic environments into core game mechanics; their focus effectively allowed the technology to follow the aesthetics of interaction.

Black Pants specializes in artfully rendered comic-style games. Two of their most successful platformers, *Tiny & Big: Grandpa's Leftovers* (2012) and *On Rusty Trails* (2016), exemplify the studio's commitment to playfully illustrated hand-crafted game worlds. In *Tiny & Big*, players must use the environment to progress through the game; the game's primary mechanics include slicing large objects with a laser tool and pulling them apart with a grappling rope. The player moves these large environmental masses around the game world to advance through each level. The environmental principle is essentially non-destructive, allowing players to interact with large parts of the environment (such as boulders) and deconstruct these into smaller fragments that maintain stable dimensions and can be used as part of gameplay. Throughout the game, players must manipulate and engage with a broad inventory of environmental objects. Most of the games developed by Black Pants are clever variations on the playful activation of the built environment. One of the key mechanics of *On Rusty Trails* is a "Switchy Suit" that allows Elvis (the game's protagonist) to shape shift between spikey and hairy forms, protecting his metallic body as he safely hops across platforms; the identity-switching suit allows Elvis to survive a series of environmental hazards, and find harmony amid the conflict of a fictional race war.

The environmental problem at the center of *Tiny & Big* was a creative challenge in need of a technical solution that has driven much of the programming work at Black Pants. The development team led with their desire to create a game that would allow players to influence the environment by destroying, reshaping or connecting large pieces of the game world; this is essentially a problem of dynamic geometry manipulation that requires a reliable plane-splitting method for convex objects. The solution is straightforward, but carries with it a degree of computational complexity: define a plane where a 3D mesh (a structural graph of a 3D object) can be segmented into meaningful parts, and dynamically wrap those parts in a convex hull (that faithfully approximates the original mesh) that can be passed through a physics engine. The Black Pants team began by experimenting with the computational parameters of two open source physics engines for simulating rigid body dynamics and material collisions as part of creating visually meaningful decompositions: the Open Dynamics Engine and the Bullet engine. The latter of these lent itself to the build of a working prototype for the Scape engine; the programmers at Black Pants steered away from early versions of Unity, as they looked for a system with fewer built-in dependencies and a more transparent architecture. The Black Pants dilemma highlights the difficulty associated with reading complex code objects; it is reflected in the desire of a small team of programmers to build a readily pulled apart modular system—a system

FIGURE 7.1 *Tiny & Big: Grandpa's Leftovers.*
Copyright 2012 Black Pants Studio.

that could also be more responsive to the needs of the studio's graphic artists. Digging more deeply, this decision also points to the language gap—of the preference of a team for building its own codebase, and for developing a workflow modeled on their own preferred language (in this case C++). The central play mechanic of *Tiny & Big*, defining boundary cuts to segment objects into multiple smaller objects, is a problem that can be solved through more than one algorithmic method. In this instance, algorithmic manipulation is an expressive conceit that connects graphic artists, level designers, programmers and players.

Black Pants does not use its proprietary game engine for all of its projects. Unity is often used to prototype games, to test and move assets by exploiting Unity's built-in physics engines, to rapidly iterate and quickly code ideas, and only then writing a native version for the Scape engine; the selective use of external design tools prevents the development workflow from being bottlenecked on the programming side, and prevents both engine and game art from setting more global technical affordances. The boundary between what is written in code and what is performed by the engine is often aligned with the know-how and approach of a studio's programmers. As the Scape engine has no functional editor, the process of translating assets and files across build environments bridges the gap between artists and coders and creates a more responsive relationship between them; the studio's artists work with external build tools while the programmers write custom build scripts that convert files into native binaries that can be loaded into Scape, where the game code is written in C++. Data moves across software packages and their associated file formats, binding together the work (and preferred visual languages) of artists and programmers, and fostering a collective and less hierarchical approach to game production. The studio's painterly graphics style is matched by its artful approach to code; and more seamless conceptual development is supported by the selective addition of external tools that meet the needs of the entire Black Pants team—its artists, designers, programmers and developers (with some of these being singular individuals).

The argument to be made about the value of the creative mechanics of *Tiny & Big* and *On Rusty Trails* is not simply in the uniqueness of the form of interaction—there are other equally innovative games that speak to players through a shared pleasure in learning how to engage with a hermetic game world, and experience new laws of physics that only seem to operate in that space. For players, there is the fascination with learning and mastering these subject-object relations and from guiding a protagonist forward using this newfound logic. The argument I am making about the mechanics of the work of Black Pants Studio is about the attachment of that fascination, of that attention to a material graphical pleasure, to the relatively immaterial syntactical pleasure (the arrangement of code) of an underlying software architecture—the Scape engine. There is a slightly alienating effect, a positive one at that, in asking a player to learn a new mechanic; this act sheds light on the mechanical consequences of a succession of quite similar control schemes for moving characters and manipulating in-game assets—associations that get embedded in the procession of engines and their associated geometries. I am simply drawing attention to a moment when a studio has seriously considered the affordances of existing engines, and at least partly opted out. Black Pants has no plans for a public release of its development platform, as the full documentation and first level support required of a public release would present the studio with an entirely new business case; I would argue that limiting the circulation of the Scape engine guarantees that it remains attached to the creative vision that drives it.

The CryEngine: Crytek

Crytek has moved in the opposite direction with its engine, licensing it with the full engine source code under a royalty-based user model and through a number of other transactional agreements (while setting restrictions on use for what the company identifies as non-game applications, including military projects, technical and scientific visualizations, architecture and serious games). As I have noted earlier, the CryEngine was licensed to Amazon for the build of the company's proprietary Lumberyard engine. The Amazon sale in 2015 and the move to a new monetization model in 2018 (with the release of CryEngine 5.5) have provided a much-needed infusion of capital to stabilize Crytek following several years of financial hardship. In 2014, the company closed its UK studio and sold the rights to its *Homefront* game property to publisher Deep Silver. In late 2016, the company announced a restructuring of its studio holdings in Bulgaria, China, Hungary, Korea and Turkey, selling its Bulgaria-based Black Sea studio to Sega the following year; and in 2018, as the company moved to a new licensing model it also reversed course on an "Engine-as-a-Service" royalty-free monthly subscription program first introduced in 2014 to help indie developers. These closures, sales and periodic changes to the company's business model follow widespread reporting in the trade press that in both 2014 and 2016 Crytek struggled to pay its staff.

Despite these course corrections, Crytek's overall software strategy reflects that of both Unity Technologies and Epic Games, in that engines are not simply proprietary software tools, they are also development platforms. When an engine is licensed, each of these companies is essentially licensing a development platform and considering what to supply in that platform—game services, repositories, team management. Unity, for example offers a range of bundled services with its engine, including the monetization and behavior frameworks Unity Ads and Analytics. This is the software-as-a-service model, where enterprise licensing often includes a range of support packages and membership levels, and can include direct access to a developer's engineers. The Crytek strategy is most analogous to that of Epic Games—building successful massive multiplayer games that run on and showcase the company's engine, as well as licensing the engine and providing access to its codebase. In part, well-played game titles provide a model use case for prospective developers, illustrating the technical features of the engine.

Crytek was founded in 1999 by the brothers Cevat, Avni and Faruk Yerli, and was built on the potential of its engine. The CryEngine was first revealed by Crytek in the technology demo *X-Isle: Dinosaur Island*, a showcase for the nascent engine that was exhibited at the 1999 Electronic Entertainment Expo (E3), where the company signed a distribution deal with computing company NVIDIA; NVIDIA licensed the demo as benchmarking software for its high-performance graphics cards. The demo led to the 2004 release of *Far Cry*, Crytek's first fully realized build with the CryEngine; expanding on the open world characteristics of the earlier demo, the game extended the core technology's ability to render richly textured environments and real-time lighting effects and shadow maps. Crytek's core mission has remained focused on its engine, both to produce its own games and to expand its portfolio of technology licenses. Each successive build of the engine requires a high degree of resource management and reliable middleware integrations, and to meet these demands the company has a broad and deep team of programmers to manage the engine as well as an expansive team of creative artists and designers to develop game assets and levels for its own titles.

In addition to its work with Amazon, Crytek has a history of porting its technology to other market sectors. Crytek's Cinebox is a specific implementation of the CryEngine built for film-based previsualization, virtual production and cinematics. Work on the Cinebox prototype began in 2008, although the technology saw limited implementation as an advanced previsualization tool before Crytek moved on to build its Film Engine, first announced in 2016. The specifications for the still-in-development Film Engine suggest more robust supports for the film industry workflow, to allow film artists to work in parallel on layout, animation, lighting, editing and related technical assets; the engine is intended to act as a hub to connect these data bundles. An initial build of the Film Engine premiered at FMX (the International Conference on Animation, Effects, Games and Immersive Media) in Stuttgart, Germany as part of Crytek's Virtual Production Stage, where the company showcased a full virtual production pipeline with support from Ncam, OptiTrack, ARRI, AMD and HP (covering visual effects, motion capture, camera and lighting, graphics and computing). The alignment of the engine with well-regarded industry partners was a noteworthy gesture for Crytek; by situating the nascent technology alongside trusted vendors, and inserting it into firmly established workflows, the company was able to document a particular use case, culled from and compliant with parallel media industries.

As technology companies innovate, it is understandable that they proceed in a calculated fashion, pushing the boundaries of longstanding industry practices while holding on to existing pipeline models, labor divisions and technologies that drive a series of intersecting media and information industries. Game developers need to consider the forward movement of computation, but also the physical object lessons of other media forms and the existing knowledge capital of media industry workers. The same holds true as digital content developers adapt the lingua franca of the tech industry.

The CryEngine was originally written in Lua, a highly customizable and expandable cross-platform programming language. The first game in the *Crysis* series, released in 2007, was designed in Lua, although the core engine mechanics run with C++. Crytek has since abandoned Lua in favor of C# and C++ although Amazon has kept building in Lua with its ongoing iteration of the CryEngine codebase for Lumberyard. Lumberyard accommodates two scripting technologies—Script Canvas, a visual scripting environment that uses readily connected graphical nodes as a visual map of game logic, and Lua, which serves as a relatively lightweight though embeddable scripting language suitable for Amazon's prospective client base. As developers license their engines, they expose their technologies to linguistic shifts, often associated with customized scripts designed for specific applications and end users. In a response to Crytek's March 2019 community spotlight, a curated (and unabashedly promotional) collection of game developer reflections on their selection of the CryEngine, a number of unsolicited online respondents criticize the company's move away from Lua toward new visual scripting tools (Flow Graph and Schematyc) and call out Crytek's failure to evolve the engine in response to their concerns (as representatives of a larger indie client base); this is noted as a failure to convey a coherent vision, to communicate that vision, and to make concessions to the independent developer community (Crytek, 2019).

While usability and stability are the core focus of evolving a game engine, a perpetual movement that is in part a response to emerging hardware standards, the push to iterate is complicated by internal conditions—the array of engine subsystems—and the deep dependencies of external user groups that have games in various stages of development. Crytek, Epic and Unity have all attempted to create community around their respective engines by providing access to their development teams and by creating online marketplaces of goods and ideas. Crytek has used Slack chat to communicate with its clients and GitHub to selectively test new versions of its engine and open its source code. Crytek also publishes a forward-looking road map to show its clients how the company plans to modify and develop the engine; the company's public release notes identify those engine enhancements and supports that are on target, at risk or delayed, and are intended to highlight the overall direction of the engine's development, outline new features, and provide target dates for stable releases. In the same way that Crytek frames its clients as a community, the company also refers to its internal development teams as a community, with engine integrations directed by feedback from the company's internal UX/UI (user experience/user interface) design group in consultation with the studio's artists; the game team and the engine team run in tandem, with the game itself as a playable manifestation of Crytek's core technology—a representation of its foundational product.

As a sizable development company that attends to both its own engine and its own game titles, Crytek has the technical resources to survive middleware transitions and dependencies, which place it at an advantage over smaller independent game studios that cannot pivot as quickly to meet ongoing shifts in third-party software and hardware markets. In July 2017, Autodesk discontinued its game middleware line—a suite that included Scaleform GFx (a tool that allowed developers to create user interfaces in Adobe Flash), HumanIK (a set of character animation tools), and Beast (a global illumination and lightmapping tool). Crytek still has Scaleform in its engine and with a full team of programmers is able to support its ongoing implementation, while Unity which featured Beast integration in 2010 with Unity 3 switched to Enlighten technology with the 2015 release of Unity 5, before moving on to a new in-house solution for global illumination in July 2019 (after Geomerics sold its interest in Enlighten to Silicon Studio in 2017). Engines are not standalone properties; their value lies in the ready integration of other resources. Independent game studios experience a high degree of vulnerability as they build games that depend on the stable engine releases of other developers, and have to be able to respond over the course of a development cycle to any number of software and hardware shifts. While larger studios are able to navigate the repeated versioning (and occasional obsolescence) of third-party middleware and industry-standard design tools, they still experience a certain degree of uncertainty, as their in-house engines always carry a range of dependencies, many of which are central to the work of their creative teams.

As they continue to negotiate changes in third-party software and hardware markets, and make the necessary adjustments to their respective codebases, larger development studios also continue to diversify their holdings and respond to emerging technology trends. In 2016, Crytek moved into virtual reality with two VR entries, *Robinson: The Journey* and *The Climb*, entering what is still an immature gaming ecosystem; *Robinson* was released for the PlayStation VR and *The Climb* was released for the Oculus Rift. The engine is a facilitator; its core provides a consistent foundation for game development and allows a studio to consider new markets without starting from scratch with a new codebase. Crytek's efforts in VR rely on the engine and reflect what is mostly a change in design intentions (and refined mechanics such as climbing) rather than an overhaul of the core software architecture. The aesthetics of immersion warrant a more nuanced and detailed approach to environmentally bounded play; level designs need to be more intimately connected and shaped as natural flows between contiguous yet varied areas of exploration. The goal is to naturalize these operations, to focus the effort on gameplay; to at once complement the aesthetics of immersion by pushing the engine's graphical capabilities, and at the same time conceal the work and the algorithmic determinacy of the engine.

It may be an oversimplification to suggest that by expanding the engine's visual logic, Crytek is attempting to amplify player agency. But this push seems to ground one of the company's more recent releases, *Hunt: Showdown*. *Hunt* is a competitive first-person multiplayer bounty hunting game structured and varied through its match-based format. The game was launched in Early Access on Steam in February 2018 and on Xbox Game Preview in May 2019. Both release formats highlight the role of the player community in a still-developing game. Expanding on the principles of its Early Access model, Valve notes:

> These are games that evolve as you play them, as you give feedback, and as the developers update and add content. We like to think of games and game development as services that grow and evolve with the involvement of customers and the community. There have been a number of prominent titles that have embraced this model of development recently and found a lot of value in the process. We like to support and encourage developers who want to ship early, involve customers, and build lasting relationships that help everyone make better games. This is the way games should be made.
>
> *(Valve Corporation, 2020)*

Player agency is inscribed as part of a feedback loop in the development cycle, as part of game design; but it does not play any particular role in the evolution of game architecture (beyond the development of new assets, new modes, new maps or new level designs, which are simply expansions of existing frameworks). The game engine remains constant in an otherwise variable equation. Against this backdrop, Crytek situates *Hunt* as more agentive, as having a more open structure of causality, turning game AI to align with the work of the player as it maps the player's imprint on the game's environment, while also wrapping AI in the modeling, rigging and skinning of the game's monsters. By varying the multiplayer experience and by shaping environment into a plot-based tool, Crytek has effectively reduced the demand for additional content, which can be one of the most expensive aspects of maintaining a game franchise. Intrinsically, players have sufficient content offered up through competitive gameplay variations, and through the nuances of their social interactions.

What binds together Crytek's properties, and ties its game titles to its technology, is the consistently high valuation of the natural environment in the first-person shooter (FPS) experience. In the same way that *Hunt* uses environmental details to signal action and progression, *Crysis* and *Far Cry* share a similar attitude toward place. *Far Cry*, the title that premiered the CryEngine, tasks the player with conquering a tropical wilderness and exploring a variety of contested open spaces. *Crysis* (built on CryEngine 2) reveals a similar comfort zone for the developer—the build of tropical islands filled with lush vegetation that feature the engine's graphical power and naturalistic lighting effects. *Hunt* (built on CryEngine 5) locates the player in the Louisiana swamps, to similarly detailed environmental effect. Consistently, Crytek has developed its engine to render rich and responsive environments, and to draft detailed outdoor spaces that also allow for large viewing distances. Crytek established its place in the game market through its engine: an engine well-equipped to render at high aesthetic thresholds, and advance the field of simulated visual effects by delivering motion blur, depth of field, volumetric lighting and fogging, and dynamic shadows. Moreover, the engine can deliver real-time physics-based environmental interactions, and is primed to deliver on the promise of endlessly varied environmental destruction. As the company moves into VR, it continues to use its engine to emphasize the player's sense of presence in the game world—a presence realized not only through the freedom of exploration, but also by expressively mapping the traces of the player on the game world—weaving both art assets and engine-based environmental mechanics into the broader work of immersive storytelling and engaged play.

While I have closed this chapter with a protracted consideration of Crytek's evolution, my goal is to draw particular attention to the company's engine in a measured way that aligns it with the technological futures of its competitors, its clients, and smaller development teams that have opted to rely on or develop other software frameworks. The balance of working within and against the affordances of a commercial engine has led a number of regional game developers to build with their own technologies and a number of regional technology companies to build around gaps in the broader ecosystem of game development, publishing, user experience and data management. These investments cannot be considered independently, and collectively they signal the conditions for balanced innovation in both media and technology—the interdependencies between software systems, the interconnectedness of programming and design, and the requisite foundations in regional infrastructure (social, political, cultural and economic) to support experimentation and to leverage and stimulate the growth of intellectual capital. By focusing on Germany here, I have not attended to the barriers that interfere with truly transnational game development, and I acknowledge that the work, talent, technology and resources outlined in this chapter are far from being evenly distributed across the globe, although some aspects of production and manufacture have migrated to less costly industrialized zones (Kerr, 2017, 3). Nevertheless, what I have outlined should provide the necessary context for the chapter that follows, as the cases that form this chapter (and the combined work of individuals, development teams and holding companies) highlight the often-overlooked tensions that drive software production. These tensions, these stops and starts in engine-based game development, can help us see software at work and understand it as a fluid enterprise; by deconstructing software, by reading software as a design process, we can properly frame it as an object lesson that cuts against the grain of technological determinism. By reading engines, we can speak to the relative presence or absence of agency in game engine culture.

8

QUEERING THE FIELD: BEYOND BINARY ENGINE CHOICES

All development tools work by trafficking in signs, in pre-determined languages. As a whole, these practices reveal the evolving contours of technobiography: they speak to the degree to which the body is a network, experience can be quantified, and technology can play a role in both the expression and construction of self. Because of their diversity, video game engines may foster an understanding of the nature of autobiographical knowledge in playable space, and the relative utility of autobiographical exchange in code-based multimedia storytelling.

This chapter considers the relative nature of free play and free expression in game development through several engagements with open source tools, contrasting entry-level and advanced toolsets. This chapter expands on the existing literature on game engine technologies, to open up a space for independent game engine developers and game designers to consider their relationship to corporate engines (such as Unity and Unreal) that are used in indie game communities by small and large development teams, and to further the interconnections between game theory and game design (as overlapping vectors of game scholarship). Moreover, this chapter proposes how a queer analysis of the work in progress and the technologies that undergird the work in progress might strengthen more generalized discussions of the representational politics of video games, their audiences and their production communities.

My focus is on game development—a site of cultural production that developers must negotiate, and where subjectivity and language are fundamentally entangled (O'Donnell, 2014). My use of the term "queer" is not limited to considerations of a counter-hegemonic impulse; more significantly, as this chapter considers game production at both the center and the periphery, I am privileging an understanding of queerness as one of semantic openness and expressive possibility that can challenge (or productively deconstruct) normative realism. This is not simply a call for more queer game designers or queer programmers, but a call for the continued investigation and expansion of code, and those obfuscations that hinder queering this terrain, some of which are standard industrial practices designed to prevent tampering, to protect intellectual property, and to increase security and stability by blocking modification. Game engine and game development pipelines can and do act as systems of oppression, to the extent that they conceal the conditions of their labor and center particular forms of knowledge; they trade in a limited currency of knowledge capital. My work here differs from existing explorations in the field of critical code studies that attempt to queer the foundational logic of programming (see, for example, Zach Blas, 2008) because this chapter focuses on the adoption of pre-existing tools (game engines) rather than artisanal (code) writing practices; as an engine is built and versioned, the otherwise latent potential of code, found in its modularity, is readily sealed over. Counter to Mark Marino's (2006) foundational claims for critical code studies, I do not believe that we can seamlessly situate code in relationship to literature, but my argument does not contradict this earlier work that suggests that the language of the programming community and the various ontological properties of code (for the programmer, modularity supports reusability and lends itself to practical efficiencies) should be used as a basis for its interpretation. Programming languages are situated practices, and their authors are situated practitioners—parts of larger software industries. The trouble with engines is that as secondary processes, as concretizations of code rather than open or unconstrained programming environments, they promote a language gap (a gap intensified by a continual process of versioning that presents complications for those independent developers trusting them as stable development environments that can nevertheless "break" their games with each new update). For most media scholars, engines have led to a certain illiteracy. Even when they are open source, game engines require a more precise understanding of specific programming languages. They take time to decode, to lay bare the particular lines of code that, taken together, produce a specific aesthetic, mechanic or functional interaction.

I do not intend to bifurcate the field of analysis between game design and development, or between narrativity and the engine (between content and code). Engine development can be considered both a creative and an industrial process, if we understand the engine as not simply software but as creative problem solving. This is most apparent in the work of independent studios, where the pleasure of creative independence is often accompanied by the associated pleasure of engine development (although most independent studios do not have the resources, interest or need to build, test and maintain their own engines). Yet we can associate some of the earliest work in computer programming with the pleasure of building solutions. Software design, as a creative process, is a fundamental part of game design.

While I have not covered the activities of modding communities, game mods (modifications) are technical, creative and often critical interventions that push the expressive limits of an otherwise hermetic culture—adopting existing game mechanics and intervening with the content. There is a rich history of "deconstructive" media development associated with machinima—creative interventions with computer game technologies that can be traced to the code-based work of the demoscene of the 1980s, when a burgeoning home computer market fueled a distinctly experimental computer art subculture. These experiments had considerable influence on the Quake (engine) movie movement of the 1990s. There are also a number of visual artists experimenting with video games who have appropriated the medium and its mechanics as part of more expansive cultural and political work—among them, Feng Mengbo has created a series of video game installations that draw from consumer game culture, and Brody Condon has produced a number of socially engaged game modifications and game-based interventions with traditional media forms that effectively hack into and transform existing game software. Indie developers and modders may be changing the aesthetics but not the mechanics of an existing property, or playing with the mechanics but not altering the engine; or, in the most aggressive pursuits, hacking and modding in an art world context that has neither penetrated nor destabilized contemporary game culture.

Many early stage game developers mimic other games; this is often an easy starting point for those teaching game design, drawing attention first to how games operate, and providing students with a pathway for making their games by simply changing the aesthetics without changing the mechanics or dynamics. Indeed, many digital natives are most interested in making games, and in this climate digital game mechanics have often taken precedence over developing personal voice and point of view, and over making a determination of what a game might express. Just changing the narrative without changing the mechanics or dynamics is a limited gesture. Game design theory grounded in MDA (mechanics, dynamics and aesthetics) teaches us that game making is not just about mechanics; instead, it should be rooted in more pervasive design methodologies focused on creative problem solving (Hunicke et al., 2004). If we accept this approach, then game building, gameplay and game criticism are connected; they are all directed toward systematic coherence. With this model in mind, we can speak to the inherent (or potential) queerness of the underlying technologies of video game development, or perhaps the queering of those technologies as they are folded into the game development pipeline. As I am focused on the critical and practical contours of game engines, I am drawn to the parallel distinctions we can make between game mechanics and game dynamics, with the former more aptly defining the codebase of an engine (program, data and algorithms) and the latter referencing the runtime components or behaviors of an engine (a temporal set of generated responses to player inputs). With this framework in mind, we can understand the game as an engine-driven feedback loop; to frame the game as a more traditional object of analysis (as a text to be read), we can follow Robin Hunicke et al.'s (2004) suggestion that "the content of a game is its behavior—not the media that streams out of it towards the player." This framework also brings game production and game labor into focus as essential elements of holistic game analysis; even if we do not possess the technical literacies to unravel the intricacies of game-related labor, we can at least be mindful of the (often undervalued) intellectual capital that is central to game production and perhaps allow the discourse of production to commingle with the discourse of cultural analysis.

Identifying with an Engine

Engine choice is driven down multiple paths—the PC and console market, the mobile market, indie distribution and commercial distribution. We can roughly approximate the indie community by examining the most popular engines featured on Itch.io, the go-to marketplace for independent developers: Unity, Construct, GameMaker, Twine and RPG Maker. These choices do not neatly align with triple-A development, if we consider several of the most popular engines on Steam, the leading video games distribution platform for the triple-A market: Unreal, Unity, Source, CryEngine, Gamebryo and id Tech. Entry-level tools such as Twine and GameMaker have become a haven for indie and queer game artists seeking alternative game languages, as both applications have broader affordances and lower skill barriers.

Gesturing toward collaboration, co-creation and community building, larger game companies have opened up their more robust development tools to independent artists. Most software developers have kept their intellectual properties open through a proprietary software development kit (SDK) while restricting the ability to publish and sell without a version license, and most have created pathways for sharing independently authored assets. Most of the major game technology companies participate in and openly advocate for some version of a sharing economy. Game engine development follows one of three business models: free open source (the engine is distributed with source code), freeware (the engine is distributed freely but without source code), and commercial (the engine is proprietary and distributed through a royalty model or commercial contract).

The Unreal Engine Marketplace launched in March 2014 with the release of the Unreal Engine 4. The Marketplace is an e-commerce platform that connects content creators with developers; the site facilitates micro-transactions of game-ready content and code (including 2D assets, characters, animations, special effects, materials and textures, environments and blueprints). With the opening of its Marketplace, developer Epic Games announced:

> Beyond the tools and source, Unreal Engine 4 provides an entire ecosystem. Chat in the forums, add to the wiki, participate in the AnswerHub Q&A,

> and join collaborative development projects via GitHub. To help you get started, we're shipping lots of ready-made content, samples, and game templates. You'll find it in the Marketplace in the Unreal Editor. Right now, it simply hosts free stuff from Epic, but its resemblance to the App Store is no coincidence: It will grow into a complete ecosystem for sharing community-created content, paid and free, and open for everyone's participation!
>
> *(Sweeney, 2014)*

The Marketplace is indicative of an emerging ecosystem approach that produces community through a series of collaborative efforts: participating in forums and wikis, sharing community-created content, and accessing common code work via GitHub.

To more properly situate code affordance and authorship, we need to consider the cultural role of indie game artists and the nature of the marketplace of ideas encouraged by open source development. If the game engine is a lynchpin for connecting code and control (as well as access, equity and inclusion), the opportunities for co-creative exploits, authentic communication and community building may be the most obvious markers of the limits of control and the operation of free play in networked space. By examining independent game production as well as the culture of modification in game development and play, we can articulate to what degree code can be broken, and whether open source engine environments act differently from closed commercial environments.

There is a broader lesson here in shifting our attention to the deeper architectures of game design while not abandoning the image altogether—a lesson that may be aligned with one of the possible futures of queer and feminist media studies. By studying software, we are unlocking our ability to be mindful of the manner in which hermetic design and delivery systems push human agency toward technocentric certitude, and we are more mindfully situating the study of representation in a richer contextual field. If we are to succeed at theorizing and building a queer game mechanic, we need to be cognizant of the nature of algorithms; they have material and cultural influence, and they operate across intersecting public and private vectors.To realize a queer game mechanic necessitates building from the ground up with an acute awareness of our cultural context—using cultural theory to inform engine design, for example. Yet the industrial frameworks of the game industry, where labor is situated within a pipeline model, and the institutional lineages of programming languages make this an inauthentic value proposition. Constructing non-normative space, creating narrative incongruity, and evoking liminality are a few collective queer tactics that have been used to reorient play, but these are punctuations in storytelling that do not pierce the systems layer. Taken together, these gestures and objects have value in that they privilege queer history and experience; but code persists and the singular pursuit of realism is well underway.

Speaking a Language

Program code, like language in general, naturally oscillates between process and expression. The call for a "QueerOS" formulated by Fiona Barnett et al. (2016) looks to the unrealized promise of self-modifying interfaces; to cut through the "skin" of the interface is to cut through the heteronormative materialities of information, to restore the transformative possibilities of code. The possibility of a queer operating system starts with the assumption that most modern interfaces are, by design, sites at which code has already coalesced—they are prescriptive in form and function, "hygienic" distillations of the material world into discrete fields of information (Barnett et al., 2016). While code may seem fluid and open, as it flows across multiple agents, it also follows a call to order. The need to execute is a non-wavering protocol that cuts across industrial sectors and functions. The call to order emanates from and satisfies multiple bodies, and conjoins machine-like humans (programmers) and human-like machines (engines) in closed-loop information systems. Programmers, as industrial agents, express themselves through their manipulation of layers of representation, including symbols, words, language and notation. The body is registered in the content (the codework itself), the human-machine reader, and the bodies of those humans involved in the production process, and there is a dynamic relation between what exists and what is possible, between past and present states, between concealing and revealing possibilities corresponding to the layers of computation itself. A significant complication in this study of bodies and languages has been explored by those opening up the overlooked queer history of computing. Jacob Gaboury's (2013) exploration of this queer genealogy, and the technical achievements of notable figures including Alan Turing reaches beyond biography into code mechanics. Gaboury's goal is to demonstrate that the structuring logic of computational systems does not fully erase queer subjectivity; any requisite semantic order cannot account for all forms of knowledge. For Gaboury and other queer scholars, queering the field of computation has less to do with the subtle mechanics of code (or radical disruptions in its operational imperatives), and more to do with the ease of communication and contact, and the production of community (Gaboury, 2013). We should understand "communication and contact" in relation to the productive sharing of limits (of the body, identity and code work), and remain open to questioning whether community can actually be produced through work. In *The Inoperative Community*, Jean-Luc Nancy (1991) suggests that the work of capital is antithetical to community, for it can only privilege the general characteristics of its products.

New media theorist Friedrich Kittler characterizes the cultural problem and importance of code by suggesting, "Programming languages have eroded the monopoly of ordinary language and grown into a new hierarchy of their own" (Kittler, 1995). Code evades perception; as it reaches from simple operations into complex languages, it also moves through several distinct assemblies, passing from the fluid production framework of programmers to the relatively fixed mechanisms of hardware controls. The programmer invariably steps out of the equation, leaving the program to run on its own; as code evades cognition by any one observer (which is code by design—it enables us to act), it also appears to write itself.

Despite my attention to code, I echo the sentiment expressed by Jennifer Malkowski and TreaAndrea Russworm (2017) in their study of game representation that code analysis if taken on its own has the tendency to silence otherness—to reconstitute margins. My goal is not to dismiss representational analysis, but to understand the complexity of its determinacy: a signature often inscribed in the codebase, at an often-overlooked point in the development pipeline. To push representational politics forward, we must understand its many origin points. This is not an either/or proposition, of studying code or image. Malkowski and Russworm note that representation is tethered to software and hardware, but this dependency does not negate the politics of the image (which in the public arena is often of greater immediacy and consequence); rather, they suggest we must situate computational and representational code side by side, and understand their specific discursive (and functional) histories. This analytical model pushes further than the "unit analysis" proposed by scholars such as Ian Bogost (2006), although what binds these approaches together is the common search for limits and the concomitant search for affordances. The critical importance of situating image and code side by side is meant to undo traditional hierarchies of labor, knowledge and value; to excavate and examine code while sacrificing any careful attention to the image is to improperly imply that representation is merely a "surface effect" (Anable, 2018, 137) of more substantive technological underpinnings.

The space for possibility, for radical queer sensibility, cuts across game layers (image, interface, the architectures of software and hardware) and shrinks through the process of development as subtle compromises are made in the selection and use of a game engine. While this is true as well in post-production praxis, in the more obvious signs of game trailers that fix meaning in parallel ways (making even the most open game a knowable, marketable property), the compromises that are made in the selection and use of a game engine are much subtler. The choices made in marketing material that set a series of limits are just as important as the default character rigs and the binary data sets that delimit "Hero_Gender_Male" or "Hero_Gender_Female."

Choosing a Writing Style

Many independent game developers, in the pursuit of efficiency, have no choice but to tie their intellectual properties to the systematized writing associated with one of several proprietary game engines, have to see their works operate less queerly, less out of bounds. There are a broad range of engines and development environments—more dominant, costly, high-powered tools such as Unity and Unreal, and alternative entry-level tools such as Twine and GameMaker that have been celebrated for their accessibility. Twine, created by Chris Klimas, is a free, open source browser-based tool that requires only basic HTML. Twine, first released in 2009, is modeled on earlier hypertext applications and has been instrumental in expanding the field of small-scale interactive storytelling and evolving the rules of gameplay; many Twine titles opt out of traditional game devices, such as fail states and reward systems, and foreground exploration and open-endedness over mastery and narrative completion. Later versions of Twine have been used for rapid prototyping rather than as native build environments, to quickly map complex narrative interactions before moving on to a more robust platform or another medium. Writer and series creator Charlie Brooker used Twine to develop the treatment for *Bandersnatch*, an interactive installment of the anthology series *Black Mirror* released by Netflix in 2018.

GameMaker, created by Mark Overmars in 1999, is primarily a 2D engine that features a drag and drop system, a proprietary scripting language (GML), and a fairly deductive build process of rooms, objects, and pre-built script events; the limitation of GameMaker lies in the simplicity of GML writing, which does not neatly align with the stricter requirements of more complex programming languages. Users of RPG Maker, a development engine for role-playing games that includes a number of pre-built assets, have formed communities of their own to overcome many of the engine's inherent physiognomic defaults or absences—such as skin tone, hair color and texture—and to support each other writing customized scripts in JavaScript or Ruby (Game Scripting System).

For queer game artists, the simpler mechanics (and alternative game languages) of Twine and GameMaker seem to facilitate qualities such as empathy, community and communicative openness. But we need to avoid understanding even the value of engine choice in such binary terms, as freedom, expressivity, multivocality and queerness are in every case delimited by software mechanics (and some game critics claim the interactive storytelling of most Twine games follows normative prose). Twine communities do not commonly intersect with Unity communities, which creates a set of linguistic (and perhaps class-based) barriers between those who have been taught to code (Unity is part of most academic interactive media programs) and those who have not. Engine choice is commonly driven by language choice and proficiency; most Unity developers write code in C# and most Unreal developers write in C++ (or marry C++ with Blueprint, the engine's visual scripting system). The affordances and relative complexities of programming languages parallel the affordances of their engines. Alison Harvey (2014) has noted that accessible open source tools such as Twine have queered the landscape of gameplay and creation by promoting game making on the periphery—expanding and diversifying communities of practice and stimulating alternative economies of production and distribution. Yet even open source development tools trade in a common vernacular and are tied to a functional pattern language. Twine developers compose with passages and links, follow the principles of HTML5, CSS and JavaScript, and build with visual structures. As they author interactive story maps, Twine artists trade in sign systems that form the relays of technobiographic practice. While Twine games may be predicated on a common structure, the sheer volume and diversity of Twine makers, many of whom are using the tool to build personal game-based experiences, have helped to erode the hard lines of common game forms; as a more responsive tool with a quicker and less labor-intensive build, Twine offers a more intimate game mechanic that allows us to see how readily its otherwise uniform build environment can yield to different forms.

The Ongoing Work of Computation

The adoption of expanded forms of AI by the game development community suggests one of several possible futures for a more expressive game mechanic, and that game scripting is a stop gap solution for the more advanced work of artificial intelligence. The contextual expertise afforded by AI in localized 3D environments has led to a number of limited experiments with real-time player-built 3D assets that trade on the autobiographical trace. *Watson and Waffles* (2016), created during an IBM sponsored hackathon uses Watson (a suite of AI services, tools and applications that are part of a growing IBM machine-learning ecosystem) to introduce a VR drawing mechanic into a pre-built Unity 3D environment (Ginn, 2018). Linking AI to the functional parameters of engine-based mechanics, the game transforms hand-drawn 2D forms into 3D objects (for example, a key, a ladder and a light bulb) that shape the field of play and form a fundamental part of puzzle-solving and progression. The 2018 launch of the IBM Watson SDK on the Unity Asset Store has fueled such early experiments by formally opening up the Unity development pipeline to integrated Watson cloud services.

Semantic openness is always relative. Game engine design, and the chronology of use and version history, limits and conceals what are otherwise mutable relations—that is the very nature of an engine. The value of the engine lies in efficiency (of labor) and re-use. As we read the engine to determine the intention behind its coded frameworks, we discover first and foremost that the need for radical clarity is a function of efficiency, reproducibility and operability. Computational space is structured to serve the organizing principles of the labor force—the seamless ability for programmers and designers to occupy their assigned positions in the production pipeline. In their discussion of code aesthetics, Michael Mateas and Nick Montfort (2005) suggest that "good" code facilitates these lived industrial relations as it "simultaneously specifies a mechanical process and talks about this mechanical process to a human reader" (153). The approach to an engine is commonly based on a studio's tools, culture and project needs. Design-friendly architectures simplify component relations and lessen the interdependence of designers and programmers; they provide flexibility without complexity, and readier modification of a game's behavior.

The experience of movement, of environment, of subject-object relations, are all bound by the engine. In gameplay, there is no transformative enactment, for there is no fundamental unmasking of the environmental mesh, no fundamental reworking of the landscape, no undoing of static and dynamic elements. There is the experience of unfolding, which itself is governed by a memory allocation subsystem—yet another mechanical layer and functional imperative of the engine. In the broadest terms, there is no fundamental understanding of the conditions that make gameplay and the game world possible. This runs counter to the impulse of computational participation (Kafai and Burke, 2015, 316), a more expansive and socially inflected frame for computational literacy that encourages us to examine the economics of cultural production, situate coding as an activity, understand programming as a matter of functional design and contextual problem solving, address the social relevance of these communicative acts (of writing and building), and ultimately restore historicity and agency. We must call into question the effects of rendering experience representable and commodified as a resource, by looking to the rendering engine and the resource manager. Media scholars must attend to the process of game design, have the foresight to pause and consider the work in progress as a by-product of an integrated software development environment, and advance a more comprehensive view of the production pipeline that acknowledges the correspondences between technology and culture, and the generative material and social conditions of the game engine, or risk effacing the labor capital of a significant body of individuals in an industry studied primarily through its sealed and marketed intellectual properties, its objects and its representations. The focus on labor is a logical extension of what Gerald Stephen Jackson (2017) refers to as the problem of complexity in software engineering that erases the collaborative creative activity of individuals within the game development pipeline—a process that substitutes mastery for agency and has no tolerance for disruption. If game development is grounded in engine choice, then computation is performed only in relation to an engine; this is relational rather than open "computational performativity" (Jackson, 2017).

There is significant value for queer game studies to advance computational literacy and to consider the relative authenticity of the transactional calls to community found in a marketplace of object-oriented ideas and solutions; beyond realizing strategies for transformative play and deciphering the contextual outlines of design (competencies that are essential to the development of more focused gaming literacy), we must be attentive to the unseen operational limits of code. Resource sharing is more often focused on collaborative problem solving (on pushing past a procedural limit) than it is on ideological decoding. This is not surprising, as code is a text most commonly understood in relation to the causal chains in machines (Tzankova and Filimowicz, 2017). Code has to work; but code is also a form of creative expression. Code is embedded in structuring transactions that foster deep cultural dependencies between organic and inorganic actors. While many queer game designers are indeed building and not simply occupying game space, and are writing code as a new form of technobiographic practice, engines are built with limits, and every development choice has its consequences.

Algorithms may be statements of machinic discourse (Goffey, 2008), but their effects are broad and real. A queer frame of reference may be fluid and intersectional, but it is not subjectless. If we understand code as the set of instructions that undergird software systems, to queer code is to understand it not simply as a functional constraint but also as a method to distribute norms. To queer code is to perceive those flashpoints where technology regulates social experience. Algorithms are overdetermined pattern agents; they depend on and foster dependencies toward pattern recognition.The push toward physiognomic (and environmental) exactness in the video game industry is tethered to the syntactic exactness of code and the operational functionality of the engine. To fully unmask normativity, we need to develop an informed critique of the commercial imperatives that fuel the engine-based mechanics of engagement. We need to continue to queer code space, but we also need to acknowledge the subjective and varied labors within the game development pipeline—where developers and publishers, artists and programmers have to arrive at a common language. Working within a localized industrial context, this language is a codebase necessarily borne of a particular moment within a protracted build cycle. To queer code space, queer game studies must consider the engine as a foundational element that delimits an otherwise mutable process. If we understand the direct mechanisms for connecting code and control, we can properly assess the limits of control and lay a more appropriate groundwork for realizing free play in networked space.

Teaching Technology

Queering the field means closely examining the expressive possibilities of an already developing engine-based culture. Against this critical backdrop, we can weigh the relative success of the educational movement aimed at teaching students to code—the goal of which should be to develop the forms of digital literacy that are required to understand, interrogate and thrive in a convergent media environment marked by increasing opaqueness and privatization. While games are often used as texts to teach a range of basic skills, advance new digital literacies, and introduce new integrated modes of teaching and learning, the underlying technologies, the engine-based imperatives that drive games, are rarely brought to the foreground in game-centered learning environments. Far from celebrating the impulse to teach students to code, we need to consider the complexity of this proposition and the systemic barriers to success that are endemic to any unilateral model of educational reform that does not attend to the unique needs of localized communities or pause to consider the intrinsic value of standardized enterprise solutions.

We need to teach to a range of computational literacies. We need to be attentive to the interdependencies between software and hardware ecosystems and the inevitable "momentum of large-scale sociotechnical systems" (Winner, 1980, 123). Video game development programs have evolved in response to the wider availability of prosumer development platforms, and they have moved beyond the purely technical domains of computer science and engineering and the decidedly critical and commonly formalist domains of media and cultural studies into broader interdisciplinary pursuits. The tools we teach often become the default choices for our students as they move into the world; students are often prematurely locked into an ecosystem of Unity or Unreal production. As we explore new modes of digital content production, such as spatial computing, the choices we make in the software layer often set the course for the choices we make in the hardware layer. At Columbia College Chicago, we have built a digital sandbox to sustain curricularly linked experimentation across extended reality platforms: HTC Vive, HoloLens, Magic Leap and Oculus Rift. In each case we have had to consider systems integration, examining the compliance of each hardware framework with an existing software ecosystem, the relative openness of each new operating system, and the long-term prospects for any early-stage (and still rapidly evolving) development environment.

By teaching students to code or by training them in engine-based mechanics, we can instill a certain degree of productive skepticism, a reflexive attitude toward software that can reset many of their adopted practices. Running counter to this impulse is an emphasis on entrepreneurial agency that aligns creative pedagogies and practices with the existing marketplace (Nicoll and Keogh, 2019, 93); this form of self-governance drives students down a well-trodden pathway, as they answer the call of industry.

In August 2019, Unity Technologies launched two classroom resources to augment its engine; Create with Code and Unity Teach broaden the reach of the Unity platform by adding context and content for the company's game creation tools. Create with Code is the educational arm of the program, a comprehensive course focused on teaching computer science through Unity, while Unity Teach is the collaborative, participatory learning platform that allows teachers to share resources and learn from one another, building community through a Unity-hosted network. The curriculum is oriented around C# and scaffolds upward through more complex Unity software builds, as it draws from pre-built 3D assets available in the Unity Asset Store. Unity has, in effect, created a hermetic system and closed the loop on a knowledge assembly in which its products affirm the values of one another.

A number of developers have added nuance to the Unity ecosystem by building custom plug-ins, and in doing so have productively expanded the field of play, working with Unity tools to shape other creative disciplines. Panoply, developed by Erik Loyer and released to the Unity Asset Store in 2016, is a plug-in for the Unity engine that fuses the visual language of comics to the dynamic visualization methods of game development. The tool alters the affordances of the Unity game engine not by hacking its codebase, but by encouraging artists to create story-driven experiences that draw attention to the graphical interface, while suppressing the logic of traditional game mechanics. This hybrid form of comics and games purposefully and poetically reinscribes the Unity engine by allowing its function to follow the form of another medium (the panel layout of graphic novels is reinterpreted as a natively digital experience); the engine works at the service of artfully choreographed interactive storytelling.

Efficiencies and economies of scale drive engine choice in education; investing in and scaling technology is an expensive proposition. Educators are asked to make difficult choices as they evaluate how well a platform aligns with universal learning outcomes that cut across discipline-specific applications, how quickly students across the educational continuum will learn and navigate a new development environment, how regularly they will move on to build an assessable prototype, and whether or not the experience will advance their career-readiness. Engine choice is guided by different concerns within distinct communities of practice, although there are a common set of criteria that guide decision-making: the centrality of the programming language, the stability of the release, the volume of documentation, the availability of support, the access to communal resources, the openness of the development environment, the adaptability and ease of use, the cost, and the relative alignment of these considerations with the overall scope and goals of the project at hand. But engine choice is inevitably circumscribed by industry.

The game development framework is a ready-built software architecture, but if we lift the hood and study the engine, we will begin to realize that what we are working with in our immediate field is a facilitator of much broader cultural production. We live in a culture of engines, of algorithmically structured design methodologies that call out particular protocols, provide certain affordances, promote unique literacies, encourage new forms of media and information flow, and circulate through platform-based business models that shape public policy and govern everyday life. Game engines may be localized software frameworks, isolated formations of informatic code, but they are part of a machinic discourse that operates beyond the boundaries of any one media industry. Engines are central to contemporary cultural production, and they are increasingly central to artificial intelligence, speeding up the development of self-learning systems.

Unity introduced the Machine Learning Agents Toolkit in 2017, and extended its investments in artificial intelligence the following year through a partnership with Google-owned DeepMind. Together, Unity and Google are moving gaming and simulation forward; the goal is to train intelligent agents in simulated physical environments, to develop new algorithms, and to use those algorithms to advance autonomous technology in the physical world. Beyond the build of the engine and the self-sufficient virtual world, the programmer lets the agent learn on its own through trial and error. *Puppo, The Corgi*, a Unity demo game released in 2018, defines the behavior and movements of its non-player character (NPC) through machine-based reinforcement learning attached to a physics engine, rather than through hard-coded scripting; as the NPC (Puppo) moves through multiple simulations (repeated fetch sessions), it builds an internal action model based on a context-dependent reward principle.

I turn to this playful example as a final thought in a volume dedicated to the critical analysis of game engine culture to signal that although game engines propagate efficiency and centralize control, they are rapidly evolving to offer up the quality of autonomy, and perhaps agency. While the development focus of the video game industry in its nascent engine-based years was on the graphical possibilities of games, the naturalness of rendered images, and the illusory promise of visual spectacle, those pleasures and practices are quickly giving way to experiments in cognitive behavior; geometric and graphical techniques are yielding to AI techniques (Dignum et al., 2009).

Game engine culture is a function of the persistence of code. Game engines are software architectures that can be readily adapted to new information contexts, new forms of governance, and new transactional imperatives. We are aware of engines to the extent that we observe their monopolizing effects on interface culture. But to truly see an engine and understand its work, we need to study its construction, its grammar and its labor. It takes considerable effort to make game engines intelligible, to properly situate them as critical cultural objects. But they are indeed formal constructs that embody design intentions. Game engines are borne from personal agency and iterated through institutional memory. They are

FIGURE 8.1 *Puppo, The Corgi.*
Copyright 2018 Unity Technologies. Used with permission of Unity Technologies. All rights reserved.

static formalizations of code that are mobilized quite purposefully. They mediate between data and embodiment, between technology and culture, between production and consumption; they are a structural lynchpin between game-based allegories of space and place and a more pervasively experienced and culturally volatile algorithmic state. Game engines modulate our sense of agency and for that reason alone, they merit our attention.

BIBLIOGRAPHY

Adorno, Theodor W. *Negative Dialectics*. Translated by E. B. Ashton. New York: Seabury Press, 1973.

Alexander, Christopher. "A City Is Not a Tree (Part I)." *Architectural Forum* 122, no. 1 (April1965): 58–62.

Alexander, Christopher, Sara Ishikawa, Murray Silverstein, Max Jacobson, Ingrid Fiksdahl-King, and Shlomo Angel. *A Pattern Language: Towns, Buildings, Construction*. New York: Oxford University Press, 1977.

Althusser, Louis. "Ideology and Ideological State Apparatuses (Notes towards an Investigation)." In *Lenin and Philosophy and Other Essays*, 127–186. Translated by Ben Brewster. New York: Monthly Review Press, 1971.

Amazon. *Alexa Design Guide*. 2019. Accessed June 27, 2019. https://developer.amazon.com/docs/alexa-design/get-started.html.

Amazon. *Alexa Skill Builder's Guide: How to Create Engaging Voice-First Games for Alexa*. Seattle, WA: Amazon, 2019.

Anable, Aubrey. "Platform Studies." *Feminist Media Histories* 4, no. 2 (Spring2018): 135–140.

Anderson, Eike Falk, Steffen Engel, Peter Comninos, and Leigh McLoughlin. "The Case for Research in Game Engine Architecture." In *Future Play '08 – Proceedings of the 2008 Conference on Future Play: Research, Play, Share*, 228–231. (Toronto, Canada, November 2008) New York: Association for Computing Machinery, 2008.

Andrejevic, Mark. "The Big Data Divide." *International Journal of Communication* 8, no. 1 (2014): 1673–1689.

Aneesh, A. *Virtual Migration: The Programming of Globalization*. Durham, NC: Duke University Press, 2006.

Anthropy, Anna. *Rise of the Videogame Zinesters: How Freaks, Normals, Amateurs, Artists, Dreamers, Drop-outs, Queers, Housewives, and People Like You Are Taking Back an Art Form*. New York: Seven Stories Press, 2012.

Aoyama, Yuko, and Hiro Izushi. "Hardware Gimmick or Cultural Innovation? Technological, Cultural, and Social Foundations of the Japanese Video Game Industry." *Research Policy* 32, no. 3 (March2003): 423–444.

Arisona, Stefan. "The CityEngine VR Experience for Unreal Engine: A Virtual Reality Experience for Urban Planning Applications." *Esri ArcGIS Blog* (July 12, 2018). Accessed September 2, 2019. www.esri.com/arcgis-blog/products/city-engine/design-planning/ce-ue4-vr-experience.

Atkins, Barry, and Tanya Krzywinska (Eds). *Videogame, Player, Text*. Manchester, UK: Manchester University Press, 2007.

Austin, Mark, Parastoo Delgoshaei, and Alan Nguyen. "Distributed System Behavior Modeling with Ontologies, Rules, and Message Passing Mechanisms." *Procedia Computer Science* 44 (December2015): 373–382.

Autodesk. "'Resident Evil 7: Biohazard' in VR – Reforming the Workflow." *AREA: Life in 3D* (July 24, 2017). Accessed September 2, 2019. https://area.autodesk.com/life-in-3d/resident-evil-7.

Bakhtin, Mikhail M. *The Dialogic Imagination*. Edited by Michael Holquist and translated by Caryl Emerson and Michael Holquist. Austin, TX: University of Texas Press, 1981.

Barnett, Fiona, Zach Blas, Micha Cárdenas, Jacob Gaboury, Jessica Marie Johnson, and Margaret Rhee. "QueerOS: A User's Manual." In *Debates in the Digital Humanities 2016*, 50–59. Edited by Matthew K. Gold and Lauren F. Klein. Minneapolis, MN: University of Minnesota Press, 2016.

Barrett, Brian. "The Year Alexa Grew Up." *Wired* (December 19, 2018). Accessed June 25, 2019. www.wired.com/story/amazon-alexa-2018-machine-learning.

Bedard, Phil. "*Terminator: Future Shock*. Review." *Computer Games Magazine* (December 17, 1997). Accessed May 30, 2019. https://web.archive.org/web/20030524212227/http://www.cdmag.com/articles/018/151/terminatorfs_review.html.

Beer, David. "The Social Power of Algorithms." *Information, Communication & Society* 20, no. 1 (2017): 1–13.

Bellomy, Ian. "What Counts: Configuring the Human in Platform Studies." *Analog Game Studies* 4, no. 2 (March 20, 2017). Accessed June 12, 2018. http://analoggamestudies.org/2017/03/what-counts/.

Bensinger, Greg. "'MissionRacer': How Amazon Turned the Tedium of Warehouse Work Into a Game." *Washington Post* (May 21, 2019). Accessed May 24, 2019. www.washingtonpost.com/technology/2019/05/21/missionracer-how-amazon-turned-tedium-warehouse-work-into-game/?noredirect=on&utm_term=.c1717900f757.

Bergen, Mark. "Why Did Google Get Rid of the Company Behind *Pokémon Go*?" *Vox* (July 12, 2016). Accessed July 1, 2019. www.vox.com/2016/7/12/12153722/google-niantic-pokemon-go-spin-out.

Berry, David M. "Iteracy: Reading, Writing and Running Code." *Stunlaw* (September 16, 2011). Accessed June 10, 2018. http://stunlaw.blogspot.com/2011/09/iteracy-reading-writing-and-running.html.

Berry, David M. *The Philosophy of Software: Code and Mediation in the Digital Age*. New York: Palgrave Macmillan, 2011.

Bertz, Matt. "The Technology Behind *The Elder Scrolls V: Skyrim*." *Game Informer* (January 17, 2011). Accessed September 10, 2019. www.gameinformer.com/games/the_elder_scrolls_v_skyrim/b/xbox360/archive/2011/01/17/the-technology-behind-elder-scrolls-v-skyrim.aspx.

Blas, Zach. "transCoder: Queer Programming Anti-Language." *transCoder* (2008). Accessed February 4, 2020. http://users.design.ucla.edu/~zblas/thesis_website/transcoder/transcoder.html.

Blevins, Tal. "*Terminator: Future Shock.* Review." *GameSpot* (May 28, 1996). Accessed May 30, 2019. www.gamespot.com/reviews/terminator-future-shock-review/1900-2533376.

Blow, Jonathan. "Game Development: Harder Than You Think." *Queue* 1, no. 10 (February2004): 29–37.

BMW Group. "BMW Opts to Incorporate HTC Vive VR Headsets and Mixed Reality Into the Development of New Vehicle Models." *BMW Group. PressClub Global* (April 7, 2016). Accessed November 1, 2019. www.press.bmwgroup.com/global/article/detail/T0258902EN/bmw-opts-to-incorporate-htc-vive-vr-headsets-and-mixed-reality-into-the-development-of-new-vehicle-models-computer-images-instead-of-laboriously-constructed-draft-models:-greater-flexibility-faster-results-and-lower-costs.

Bogost, Ian. *Persuasive Games: The Expressive Power of Videogames.* Cambridge, MA: MIT Press, 2007.

Bogost, Ian. "Procedural Literacy: Problem Solving with Programming, Systems, & Play." *Telemedium* 52, nos. 1–2 (Winter/Spring2005): 32–36.

Bogost, Ian. *Unit Operations: An Approach to Videogame Criticism.* Cambridge, MA: MIT Press, 2006.

Bogost, Ian. "Videogames and the Future of Education." *On the Horizon* 13, no. 2 (2005): 119–125.

Bogost, Ian, and Nick Montfort. "Platform Studies: Frequently Questioned Answers." In *Proceedings of the Digital Arts and Culture Conference 2009.* (Irvine, CA, December 2009) Accessed April 9, 2018. https://escholarship.org/uc/item/01r0k9br.

Bohman, James. "Practical Reason and Cultural Constraint: Agency in Bourdieu's Theory of Practice." In *Bourdieu: A Critical Reader*, 129–152. Edited by Richard Shusterman. Malden, MA: Blackwell Publishers, 1999.

Boluk, Stephanie, and Patrick Lemieux. *Metagaming: Playing, Competing, Spectating, Cheating, Trading, Making, and Breaking Videogames.* Minneapolis: University of Minnesota Press, 2017.

BOP Consulting. *Mapping the Creative Industries: A Toolkit.* London: British Council, 2010.

Bourdieu, Pierre. "The Forms of Capital." In *Handbook of Theory and Research for the Sociology of Education*, 241–258. Edited by John G. Richardson. New York: Greenwood Press, 1986.

Bredl, Klaus, and Wolfgang Bösche (Eds). *Serious Games and Virtual Worlds in Education, Professional Development, and Healthcare.* Hershey, PA: IGI Global, 2013.

Brooks, Anthony Lewis, Sheryl Brahnam, Bill Kapralos, and Lakhmi C. Jain (Eds). *Recent Advances in Technologies for Inclusive Well-Being: From Worn to Off-body Sensing, Virtual Worlds, and Games for Serious Applications.* New York: Springer, 2017.

Burrows, Roger, and Nick Ellison. "Sorting Places Out? Toward a Social Politics of Neighborhood Informatization." *Information, Community & Society* 7, no. 3 (2004): 321–336.

Bush, Vannevar. "As We May Think." *The Atlantic Monthly* (July1945): 101–108.

Callele, David, Eric Neufeld, and Kevin Schneider. "Requirements Engineering and the Creative Process in the Video Game Industry." In *Proceedings of the 13th IEEE International Conference on Requirements Engineering (RE'05)*, 240–250. (Paris, France, August–September 2005) Los Alamitos, CA: IEEE, 2005.

Callon, Michel. "Techno-economic Networks and Irreversibility." In *A Sociology of Monsters: Essays on Power, Technology and Domination*, 132–161. Edited by John Law. New York: Routledge, 1991.

Campbell, Angela J., and Lindsey Barrett. "Request for Investigation of Amazon, Inc.'s Echo Dot Kids Edition for Violating the Children's Online Privacy Protection Act." (May 9, 2019). Accessed May 10, 2019. www.law.georgetown.edu/wp-content/uploads/2019/05/Echo-Dot-Complaint-FINAL-1.pdf.

Capcom. Capcom Integrated Report 2017. Accessed May 24, 2019. www.capcom.co.jp/ir/english/data/annual.html.

Capcom. Capcom Integrated Report 2018. Accessed May 24, 2019. www.capcom.co.jp/ir/english/data/oar/2018.

Capcom. "Ten Years in the Making: Pushing Stylish Action and Beautiful Graphics to the Limits in *Devil May Cry 5*." *Capcom Investor Relations Developer Interviews 2018* 3 (November 2, 2018). Accessed September 17, 2019. www.capcom.co.jp/ir/english/interview/2018/vol03.

Carpenter, Nicole. "*Harry Potter: Wizards Unite* Is the Next Step Forward for Augmented Reality Games." *Polygon* (June 20, 2019). Accessed July 1, 2019. www.polygon.com/2019/6/20/18683450/harry-potter-wizards-unite-preview-augmented-reality-games-niantic.

Carpentier, Giliamde, and Kohei Ishiyama. "Decima Engine: Advances in Lighting and AA." *SIGGRAPH 2017: Advances in Real-Time Rendering in Games*. (July 31, 2017). Accessed May 19, 2018. www.guerrilla-games.com/read/decima-engine-advances-in-lighting-and-aa.

Carstens, Adam, and John Beck. "Get Ready for the Gamer Generation." *TechTrends* 49, no. 3 (May/June2005): 22–25.

Castells, Manuel. *The Rise of the Network Society*. Oxford, UK: Blackwell, 1996.

Certeau, Michel de. *The Practice of Everyday Life*. Translated by Steven F. Rendall. Berkeley, CA: University of California Press, 1984.

Champagne, Rick. "Walt Disney Imagineering, NVIDIA Develop New Tech to Enable Star Wars: Galaxy's Edge Millennium Falcon Attraction for Disney Parks." *NVIDIA Blog* (March 28, 2018). Accessed July 2, 2019. https://blogs.nvidia.com/blog/2018/03/28/walt-disney-imagineering-nvidia-star-wars-galaxys-edge-millennium-falcon.

Chang, Edmond Y. "Love Is in the Air: Queer (Im)Possibility and Straightwashing in *FrontierVille* and *World of Warcraft*." *QED: A Journal in GLBTQ Worldmaking* 2, no. 2 (Summer2015): 6–31.

Charrieras, Damien, and Nevena Ivanova. "Emergence in Video Game Production: Video Game Engines as Technical Individuals." *Social Science Information* 55, no. 3 (2016): 337–356.

Che Mat, Ruzinoor, Abdul Rashid Mohammed Shariff, Abdul Nasir Zulkifli, Mohd Shafry, Mohd Rahim, and Mohd Hafiz Mahayudin. "Using Game Engine for 3D Terrain Visualization of GIS Data: A Review." *IOP Conference Series: Earth and Environmental Science* 20, no. 1, article 012037 (2014): 1–11.

Chun, Wendy Hui Kyong. *Control and Freedom: Power and Paranoia in the Age of Fiber Optics*. Cambridge, MA: MIT Press, 2006.

Chun, Wendy Hui Kyong. "On Software, or the Persistence of Visual Knowledge." *Grey Room* 18 (Winter2004): 26–51.

Chun, Wendy Hui Kyong. *Programmed Visions: Software and Memory*. Cambridge, MA: MIT Press, 2011.

Chutko, Christopher. "Pokémon Go-style Augmented Reality Harry Potter Wizards Game Poised to be a Mega-hit." *CNBC* (May 19, 2019). Accessed July 1, 2019. www.cnbc.com/2019/05/17/niantics-harry-potter-wizards-unite-game-poised-to-be-a-mega-hit.html.

Colman, Felicity, Vera Bühlmann, Aislinn O'Donnell, and Iris van der Tuin. "Ethics of Coding: A Report on the Algorithmic Condition." H2020-EU.2.1.1. – Industrial Leadership – Leadership in enabling and industrial technologies – Information and

Communication Technologies. Brussels: European Commission (Project Number 732407), 2018. https://cordis.europa.eu/project/rcn/207025_en.html.

Conn, Matt. "Gaming's Untapped Queer Potential as Art." *QED: A Journal in GLBTQ Worldmaking* 2, no. 2 (Summer2015): 1–5.

Consalvo, Mia. *Atari to Zelda: Japan's Videogames in Global Contexts*. Cambridge, MA: MIT Press, 2016.

Consalvo, Mia. *Cheating: Gaining Advantage in Videogames*. Cambridge, MA: MIT Press, 2007.

Conway, Kevin R. "Game Mods, Engines, and Architecture." In *Game Mods: Design, Theory and Criticism*, 87–111. Edited by Erik Champion. Pittsburgh, PA: Carnegie Mellon University ETC Press, 2012.

Cooper, Kendra M. L., and Walt Scacchi (Eds). *Computer Games and Software Engineering*. Boca Raton, FL: CRC Press, 2015.

Coppock, Patrick. "Are Computer Games Real?" In *The Philosophy of Computer Games*, 259–277. Edited by John Richard Sageng, Hallvard Fossheim, and Tarjei Mandt Larsen. London: Springer, 2012.

Costa, Carlos J., and Manuela Aparicio. "Computer Games Development Process – Producing an Education Games for the Web." In *Proceedings of the IADIS International Conference on WWW/Internet*, 313–320. (Murcia, Spain, October 5–8, 2006) Edited by Miguel Baptista Nunes, Pedro Isaías, and Inmaculada J. Martínez. Accessed June 17, 2018. www.researchgate.net/publication/264881804.

Cox, Geoff, and Alex McLean. *Speaking Code: Coding as Aesthetic and Political Expression*. Cambridge, MA: MIT Press, 2013.

Cox, Geoff, Alex McLean, and Adrian Ward. "The Aesthetics of Generative Code." Generative Art Conference, Politecnico di Milano, Italy (2000). Accessed June 17, 2018. www.generativeart.com.

Crampton, Jeremy W. "Keyhole, Google Earth, and 3D Worlds: An Interview with Avi Bar-Zeev." *Cartographica* 43, no. 2 (Summer2008): 85–93.

Crawford, Kate, Kate Miltner, and Mary L. Gray. "Critiquing Big Data: Politics, Ethics, Epistemology." *International Journal of Communication* 8 (2014): 1663–1672.

Crecente, Brian. "Their Future is Epic: The Evolution of a Gaming Giant." *Polygon* (May 1, 2016). Accessed July 1, 2019. www.polygon.com/a/epic-4-0.

Crytek. "Why Developers Choose CRYENGINE – Part 5. CRYENGINE: Community Spotlight. Developer Quotes #5." (March 6, 2019). Accessed September 2, 2019. www.cryengine.com/news/why-developers-choose-cryengine-part-5.

Cutsinger, Paul. *Situational Design: How to Shift from Screen-First to Voice-First Design*. Seattle, WA: Amazon, 2018.

Damsgaard, Jan, and Jan Karlsbjerg. "Seven Principles for Selecting Software Packages." *Communications of the ACM* 53, no. 8 (August2010): 63–71.

Davidson, Drew. "Games by Degrees: Playing with Programs." *On the Horizon* 13, no. 2 (2005): 70–74.

Davidson, Drew (Ed). *Beyond Fun: Serious Games and Media*. Pittsburgh, PA: Carnegie Mellon University ETC Press, 2008.

Davis, Ray. "Unreal Engine 4 Goes Free for Academic Use." *Epic Games Unreal Engine Blog* (September 4, 2014). Accessed May 23, 2019. www.unrealengine.com/en-US/blog/unreal-engine-4-goes-free-for-academic-use.

De Koven, Bernard. *The Well-Played Game: A Player's Philosophy*. Cambridge, MA: MIT Press, 2013.

De Michelis, Giorgio. "Situated Computing." In *Designing Socially Embedded Technologies in the Real-World*, 65–77. Edited by Volker Wulf, Kjeld Schmidt, and David Randall. London: Springer, 2015.

De Prato, Giuditta, Claudio Feijóo, Daniel Nepelski, Marc Bogdanowicz, and Jean-Paul Simon. *Born Digital/Grown Digital: Assessing the Future Competitiveness of the EU Video Games Software Industry* (A Report of the European Commission Joint Research Centre, Institute for Prospective Technological Studies). Luxembourg: Publication Office of the European Union, 2010.

De Prato, Giuditta, Sven Lindmark, and Jean-Paul Simon. "The Evolving European Video Game Software Ecosystem." In *The Video Game Industry: Formation, Present State, and Future*, 221–243. Edited by Peter Zackariasson and Timothy L. Wilson. New York: Routledge, 2012.

Deleuze, Gilles. "Postscript on the Societies of Control." *October* 59 (Winter 1992): 3–7.

DePietro, Peter. *Transforming Education with New Media: Participatory Pedagogy, Interactive Learning, and Web 2.0*. New York: Peter Lang, 2013.

Deuze, Mark, Chase Bowen Martin, and Christian Allen. "The Professional Identity of Gameworkers." *Convergence* 13, no. 4 (November2007): 335–353.

Dickson, Paul E. "Using Unity to Teach Game Development: When You've Never Written a Game." In *ITiCSE '15: Proceedings of the 2015 ACM Conference on Innovation and Technology in Computer Science Education*, 75–80. (Vilnius, Lithuania, July 6–8, 2015) New York: Association for Computing Machinery, 2015.

Dignum, Frank, Joost Westra, Willem A. van Doesburg, and Maaike Harbers. "Games and Agents: Designing Intelligent Gameplay." *International Journal of Computer Games Technology* (March2009): 1–18.

Dodge, Martin, and Rob Kitchin. "Code and the Transduction of Space." *Annals of the Association of American Geographers* 95, no. 1 (2005): 162–180.

Donovan, Tristan. *Replay: The History of Video Games*. Lewes, UK: Yellow Ant, 2010.

Dormans, Joris. *Engineering Emergence: Applied Theory for Game Design*. PhD dissertation, University of Amsterdam. Amsterdam, Netherlands: Creative Commons, 2012.

Dourish, Paul. *The Stuff of Bits: An Essay on the Materialities of Information*. Cambridge, MA: MIT Press, 2017.

Dourish, Paul, and Genevieve Bell. *Divining a Digital Future: Mess and Mythology in Ubiquitous Computing*. Cambridge, MA: MIT Press, 2011.

Dourish, Paul, and Genevieve Bell. "The Infrastructure of Experience and the Experience of Infrastructure: Meaning and Structure in Everyday Encounters with Space." *Environment and Planning B: Planning and Design* 34, no. 3 (June2007): 414–430.

Dourish, Paul, and Melissa Mazmanian. "Media as Material: Information Representations as Material Foundations for Organizational Practice." (Working paper for Third International Symposium on Process Organization Studies. (Corfu, Greece, 16–18 June 2011)) In *How Matter Matters: Objects, Artifacts, and Materiality in Organization Studies*, 92–118. Edited by Paul R. Carlile, Davide Nicolini, Ann Langley, and Haridimos Tsoukas. Oxford, UK: Oxford University Press, 2013.

Duany, Andres, Sandy Sorlien, and William Wright. *SmartCode Version 9 and Manual*. Ithaca, NY: New Urban News Publications, 2008.

Dutta, Suhail. "Bringing Connected Games Within Reach with Google Cloud." *Unity Blog* (June 21, 2018). Accessed June 25, 2019. https://blogs.unity3d.com/2018/06/21/bringing-connected-games-within-reach-with-google-cloud.

Dyer-Witheford, Nick. "Digital Labour, Species-becoming and the Global Worker." *Ephemera* 10, no. 3/4 (November2010): 484–503.

Dyer-Witheford, Nick, and Greig de Peuter. *Games of Empire: Global Capitalism and Video Games*. Minneapolis, MN: University of Minnesota Press, 2009.

El-Nasr, Magy Seif, and Brian K. Smith. "Learning Through Game Modding." *ACM Computers in Entertainment* 4, no. 1 (January2006): 1–20.

Eller, Christian, Timo Bittner, Marcus Dombois, and Uwe Rüppel. "Collaborative Immersive Planning and Training Scenarios in VR." In *Advanced Computing Strategies for Engineering: 25th EG-ICE International Workshop 2018, Proceedings, Part I*, 164–185. (Lausanne, Switzerland, June 10–13, 2018) Edited by Ian F. C. Smith and Bernd Domer. Cham, Switzerland: Springer, 2018.

Ellison, Cara. "Anna Anthropy and the Twine Revolution." *The Guardian* (April 10, 2013). Accessed May 23, 2019. www.theguardian.com/technology/gamesblog/2013/apr/10/anna-anthropy-twine-revolution.

Ellison, Nick, and Roger Burrows. "New Spaces of (Dis)engagement? Social Politics, Urban Technologies and the Rezoning of the City." *Housing Studies* 22, no. 3 (May2007): 295–312.

Engel, Maureen. "Perverting Play: Theorizing a Queer Game Mechanic." *Television & New Media* 18, no. 4 (May2017): 351–360.

Engelbart, Douglas C., and William K. English. "A Research Center for Augmenting Human Intellect." In *AFIPS Conference Proceedings of the Fall Joint Computer Conference*, 395–410. (San Francisco, CA, December 1968) Washington, DC: Thomas Book Company, 1968.

Engeli, Maia. "Playful Play with Games: Linking Level Editing to Learning in Art and Design." In *DiGRA '05 – Proceedings of the 2005 Digital Games Research Association International Conference: Changing Views: Worlds in Play*, Volume 3. (Vancouver, Canada, June 16–20, 2005) Accessed June 12, 2018. www.digra.org/wp-content/uploads/digital-library/06276.54243.pdf.

Evans, Sarah Beth, and Elyse Janish. "#INeedDiverseGames: How the Queer Backlash to GamerGate Enables Nonbinary Coalition." *QED: A Journal in GLBTQ Worldmaking* 2, no. 2 (Summer 2015): 125–150.

Fabricius, Taisha. "Make Game Maps With CityEngine." *Esri ArcGIS Blog* (November 21, 2018). Accessed September 10, 2019. www.esri.com/arcgis-blog/products/city-engine/3d-gis/make-game-maps-with-cityengine.

Finn, Ed. *What Algorithms Want: Imagination in the Age of Computing*. Cambridge, MA: MIT Press, 2017.

Finn, Mark. "Console Games in the Age of Convergence." In *Computer Games and Digital Cultures Conference Proceedings*, Volume 1, 45–58. (Tampere, Finland, June 6–8, 2002) Edited by Frans Mäyrä. Tampere, Finland: Tampere University Press, 2002.

Flanagan, Mary, and Helen Nissenbaum. *Values at Play in Digital Games*. Cambridge, MA: MIT Press, 2014.

Fleming, Jeffrey. "Down the Hyper-Spatial Tube: Spacewar and the Birth of Digital Game Culture." *Gamasutra* (June 1, 2007). Accessed June 22, 2018. www.gamasutra.com/view/feature/1433.

Flew, Terry, and Stuart Cunningham. "Creative Industries After the First Decade of Debate." *The Information Society* 26, no. 2 (2010): 113–123.

Folmer, Eelke. "Component Based Game Development – A Solution to Escalating Costs and Expanding Deadlines?" In *Component-Based Software Engineering: Proceedings of the 10th International Symposium, CBSE 2007*, 66–73. (Medford, MA, July 9–11, 2007)

Edited by Heinz W. Schmidt, Ivica Crnkovic, George T. Heineman, and Judith A. Stafford. Berlin, Heidelberg, Germany: Springer, 2007.

Foresiepi, Taama. "Building a Super Model." *Innovate* (Fall/Winter2004): 32–35.

Freedman, Eric. "Engineering Queerness in the Game Development Pipeline." *Game Studies: The International Journal of Computer Game Research* 18, no. 3 (December2018): http://gamestudies.org/1803/articles/ericfreedman.

Freedman, Eric. "Software." In *The Craft of Criticism: Critical Media Studies in Practice*, 318–330. Edited by Michael Kackman and Mary Kearney. New York: Routledge, 2018.

Freedman, Eric. "Technobiography: Industry, Agency and the Networked Body." In *Produsing Theory in a Digital World: The Intersection of Audiences and Production in Contemporary Theory*, 51–68. Edited by Rebecca Ann Lind. New York: Peter Lang, 2012.

Freedman, Eric. *Transient Images: Personal Media in Public Frameworks*. Philadelphia, PA: Temple University Press, 2011.

Friedman, Ted. "Civilization and its Discontents: Simulation, Subjectivity, and Space." In *On a Silver Platter: CD-ROMs and the Promises of a New Technology*, 132–150. Edited by Greg M. Smith. New York: New York University Press, 1999.

Fuller, Matthew. *Behind the Blip: Essays on the Culture of Software*. Brooklyn, NY: Autonomedia, 2003.

Gaboury, Jacob. "Hidden Surface Problems: On the Digital Image as Material Object." *Journal of Visual Culture* 14, no. 1 (2015): 40–60.

Gaboury, Jacob. "A Queer History of Computing." *Rhizome* (February 19, 2013). Accessed June 10, 2018. http://rhizome.org/editorial/2013/feb/19/queer-computing-1/.

Galloway, Alexander R. *Gaming: Essays on Algorithmic Culture*. Minneapolis, MN: University of Minnesota Press, 2006.

Galloway, Alexander R. *The Interface Effect*. Malden, MA: Polity, 2012.

Galloway, Alexander R. "Language Wants to be Overlooked: On Software and Ideology." *Journal of Visual Culture* 5, no. 3 (2006): 315–331.

Galloway, Alexander R. *Protocol: How Control Exists After Decentralization*. Cambridge, MA: MIT Press, 2004.

Galloway, Alexander R. "Social Realism in Gaming." *Game Studies* 4, no. 1 (November2004). Accessed June 10, 2018. www.gamestudies.org/0401/galloway.

Galloway, Susan, and Stewart Dunlop. "Deconstructing the Concept of 'Creative Industries.'" In *Cultural Industries: The British Experience in International Perspective*, 33–52. Edited by Christiane Eisenberg, Rita Gerlach, and Christian Handke. Berlin, Germany: Humboldt University, 2006.

Gamma, Erich, Richard Helm, Ralph Johnson, and John Vlissides. *Design Patterns: Elements of Reusable Object-Oriented Software*. Boston, MA: Addison-Wesley, 1995.

GarageGames. *Torque 3D Documentation: Release 3.5.1*. Garage Games, February 4, 2017.

Garlan, David, and Mary Shaw. "An Introduction to Software Architecture." In *Advances in Software Engineering and Knowledge Engineering*, 1–39. Edited by Vincenzo Ambriola and Genoveffa Tortora. River Edge, NJ: World Scientific Publishing Company, 1993.

Garrelts, Nate (Ed). *Understanding Minecraft: Essays on Play, Community and Possibilities*. Jefferson, NC: McFarland, 2014.

German Games Industry Association. "Despite Strong Market Growth, Employee Number in German Games Industry Drops." *game* (August 7, 2019). Accessed September 2, 2019. www.game.de/en/despite-strong-market-growth-employee-number-in-german-games-industry-drops.

German Games Industry Association. *The German Games Industry: Insights, Facts and Reports*. Berlin, Germany: German Games Industry Association, 2019.

Germany Trade and Invest (GTAI). *The Gaming Industry in Germany: Issue 2016/2017*. Berlin, Germany: Germany Trade and Invest, 2016.

Gershman, Anatole V., Joseph F. McCarthy, and Andrew E. Fano. "Situated Computing: Bridging the Gap between Intention and Action." In *Proceedings of the 3rd IEEE International Symposium on Wearable Computers (ISWC '99)*, 3–9. (San Francisco, CA, October 18–19, 1999) Washington, DC: IEEE Computer Society, 1999.

Gibson, James J. *The Ecological Approach to Visual Perception*. Boston, MA: Houghton Mifflin, 1979.

Giddings, Seth, and HelenW. Kennedy. "Little Jesuses and *@#?-off Robots: On Cybernetics, Aesthetics, and Not Being Very Good at *Lego Star Wars*." In *The Pleasures of Computer Gaming: Essays on Cultural History, Theory, and Aesthetics*, 13–32. Edited by Melanie Swalwell and Jason Wilson. Jefferson, NC: McFarland, 2008.

Ginn, Crystal. "IBM & Unity Partner to Bring the Power of AI to Developers." *IBM DeveloperWorks Blog* (May 3, 2018). Accessed August 31, 2018. https://developer.ibm.com/dwblog/2018/ibm-watson-unity-sdk-developers-ai-ar-vr-speech-gaming.

Goffey, Andrew. "Algorithm." In *Software Studies: A Lexicon*, 15–20. Edited by Matthew Fuller. Cambridge, MA: MIT Press, 2008.

Goffey, Andrew. "Technology, Logistics and Logic: Rethinking the Problem of Fun in Software." In *Fun and Software: Exploring Pleasure, Paradox and Pain in Computing*, 21–40. Edited by Olga Goriunova. New York: Bloomsbury, 2014.

Goffman, Erving. *Behavior in Public Places: Notes on the Social Organization of Gatherings*. New York: The Free Press, 1963.

Goldsmith, Stephen, and Susan Crawford. *The Responsive City: Engaging Communities Through Data-Smart Governance*. San Francisco, CA: Jossey-Bass, 2014.

Golumbia, David. *The Cultural Logic of Computation*. Cambridge, MA: Harvard University Press, 2009.

Gordon, Eric, and Paul Mihailidis (Eds). *Civic Media: Technology, Design, Practice*. Cambridge, MA: MIT Press, 2016.

Green, Ben. *The Smart Enough City: Putting Technology in Its Place to Reclaim Our Urban Future*. Cambridge, MA: MIT Press, 2019.

Greenfield, Adam. *Radical Technologies: The Design of Everyday Life*. Brooklyn, NY: Verso, 2017.

Gregersen, Andreas, and Torben Grodal. "Embodiment and Interface." In *The Video Game Theory Reader 2*, 65–83. Edited by Bernard Perron and Mark J. P. Wolf. New York: Routledge, 2009.

Gregory, Jason. *Game Engine Architecture*. Natick, MA: A K Peters, 2009.

Griffiths, Daniel Nye. "How Video Games Have the Power to Change Real Lives." *The Guardian* (August 6, 2014). Accessed May 24, 2019. www.theguardian.com/technology/2014/aug/06/how-video-games-have-the-power-to-change-real-lives.

Grizioti, Marianthi, and Chronis Kynigos. "Game Modding for Computational Thinking: An Integrated Design Approach." In *Proceedings of the 17th ACM Conference on Interaction Design and Children (IDC '18)*, 687–692. (Trondheim, Norway, June 2018) New York: Association for Computing Machinery, 2018.

Guins, Raiford. *Game After: A Cultural Study of Video Game Afterlife*. Cambridge, MA: MIT Press, 2014.

Hall, Charlie. "Nintendo is Using Unreal Engine 4, and Miyamoto Says They Have It 'Mastered'." *Polygon* (February 7, 2017). Accessed January 10, 2019. www.polygon.com/2017/2/7/14533324/nintendo-switch-unreal-engine-miyamoto.

Hall, Jeremy J. S. B. "Customizing Business Simulations: An Exploration and a Hierarchy." *Developments in Business Simulation and Experiential Learning* 40 (2013): 146–153.

Hall, Jeremy J. S. B. "Existing and Emerging Business Simulation-Game Design Movements." *Developments in Business Simulation and Experiential Learning* 36 (2009): 132–136.

Halpern, Sue. "Virtual Iraq: Using Simulation to Treat a New Generation of Traumatized Veterans." *The New Yorker* (May 12, 2008). Accessed June 10, 2011. www.newyorker.com/magazine/2008/05/19/virtual-iraq.

Harrigan, Pat, and Matthew G. Kirschenbaum (Eds). *Zones of Control: Perspectives on Wargaming*. Cambridge, MA: MIT Press, 2016.

Harvey, Alison. "Twine's Revolution: Democratization, Depoliticization, and the Queering of Game Design." *GAME: The Italian Journal of Game Studies* 3 (2014): 95–107.

Heath, Stephen. *Questions of Cinema*. Bloomington, IN: Indiana University Press, 1981.

Herz, J. C. "Game Theory: For Game Maker, There's Gold in the Code." *New York Times* (December 2, 1999). Accessed May 23, 2018. www.nytimes.com/1999/12/02/technology/game-theory-for-game-maker-there-s-gold-in-the-code.html.

Hoover, Amy K., Jackie Barnes, Borna Fatehi, Jesús Moreno-León, Gillian Puttick, Eli Tucker-Raymond, and Casper Harteveld. "Assessing Computational Thinking in Students' Game Designs." In *CHI PLAY Companion '16: Proceedings of the 2016 Annual Symposium on Computer-Human Interaction in Play Companion. Extended Abstracts*, 173–179. (Austin, TX, October 2016) New York: Association for Computing Machinery, 2016.

Hudlicka, Eva. "Affective Game Engines: Motivation and Requirements." In *FDG '09: Proceedings of the 4th International Conference on Foundations of Digital Games*, 299–306. (Orlando, FL, April 2009) New York: Association for Computing Machinery, 2009.

Hudson, Laura. "Twine, the Video-Game Technology for All." *New York Times Magazine* (November 19, 2014). Accessed May 23, 2019. www.nytimes.com/2014/11/23/magazine/twine-the-video-game-technology-for-all.html.

Huizinga, Johan. *Homo Ludens: A Study of the Play-Element in Culture*. London: Routledge & Kegan Paul, 1949.

Hunicke, Robin, Marc LeBlanc, and Robert Zubek. "MDA: A Formal Approach to Game Design and Game Research." In *Proceedings of the Challenges in Game AI Workshop, Nineteenth National Conference on Artificial Intelligence*. (San Jose, CA, 2004) Accessed August 9, 2009. http://users.cs.northwestern.edu/~hunicke/pubs/MDA.pdf.

Huntemann, Nina B., and Matthew Thomas Payne (Eds). *Joystick Soldiers: The Politics of Play in Military Video Games*. New York: Routledge, 2010.

Isbister, Katherine. *How Games Move Us: Emotion by Design*. Cambridge, MA: MIT Press, 2016.

Ishida, Tomofumi. "Technologies Underpinning the Development of *Resident Evil 7: Biohazard*, RE Engine." *Capcom Integrated Report 2016 (The Latest Development Report)*, 5–6. Osaka, Japan: Capcom, 2016.

Ito, Mizuko. *Engineering Play: A Cultural History of Children's Software*. Cambridge, MA: MIT Press, 2009.

Jackson, Gerald Stephen. "Transcoding Sexuality: Computational Performativity and Queer Code Practices." *QED: A Journal in GLBTQ Worldmaking* 4, no. 2 (Summer2017): 1–25.

Jenkins, Henry. "Confronting the Challenges of Participatory Culture: Media Education for the 21st Century." Chicago, IL: The MacArthur Foundation, 2006. Accessed June 11, 2018. www.macfound.org/media/article_pdfs/JENKINS_WHITE_PAPER.PDF.

Jennings, Ken. *Maphead: Charting the Wide, Weird World of Geography Wonks*. New York: Scribner, 2011.

Johnson, Jessica Marie, and Mark Anthony Neal. "Introduction: Wild Seed in the Machine." *The Black Scholar* 47, no. 3 (2017): 1–2.

Joint Chiefs of Staff. *Joint Vision 2020*. Washington, DC: United States, Government Printing Office, 2000.

Jones, Steven E. *The Meaning of Video Games: Gaming and Textual Strategies*. New York: Routledge, 2008.

Juul, Jesper. *The Art of Failure: An Essay on the Pain of Playing Video Games*. Cambridge, MA: MIT Press, 2013.

Juul, Jesper. *Half-Real: Video Games between Real Rules and Fictional Worlds*. Cambridge, MA: MIT Press, 2005.

Juul, Jesper. "The Magic Circle and the Puzzle Piece." In *Conference Proceedings of the Philosophy of Computer Games 2008*, 56–67. (Potsdam, Germany, May 8–10, 2008) Edited by Stephan Günzel, Michael Liebe, and Dieter Mersch. Potsdam, Germany: Potsdam University Press, 2008.

Kafai, Yasmin B., and Quinn Burke. *Connected Gaming: What Making Video Games Can Teach Us about Learning and Literacy*. Cambridge, MA: MIT Press, 2016.

Kafai, Yasmin B., and Quinn Burke. "Constructionist Gaming: Understanding the Benefits of Making Games for Learning." *Educational Psychologist* 50, no. 4 (2015): 313–334.

Kasurinen, Jussi, Andrey Maglyas, and Kari Smolander. "Is Requirements Engineering Useless in Game Development?" In *Requirements Engineering: Foundation for Software Quality, Proceedings of the 20th International Working Conference, REFSQ 2014*, 1–16. (Essen, Germany, April 7–10, 2014) Edited by Camille Salinesi and Inge van de Weerd. Cham, Switzerland: Springer, 2014.

Kayser, Daniel. "The Weather Channel Taps The Future Group to Provide Revolutionary Mixed-Reality Capabilities." *Unreal Engine* (April 5, 2018). Accessed September 15, 2018. www.unrealengine.com/en-US/spotlights/the-weather-channel-taps-the-future-group-to-provide-revolutionary-mixed-reality-capabilities.

Kennedy, Helen W., and Seth Giddings. "Just Gaming? Seth Giddings and Helen Kennedy on studying games." *Three_D: News and Comment from the UK Media, Communication and Cultural Studies Association* 7 (April 1, 2016): 10–11.

Kent, Steven L. "Engines and Engineering: What to Expect in the Future of PC Games." *GameSpy* (October 31, 2002). Accessed June 3, 2019. https://web.archive.org/web/20031219133746/http://www.gamespy.com/futureofgaming/engines/index3.shtml.

Kerr, Aphra. *The Business and Culture of Digital Games: Gamework/Gameplay*. London: Sage, 2006.

Kerr, Aphra. *Global Games: Production, Circulation and Policy in the Networked Era*. New York: Routledge, 2017.

Kerr, Aphra, and Anthony Cawley. "The Spatialisation of the Digital Games Industry: Lessons from Ireland." *International Journal of Cultural Policy* 18, no. 4 (September2012): 398–418.

King, Geoff, and Tanya Krzywinska (Eds). *ScreenPlay: Cinema/Videogames/Interfaces*. London: Wallflower Press, 2002.

Kinsella, Bret. "A *Fortnite* Player Created an Alexa Skill to Assist His Gameplay." *Voicebot* (December 7, 2018). Accessed June 26, 2019. https://voicebot.ai/2018/12/07/a-fortnite-player-created-an-alexa-skill-to-assist-his-gameplay.

Kirkpatrick, Graeme. *Computer Games and the Social Imaginary*. Cambridge, UK: Polity Press, 2013.

Kitchin, Rob, and Martin Dodge. *Code/Space: Software and Everyday Life*. Cambridge, MA: MIT Press, 2011.

Kittler, Friedrich. "There is No Software." *CTHEORY*, a032 (October 18, 1995). Accessed February 3, 2014. www.ctheory.net/articles.aspx?id=74.

Kline, Stephen. "The Ends of History and the Tyranny of the Algorithm." In *Kinephanos, History of Games International Conference Proceedings*, 12–42. Edited by Carl Therrien, Henry Lowood, and Martin Picard, 2014.

Kline, Stephen, Nick Dyer-Witheford, and Greig de Peuter. *Digital Play: The Interaction of Technology, Culture, and Marketing*. Montreal: McGill-Queen's University Press, 2003.

Kocurek, Carly A. "Tabled for Discussion: A Conversation with Game Designer Michael De Anda." *QED: A Journal in GLBTQ Worldmaking* 2, no. 2 (Summer2015): 151–172.

Kuhlmann, Johannes. "In-house Engine Development: Process Tips." *Gamasutra Blogs* (April 4, 2017). Accessed July 14, 2017. www.gamasutra.com/blogs/JohannesKuhlmann/20170404/294327/InHouse_Engine_Development_Process_Tips.php.

Kuhlmann, Johannes. "The Road to Abyss Engine 4.0." *MCV* (September 29, 2016). Accessed July 14, 2017. www.mcvuk.com/the-road-to-abyss-engine-4-0.

Kultima, Annakaisa, and Mirva Peltoniemi (Eds). *Games and Innovation Research Seminar 2011 Working Papers* (*TRIM Research Reports* 7). Tampere, Finland: University of Tampere, 2012.

Kushner, David. *Masters of Doom: How Two Guys Created an Empire and Transformed Pop Culture*. New York: Random House, 2003.

Lafortune, Eric. *Mathematical Models and Monte Carlo Algorithms for Physically Based Rendering*. PhD dissertation, Catholic University of Leuven, Belgium. 1996.

Lafortune, Eric, and Yves Willems. "A Theoretical Framework for Physically Based Rendering." *Computer Graphics Forum* 13, no. 2 (1994): 97–107.

Lahti, Martti. "As We Become Machines: Corporealized Pleasures in Video Games." In *The Video Game Theory Reader*, 157–170. Edited by Mark J. P. Wolf and Bernard Perron. New York: Routledge, 2003.

Laidlaw, Marc. "The Egos at Id." *Wired* (August 1, 1996). Accessed May 30, 2019. www.wired.com/1996/08/id.

Latour, Bruno. "Visualization and Cognition: Thinking with Eyes and Hands." *Knowledge and Society: Studies in the Sociology of Culture Past and Present* 6 (1986): 1–40.

Leadbeater, Charles, and Kate Oakley. *The Independents: Britain's New Cultural Entrepreneur*. London: Demos, 1999.

Lee, Mark, Brian Green, Feng Xie, and Eric Tabellion. "Vectorized Production Path Tracing." In *HPG '17: Proceedings of High Performance Graphics*, 1–11. (Los Angeles, CA, July 2017) New York: Association for Computing Machinery, 2017.

Lessig, Lawrence. *Code and Other Laws of Cyberspace*. New York: Basic Books, 1999.

Levant, Yves, Michel Coulmont, and Raluca Sandu. "Business Simulation as an Active Learning Activity for Developing Soft Skills." *Accounting Education* 25, no. 4 (2016): 368–395.

Lewis, Michael, and Jeffrey Jacobson. "Game Engines in Scientific Research." *Communications of the ACM* 45, no. 1 (January2002): 27–31.

Licklider, J. C. R. "Man-Computer Symbiosis." *IRE Transactions on Human Factors in Electronics* (March 1960): 4–11.

Liu, Rong, Hao Zhang, and James Busby. "Convex Hull Covering of Polygonal Scenes for Accurate Collision Detection in Games." In *GI '08: Proceedings of Graphics Interface 2008*, 203–210. (Windsor, Canada, May 28–30, 2008) Mississauga, Canada: Canadian Information Processing Society, 2008.

Losh, Elizabeth. *The War on Learning: Gaining Ground in the Digital University*. Cambridge, MA: MIT Press, 2014.

Lowood, Henry. "Game Engine." In *Debugging Game History: A Critical Lexicon*, 203–209. Edited by Henry Lowood and Raiford Guins. Cambridge, MA: MIT Press, 2016.

Lowood, Henry. "Game Engines and Game History." In *Kinephanos, History of Games International Conference Proceedings*, 179–198. Edited by Carl Therrien, Henry Lowood, and Martin Picard, 2014.

Lugrin, Jean-Luc, Fred Charles, Marc Cavazza, Marc Le Renard, Jonathan Freeman, and Jane Lessiter. "CaveUDK: A VR Game Engine Middleware." In *VRST '12 – Proceedings of the 18th ACM Symposium on Virtual Reality Software and Technology*, 137–144. (Toronto, Canada, December 2012) New York: Association for Computing Machinery, 2012.

Lukas, Scott A. *A Reader in Themed and Immersive Spaces*. Pittsburgh, PA: ETC Press, 2016.

Mackenzie, Adrian. *Cutting Code: Software and Sociality*. New York: Peter Lang, 2006.

Mackenzie, Adrian. *Transduction: Invention, Innovation and Collective Life*. Unpublished manuscript, 2003. Accessed July 1, 2019. www.lancaster.ac.uk/staff/mackenza/papers/transduction.pdf.

Mackenzie, Adrian. *Transductions: Bodies and Machines at Speed*. London: Continuum, 2002.

Malfatti, Silvano Maneck, Selan Rodrigues dos Santos, Luciane Machado Fraga, Claudia Marcela Justel, Paulo Fernando Ferreira Rosa, and Jauvane Cavalvante de Oliveira. "The Design of a Graphics Engine for the Development of Virtual Reality Applications." *RITA* 15, no. 3 (2008): 25–45.

Malkowski, Jennifer, and TreaAndrea M. Russworm. "Introduction: Identity, Representation, and Video Game Studies Beyond the Politics of the Image." In *Gaming Representation: Race, Gender, and Sexuality in Videogames*, 1–16. Edited by Jennifer Malkowski and TreaAndrea M. Russworm. Bloomington, IN: Indiana University Press, 2017.

Manaugh, Geoff, and Nicola Twilley. "The Philosophy of *SimCity*: An Interview With the Game's Lead Designer." *The Atlantic* (May 9, 2013). Accessed September 13, 2019. www.theatlantic.com/technology/archive/2013/05/the-philosophy-of-simcity-an-interview-with-the-games-lead-designer/275724.

Manovich, Lev. *The Language of New Media*. Cambridge, MA: MIT Press, 2001.

Manovich, Lev. *Software Takes Command*. New York: Bloomsbury, 2013.

Marcuse, Herbert. *One-Dimensional Man: Studies in the Ideology of Advanced Industrial Society*. Boston: Beacon Press, 1964.

Marino, Mark. "Critical Code Studies." *Electronic Book Review* (December 4, 2006). Accessed June 10, 2018. www.electronicbookreview.com/thread/electropoetics/codology.

Marino, Mark. "Critical Code Studies and the *Electronic Book Review*: An Introduction." *Electronic Book Review* (September 15, 2010). Accessed June 10, 2018. www.electronicbookreview.com/thread/firstperson/ningislanded#.

Marino, Mark. "Field Report for Critical Code Studies, 2014." *Computational Culture* (November 9, 2014). Accessed June 10, 2018. http://computationalculture.net/field-report-for-critical-code-studies-2014%E2%80%A8.

Mateas, Michael. "Procedural Literacy: Educating the New Media Practitioner." *On the Horizon* 13, no. 2 (2005): 101–111.

Mateas, Michael, and Nick Montfort. "A Box, Darkly: Obfuscation, Weird Languages, and Code Aesthetics." In *Proceedings of the 6th Digital Arts and Culture Conference*, 144–153. (College Park, MD, November 15, 2005) College Park, MD: Maryland Institute for Technology in the Humanities, 2005.

Max73. "*Mass Effect*: Interview with Casey Hudson." *Xbox Gazette* (August 21, 2007). Accessed May 24, 2019. www.xboxgazette.com/interview_mass_effect_en.php.

McAllister, Ken S. *Game Work: Language, Power, and Computer Game Culture*. Tuscaloosa, AL: University of Alabama Press, 2004.
McCracken, Harry. "A First Look Deep Inside Amazon Game Studios." *Fast Company* (October 14, 2014). Accessed June 15, 2019. www.fastcompany.com/3037064/amazon-game-studios.
McDonald, Heidi. "Romance in Games: What It Is, How It Is, and How Developers Can Improve It." *QED: A Journal in GLBTQ Worldmaking* 2, no. 2 (Summer2015): 32–63.
McDonald, T. Liam. "Game Theory." *Maximum PC* 3, no. 10 (November1998): 43.
McGowan, Chris. "The World of Theme Parks and VFX." *VFX Voice* 2, no. 4 (Fall2018): 46–57.
McPherson, Tara. "U.S. Operating Systems at Mid-Century: The Intertwining of Race and UNIX." In *Race After the Internet*, 21–35. Edited by Lisa Nakamura and Peter A. Chow-White. New York: Routledge, 2012.
MCV Staff. "The Rise of Middleware 2.0." *MCV* (July 6, 2007). Accessed August 25, 2019. www.mcvuk.com/the-rise-of-middleware-2-0.
Microsoft. "Lockheed Martin-Microsoft Agreement to Bring Better Training to Warfighters." *Microsoft News* (November 30, 2009). Accessed September 16, 2018. https://news.microsoft.com/2009/11/30/lockheed-martin-microsoft-agreement-to-bring-better-training-to-warfighters.
Microsoft. "Microsoft ESP Debuts as a Platform for Visual Simulation." *Microsoft News* (November 14, 2007). Accessed September 16, 2018. https://news.microsoft.com/2007/11/14/microsoft-esp-debuts-as-a-platform-for-visual-simulation/.
Milburn, Colin. *Mondo Nano: Fun and Games in the World of Digital Matter*. Durham, NC: Duke University Press, 2015.
Miller, Matt. "Decrypting *The Elder Scrolls*." *Game Informer* (December 26, 2010). Accessed May 30, 2019. www.gameinformer.com/b/features/archive/2010/12/26/decrypting-the-elder-scrolls.aspx.
Mitropoulou, Ioanna, Stefan Arisona, and Taisha Fabricius. "From CityEngine to Unreal Studio: The Journey from First Design Steps to High-quality Real-time Visualization." *GeoNet: The Esri Community* (May 23, 2019). Accessed September 2, 2019. https://community.esri.com/docs/DOC-13480.
Montford, Nick. "Obfuscated Code." In *Software Studies: A Lexicon*, 193–199. Edited by Matthew Fuller. Cambridge, MA: MIT Press, 2008.
Montfort, Nick, and Ian Bogost. *Racing the Beam: The Atari Video Computer System*. Cambridge, MA: MIT Press, 2009.
Murnane, Kevin. "Google's Got Game: Collaboration with Unity Could Be a Game Changer." *Forbes* (June 20, 2018). Accessed June 25, 2019. www.forbes.com/sites/kevinmurnane/2018/06/20/google-cloud-hosting-for-unity-engine-games-is-another-game-changer/#59d2c251e92b.
Murray, Janet H. *Hamlet on the Holodeck: The Future of Narrative in Cyberspace*. New York: The Free Press, 1997.
Nakamura, Lisa. "Queer Female of Color: The Highest Difficulty Setting There Is? Gaming Rhetoric as Gender Capital." *Ada: A Journal of Gender, New Media, and Technology* 1 (November 15, 2012). Accessed June 18, 2018. https://adanewmedia.org/2012/11/issue1-nakamura/.
Nakevska, Marija, Alex Juarez, and Jun Hu. "CryVE: Modding the CryEngine2 to Create a CAVE System." In *Game Mods: Design, Theory and Criticism*, 167–193. Edited by Erik Champion. Pittsburgh, PA: Carnegie Mellon University ETC Press, 2012.

Nancy, Jean-Luc. *The Inoperative Community*. Edited by Peter Connor. Translated by Peter Conner *et al.*Minneapolis, MN: University of Minnesota Press, 1991.

NASA. NetworKing Game Manual. (2019). Accessed March 22, 2012. https://nasa3d.arc.nasa.gov/visualizations/networking/manual.

Nelson, Theodor H. "Complex Information Processing: A File Structure for the Complex, the Changing and the Indeterminate." In *Association for Computing Machinery: Proceedings of the 20th National Conference*, 84–100. Edited by Lewis Winner. New York: Association for Computing Machinery, 1965.

Newman, James. *Playing with Videogames*. New York: Routledge, 2008.

Newzoo. Global Games Market Report 2019 (Light Version). Accessed September 7, 2019. https://newzoo.com/insights/trend-reports/newzoo-global-games-market-report-2019-light-version.

Next Games. "The Walking Dead: Our World." Accessed February 3, 2020. www.thewalkingdeadourworld.com.

Next Generation. "3D Realms." *Next Generation* 1, no. 10 (October1995): 99–102.

Niantic. "Designing a Planet-scale Real-world AR Platform." *Niantic Blog* (February 27, 2019). Accessed July 1, 2019. https://nianticlabs.com/blog/nrwp-update.

Niantic. "The Niantic Story: A History of Viewing the World Differently." *About Niantic* (2015–2020). Accessed February 3, 2020. https://nianticlabs.com/about/.

Niantic. "A Peek Inside the Niantic Real World Platform." *Niantic Blog* (June 28, 2018). Accessed July 1, 2019. https://nianticlabs.com/blog/nianticrealworldplatform.

Nickelodeon. "Nickelodeon Breaks Ground with Development of Virtual and Augmented Reality Series for TV." *Nickelodeon Press* (August 2, 2018). Accessed August 23, 2019. www.nickpress.com/press-releases/2018/08/02/nickelodeon-breaks-ground-with-development-of-virtual-and-augmented-reality-series-for-tv.

Nicoll, Benjamin, and Brendan Keogh. *The Unity Game Engine and the Circuits of Cultural Software*. Cham, Switzerland: Palgrave Macmillan, 2019.

Nideffer, Robert F. "Game Engines as Embedded Systems." In *Database Aesthetics: Art in the Age of Information Overflow*, 211–232. Edited by Victoria Vesna. Minneapolis, MN: University of Minnesota Press, 2007.

Norman, Don. *The Design of Everyday Things*. New York: Basic Books, 2013.

O'Donnell, Casey. *Developer's Dilemma: The Secret World of Videogame Creators*. Cambridge, MA: MIT Press, 2014.

Oreskovic, Alexei. "Why EA's Former Boss Believes the 3D Tech that Powers Video Games Will Make Way More Money Outside of Gaming." *Business Insider* (September 14, 2018). Accessed April 2, 2019. www.businessinsider.com/unity-ceo-john-riccitiello-opportunity-beyond-gaming-2018-9.

Parisi, David. "Game Interfaces as Disabling Infrastructures." *Analog Game Studies 4*, no. 3 (May 30, 2017). AccessedJune 12, 2018. http://analoggamestudies.org/byline/david-parisi.

Pasquale, Frank. *The Black Box Society: The Secret Algorithms That Control Money and Information*. Cambridge, MA: Harvard University Press, 2015.

Paula, Bruno Henrique de, Andrew Burn, Richard Noss, and José Armando Valente. "Playing *Beowulf*: Bridging computational thinking, arts and literature through game-making." *International Journal of Child-Computer Interaction* 16 (2018): 39–46.

Pedersen, Roger E. *Game Design Foundations*. Plano, TX: Wordware Publishing, 2003.

Petrillo, Fábio, Marcelo Pimenta, Francisco Trindade, and Carlos Dietrich. "What Went Wrong? A Survey of Problems in Game Development." *ACM Computers in Entertainment* 7, no. 1, (February2009) Article 13: 1–22.

Piccinini, Gualtiero. "Computationalism in the Philosophy of Mind." *Philosophy Compass* 4, no. 3 (2009): 515–532.

Pimentel, Ken. "HOK on Architectural Visualization: Aggregate, Iterate, Communicate." *Epic Games Unreal Engine Blog* (March 13, 2019). Accessed October 1, 2019. www.unrealengine.com/en-US/spotlights/hok-architectural-visualization-aggregate-iterate-communicate.

Poretski, Leo, and Ofer Arazy. "Placing Value on Community Co-creations: A Study of a Video Game 'Modding' Community." In *CSCW '17 – Proceedings of the 2017 ACM Conference on Computer Supported Cooperative Work and Social Computing*, 480–490. (Portland, OR, February–March 2017) New York: Association for Computing Machinery, 2017.

Pratt, Andy C. "The Cultural Industries Production System: A Case Study of Employment Change in Britain, 1984–1991." *Environment and Planning A* 29, no. 11 (1997): 1953–1974.

Pratt, Andy C., Rosalind Gill, and Volker Spelthann. "Work and the City in the e-Society: A Critical Investigation of the Sociospatially Situated Character of Economic Production in the Digital Content Industries in the UK." *Information, Communication & Society* 10, no. 6 (2007): 922–942.

Prax, Patrick. *Co-creative Game Design as Participatory Alternative Media*. PhD dissertation, Uppsala University, 2016.

Reddi, Vijay Janapa, Dan Connors, and Robert S. Cohn. "Persistence in Dynamic Code Transformation Systems." *ACM SIGARCH Computer Architecture News* 33, no. 5 (November2005): 69–74.

Reed, Alison, and Amanda Phillips. "Additive Race: Colorblind Discourses of Realism in Performance Capture Technologies." *Digital Creativity* 24, no. 2 (2013): 130–144.

Refenes, Tommy. "The Engine Sandwich: Made with Super Meat." In *Behind the Black Box: Sessions with Game Engine Programmers*, 88–97. Edited by Caleb Biasco, Jared Ettinger, Jacob Wilson, Chaojie Zhu, and Yidi Zhu. Pittsburgh, PA: Carnegie Mellon University ETC Press, 2018.

Reisenleitner, Markus. "Resetting the Clock: Theme Parks, New Urbanism, and Smart Cities." In *A Reader in Themed and Immersive Spaces*, 279–287. Edited by Scott A. Lukas. Pittsburgh, PA: ETC Press, 2016.

Renardson, Adam. "The Hideo Kojima *Death Stranding* Interview: Strands, Decima and Guerrilla Games." *PlayStation Blog* (February 23, 2017). Accessed September 7, 2019. https://blog.us.playstation.com/2017/02/23/the-hideo-kojima-death-stranding-interview-strands-decima-and-guerrilla-games/.

Resnick, Mitchel, and Brian Silverman. "Some Reflections on Designing Construction Kits for Kids." In *IDC '05 – Proceedings of the 2005 Conference on Interaction Design and Children*, 117–122. (Boulder, Colorado, June 2005) New York: Association for Computing Machinery, 2005.

Reyes, Ian, and Suellen Adams. "Screening Play: Rules, Wares, and Representations in 'Realistic' Video Games." *Eludamos: Journal for Computer Game Culture* 4, no. 2 (2010): 149–166.

Roberts, Samuel. "Valve Reflects on *The Orange Box*, Ten Years Later." *PC Gamer* (October 10, 2017). Accessed May 25, 2019. www.pcgamer.com/valve-reflects-on-the-orange-box-ten-years-later.

Rodden, Tom, Andy Crabtree, Terry Hemmings, Boriana Koleva, Jan Humble, Karl-Petter Åkesson, and Pär Hansson. "Between the Dazzle of a New Building and its Eventual Corpse: Assembling the Ubiquitous Home." In *DIS '04 – Proceedings of the 5th Conference on Designing Interactive Systems: Processes, Practices, Methods, and Techniques*, 71–80. (Cambridge, MA, August 2004) New York: Association for Computing Machinery, 2004.

Roodhouse, Simon. "The Creative Industries: Definitions, Quantification and Practice." In *Cultural Industries: The British Experience in International Perspective*, 13–32. Edited by Christiane Eisenberg, Rita Gerlach, and Christian Handke. Berlin: Humboldt University, 2006.

Rosen, Jeffrey. "Silicon Valley's Spy Game." *New York Times Magazine* (April 14, 2002): 46–51.

Ross, Alec. *The Industries of the Future*. New York: Simon & Schuster, 2016.

Ruberg, Bonnie. "No Fun: The Queer Potential of Video Games that Annoy, Anger, Disappoint, Sadden, and Hurt." *QED: A Journal in GLBTQ Worldmaking* 2, no. 2 (Summer2015): 108–124.

Ruberg, Bonnie, and Adrienne Shaw (Eds). *Queer Game Studies*. Minneapolis, MN: University of Minnesota Press, 2017.

Salen, Katie. "Gaming Literacies: A Game Design Study in Action." *Journal of Educational Multimedia and Hypermedia* 16, no. 3 (2007): 301–322.

Salen, Katie, and Eric Zimmerman. *Rules of Play: Game Design Fundamentals*. Cambridge, MA: MIT Press, 2004.

Salen, Katie, and Eric Zimmerman (Eds). *The Game Design Reader: A Rules of Play Anthology*. Cambridge, MA: MIT Press, 2006.

Sample, Mark. "Code." In *Debugging Game History: A Critical Lexicon*, 53–62. Edited by Henry Lowood and Raiford Guins. Cambridge, MA: MIT Press, 2016.

Sample, Mark L. "Criminal Code: Procedural Logic and Rhetorical Excess in Videogames." *Digital Humanities Quarterly* 7, no. 1 (2013). Accessed June 10, 2018. www.digitalhumanities.org/dhq/vol/7/1/000153/000153.html.

Sampson, Robert J. *Great American City: Chicago and the Enduring Neighborhood Effect*. Chicago, IL: University of Chicago Press, 2012.

Sanglard, Fabien. *Game Engine Black Book: Doom*. CreateSpace Independent Publishing Platform, 2018.

Sanglard, Fabien. *Game Engine Black Book: Wolfenstein 3D* (Second Edition). CreateSpace Independent Publishing Platform, 2018.

Scacchi, Walt. "Computer Game Mods, Modders, Modding, and the Mod Scene." *First Monday* 15, no. 5 (May2010). Accessed June 18, 2018. http://firstmonday.org/ojs/index.php/fm/article/view/2965/2526.

Scacchi, Walt. "Free and Open Source Development Practices in the Game Community." *IEEE Software* 21, no. 1 (January2004): 59–66.

Scacchi, Walt. "Modding as a Basis for Developing Game Systems." In *GAS '11 – Proceedings of the 1st International Workshop on Games and Software Engineering*, 5–8 (Waikiki, Honolulu HI, May 2011) New York: Association for Computing Machinery, 2011.

Scacchi, Walt. "Practices and Technologies in Computer Game Software Engineering." *IEEE Software* 34, no. 1 (January/February2017): 110–116.

Schreier, Jason. "Amazon Lays Off Dozens of Game Developers During E3." *Kotaku* (June 14, 2019). Accessed June 15, 2019. https://kotaku.com/amazon-lays-off-dozens-of-game-developers-during-e3-1835523460.

Sens, Jeffrey. "Queer Worldmaking Games: A Portland Indie Experiment." *QED: A Journal in GLBTQ Worldmaking* 2, no. 2 (Summer2015): 98–107.

Serdar, Adam. "The Definition and Beginning of a Game Engine." In *Behind the Black Box: Sessions with Game Engine Programmers*, 35–43. Edited by Caleb Biasco, Jared Ettinger, Jacob Wilson, Chaojie Zhu, and Yidi Zhu. Pittsburgh, PA: Carnegie Mellon University ETC Press, 2018.

Shannon, Claude E. "A Mathematical Theory of Communication." *The Bell System Technical Journal* 27 (July, October1948): 379–423, 623–656.

Shaw, Adrienne. "Circles, Charmed and Magic: Queering Game Studies." *QED: A Journal in GLBTQ Worldmaking* 2, no. 2 (Summer2015): 64–97.

Shaw, Adrienne, and Elizaveta Friesem. "Where is the Queerness in Games? Types of Lesbian, Gay, Bisexual, Transgender, and Queer Content in Digital Games." *International Journal of Communication* 10 (2016): 3877–3889.

Shepherd, Jeremiah, Jijun Tang, and Roger Dougal. "The Simulation and Data Visualization Potential of Microsoft's XNA." In *GCMS '10 – Proceedings of the 2010 Conference on Grand Challenges in Modeling and Simulation*, 306–310. (Ottawa, Canada, July 2010) Vista, CA: Society for Modeling & Simulation International, 2010.

Sicart, Miguel. "The Ethics of Computer Game Design." In *DiGRA '05 – Proceedings of the 2005 Digital Games Research Association International Conference: Changing Views: Worlds in Play*, Volume 3. (Vancouver, Canada, June 16–20, 2005) Accessed June 12, 2018. www.digra.org/wp-content/uploads/digital-library/06276.55524.pdf.

Sicart, Miguel. *The Ethics of Computer Games*. Cambridge, MA: MIT Press, 2009.

Sicart, Miguel. "Game, Player, Ethics: A Virtue Ethics Approach to Computer Games." *International Review of Information Ethics* 4 (December2005): 13–18.

Sicart, Miguel. "Queering the Controller." *Analog Game Studies* 4, no. 4 (July 31, 2017). Accessed June 12, 2018. http://analoggamestudies.org/2017/07/queering-the-controller.

Simon, Bart. "Indie Eh? Some Kind of Game Studies." *Loading... The Journal of the Canadian Game Studies Association* 7, no. 11 (2013): 1–7.

Simpson, Jake. "Game Engine Anatomy 101." *ExtremeTech* (April 12, 2002). Accessed June 22, 2018. www.extremetech.com/computing/50938-game-engine-anatomy-101.

Squire, Kurt D. "Toward a Media Literacy for Games." *Telemedium* 52, nos. 1–2 (Winter/Spring2005): 9–15.

Star, Susan Leigh. "The Ethnography of Infrastructure." *American Behavioral Scientist* 43, no. 3 (November1999): 377–391.

Star, Susan Leigh, and Karen Ruhleder. "Steps Toward an Ecology of Infrastructure: Design and Access for Large Information Spaces." *Information Systems Research* 7, no. 1 (March1996): 111–134.

Stenros, Jaakko. "The Game Definition Game: A Review." *Games and Culture* 12, no. 6 (2017): 499–520.

Stokes, Benjamin, Samantha Dols, and Aubrey Hill. "Cities Remix a Playful Platform: Experiments to Embed *Pokémon GO*, from Open Street Festivals to Neighborhood Libraries." A Report from the Playful Cities Group, with American University Game Lab and the Center for Media and Social Impact, June 29, 2018. Accessed February 11, 2019. https://playfulcity.net/go/pokemon-report/.

Strivr. *Transforming Employee Experience with Immersive Learning*. Ebook. 2019.

Stuart, Keith. "The Hidden Story of the 3D Engine – By the People Who Write Them." *The Guardian* (December 14, 2009). Accessed September 16, 2018. https://www.theguardian.com/technology/gamesblog/2009/dec/14/games-gameculture.

Švelch, Jan. "Exploring the Myth of the Representative Video Game Trailer." *Kinephanos* 7, no. 1 (November2017): 7–36.

Sweeney, Tim. "Welcome to Unreal Engine 4." *Unreal Engine Blog* (March 19, 2014). Accessed February 1, 2020. www.unrealengine.com/en-US/blog/welcome-to-unreal-engine-4.

Tabellion, Eric, and Arnauld Lamorlette. "An Approximate Global Illumination System for Computer Generated Films." *ACM Transactions on Graphics* 23, no. 3 (August2004): 469–476.

Tagliasacchi, Andrea, Ryan Dickie, Alex Couture-Beil, Micah J. Best, Alexandra Fedorova, and Andrew Brownsword. "Cascade: A Parallel Programming Framework for Video Game Engines." In *Proceedings of the Workshop on Parallel Execution of Sequential Programs on Multi-core Architectures*, 47–54. Beijing, China, 2008.

Taylor, Astra. *The People's Platform: Taking Back Power and Culture in the Digital Age*. New York: Metropolitan Books, 2014.

Taylor, Mark, Mike Baskett, Denis Reilly, and Somasundaram Ravindran. "Game Theory for Computer Games Design." *Games and Culture* (November2017). Accessed June 19, 2018. http://journals.sagepub.com/doi/pdf/10.1177/1555412017740497.

Taylor, Mark J., David Gresty, and Michael Baskett. "Computer Game-Flow Design." *ACM Computers in Entertainment* 4, no. 1, Article 3A (January2006): 1–10.

Thompson, Joseph. "Games, Glitches, Ghosts: Giving Voice to Enchantment in the Gamic Assemblage." *The International Journal of Technology, Knowledge, and Society* 8 (2012): 85–93.

Thomsen, Mike. "History of the Unreal Engine." *IGN* (February 23, 2010). Accessed May 21, 2019. www.ign.com/articles/2010/02/23/history-of-the-unreal-engine.

Tulip, James, James Bekkema, and Keith Nesbitt. "Multi-threaded Game Engine Design." In *IE 2006: Proceedings of the 3rd Australasian Conference on Interactive Entertainment*, 9–14. (Perth, Australia, December 2006) Murdoch, Australia: Murdoch University, 2006.

Turing, Alan M. "Computing Machinery and Intelligence." *Mind: A Quarterly Review of Psychology and Philosophy* 59, no. 236 (1950): 433–460.

Turkle, Sherry. *The Second Self: Computers and the Human Spirit*. Cambridge, MA: MIT Press, 2005.

Tzankova, Veronika, and Michael Filimowicz. "Introduction: Pedagogies at the Intersection of Disciplines." In *Teaching Computational Creativity*, 1–17. Edited by Veronika Tzankova and Michael Filimowicz. New York: Cambridge University Press, 2017.

Unity Technologies. "Fast Company Names Unity Technologies Among World's Top 10 Most Innovative Companies in Virtual and Augmented Reality." *Unity PR* (February 20, 2018). Accessed May 23, 2019. https://unity3d.com/company/public-relations/news/fast-company-names-unity-technologies-among-worlds-top-10-most.

Unity Technologies. "Unity Development Platform and Web Player Certified by the US Army and Air Force." *Marketwire* (May 9, 2011). Accessed November 29, 2014. www.marketwired.com/press-release/unity-development-platform-and-web-player-certi fied-by-the-us-army-and-air-force-1511958.htm.

Valve Corporation. "Early Access Games." *Steam: Introducing Early Access* (2020). Accessed February 4, 2020. https://store.steampowered.com/earlyaccessfaq/?snr=1_200_200_Early+Access.

Vanhatupa, Juha-Matti. "Game Engines in Game Programming Education – Experiences from Use of the CAGE Game Engine." In *Koli Calling '11 – Proceedings of the 11th Koli Calling International Conference on Computing Education Research*, 118–119. (Koli, Finland, November 2011) New York: Association for Computing Machinery, 2011.

Vella, Matt. "Unreal Architecture: Powerhouse Dallas Architecture Firm HKS is Licensing a Popular Video Game Engine to Wow Potential Clients." *Bloomberg* (December 21, 2007). Accessed September 16, 2018. www.bloomberg.com/news/articles/2007-12-21/unreal-architecturebusinessweek-business-news-stock-market-and-financial-advice.

Waltemate, Thomas, Felix Hülsmann, Thies Pfeiffer, Stefan Kopp, and Mario Botsch. "Realizing a Low-latency Virtual Reality Environment for Motor Learning." In *VRST '15: Proceedings of the 21st ACM Symposium on Virtual Reality Software and Technology*, 139–147. (Beijing, China, November 2015) New York: Association for Computing Machinery, 2015.

Wardrip-Fruin, Noah. *Expressive Processing: Digital Fictions, Computer Games, and Software Studies*. Cambridge, MA: MIT Press, 2009.

Wark, McKenzie. *Gamer Theory*. Cambridge, MA: Harvard University Press, 2007.

Webb, Amy. *The Signals are Talking: Why Today's Fringe is Tomorrow's Mainstream*. New York: Public Affairs, 2016.

Weintrop, David, Nathan Holbert, Michael S. Horn, and Uri Wilensky. "Computational Thinking in Constructionist Video Games." *International Journal of Game-Based Learning* 6, no. 1 (January–March2016): 1–17.

Weiser, Mark. "The Computer for the 21st Century." *Scientific American* (September1991): 94–104.

Weiss, Tara. "The Interactive Frontier of Kids Programming." *Viacom News* (September 4, 2018). Accessed August 23, 2019. www.viacom.com/news/interactive-frontier-kids-p rogramming.

Whitson, Jennifer R. "Gaming the Quantified Self." *Surveillance & Society* 11, nos. 1–2 (2013): 163–176.

Wiebusch, Dennis, and Marc Erich Latoschik. "Decoupling the Entity-component-system Pattern Using Semantic Traits for Reusable Realtime Interactive Systems." In *2015 IEEE 8th Workshop on Software Engineering and Architectures for Realtime Interactive Systems (SEARIS)*, 25–32. (Arles, France, March 24, 2015) IEEE, 2015.

Wing, Jeannette M. "Computational Thinking." *Communications of the ACM* 49, no. 3 (March2006): 33–35.

Winner, Langdon. "Do Artifacts Have Politics?" *Daedalus* 109, no. 1 (Winter1980): 121–136.

Withers, Rachel. "The Weather Channel Uses Video Game Simulation to Convey the Severity of the Hurricane Threat." *Slate* (September 13, 2018). Accessed September 15, 2018. https://slate.com/technology/2018/09/weather-channel-hurricane-florence-flood-simulation.html.

Wolverton, Troy. "One of the Leading Companies in the Video-Game Business is Gunning to Take Over the Enterprise Software Industry." *Business Insider* (September 14, 2018). Accessed April 2, 2019. www.businessinsider.com/unity-technologies-sees-big-opportuni ties-outside-of-video-games-2018-9.

World Video Game Hall of Fame. *A History of Video Games in 64 Objects*. New York: Dey Street Books, 2018.

Wyeld, Theodor G., Joti Carroll, Brendan Ledwich, Brett Leavy, Craig Gibbons, and James Hills. "The Ethics of Indigenous Storytelling: Using the Torque Game Engine to Support Australian Aboriginal Cultural Heritage." In *DiGRA '07 – Proceedings of the 2007 Digital Games Research Association International Conference: Situated Play*, 261–268. (Tokyo, Japan, September 24–28, 2007) Digital Games Research Association, 2007.

Yahagi, Taro. "How *Dragon's Dogma* Changed the MT Framework." *GregaMan Blog* (April 5, 2012). Retrieved August 31, 2018. www.capcom-unity.com/gregaman/blog/2012/04/05/how_dragons_dogma_changed_the_mt_framework.

Yang, Robert. "On 'FeministWhorePurna' and the Ludo-material Politics of Gendered Damage Power-ups in Open-World RPG Video Games." In *Queer Game Studies*, 97–108. Edited by Bonnie Ruberg and Adrienne Shaw. Minneapolis, MN: University of Minnesota Press, 2017.

Yiannoutsou, Nikoleta, Maria Daskolia, and Chronis Kynigos. "Constructionist Designs in Game Modding: The Case of Learning About Sustainability." Paper presented at *Constructionism 2014: Constructionism and Creativity*. Vienna, Austria, August 19–23, 2014.

Yiannoutsou, Nikoleta, and Chronis Kynigos. "Game Kits: Metadesign Considerations on Game Modding for Learning." In *IDC '16 – Proceedings of the 15th International Conference on Interaction Design and Children*, 583–588. (Manchester, UK, June 2016) New York: Association for Computing Machinery, 2016.

Zagal, José P., Michael Mateas, Clara Fernández-Vara, Brian Hochhalter, and Nolan Lichti. "Towards an Ontological Language for Game Analysis." In *DiGRA '05 – Proceedings of the 2005 Digital Games Research Association International Conference: Changing Views: Worlds in Play*, Volume 3. (Vancouver, Canada, June 16–20, 2005). Accessed June 12, 2018. www.digra.org/wp-content/uploads/digital-library/06276.09313.pdf.

Zhu, Meng, Alf Inge Wang, and Hallvard Traetteberg. "Engine– Cooperative Game Modeling (ECGM): Bridge Model-Driven Game Development and Game Engine Tool-chains." In *ACE '16 – Proceedings of the 13th International Conference on Advances in Computer Entertainment Technology*, 1–10. (Osaka Japan, November 2016) New York: Association for Computing Machinery, 2016.

Ziarek, Krysztof. *The Historicity of Experience: Modernity, the Avant-Garde and the Event*. Evanston, IL: Northwestern University Press, 2001.

Zimmerman, Eric. "Gaming Literacy: Game Design as a Model for Literacy in the Twenty-First Century." In *The Video Game Theory Reader 2*, 23–31. Edited by Bernard Perron and Mark J. P. Wolf. New York: Routledge, 2009.

INDEX

Taylor & Francis Group
an **informa** business

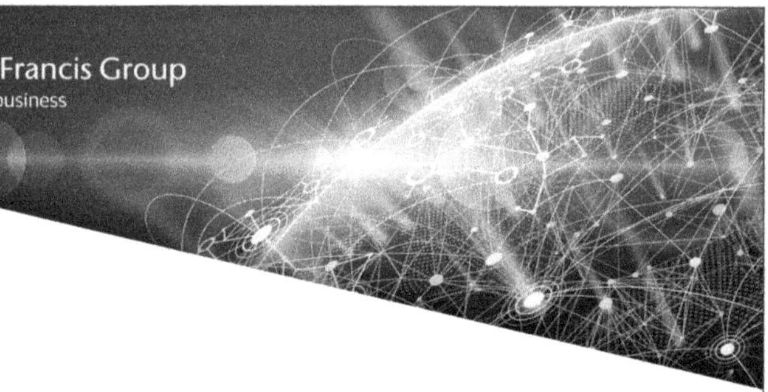

Taylor & Francis eBooks

www.taylorfrancis.com

A single destination for eBooks from Taylor & Francis with increased functionality and an improved user experience to meet the needs of our customers.

90,000+ eBooks of award-winning academic content in Humanities, Social Science, Science, Technology, Engineering, and Medical written by a global network of editors and authors.

TAYLOR & FRANCIS EBOOKS OFFERS:

- A streamlined experience for our library customers
- A single point of discovery for all of our eBook content
- Improved search and discovery of content at both book and chapter level

REQUEST A FREE TRIAL

support@taylorfrancis.com

Routledge
Taylor & Francis Group

CRC Press
Taylor & Francis Group

For Product Safety Concerns and Information please contact our EU
representative GPSR@taylorandfrancis.com
Taylor & Francis Verlag GmbH, Kaufingerstraße 24, 80331 München, Germany

www.ingramcontent.com/pod-product-compliance
Ingram Content Group UK Ltd.
Pitfield, Milton Keynes, MK11 3LW, UK
UKHW021855031125
464675UK00007B/83

* 9 7 8 1 1 3 8 3 5 3 3 8 1 *